D1610142

Better Against a Wall

Better Against a Wall

Garden Writings

Ursula Buchan

JOHN MURRAY

To CTW, ESBW and TNBW
with love

'A Green Song' from *Serious Concerns* by Wendy Cope is
reproduced by kind permission of Faber & Faber Ltd.

Introduction, selection and editorial matter © Ursula Buchan 2003
Articles © Ursula Buchan 1988, 1990, 1991, 1993, 1994, 1997, 1999,
2000, 2001, 2002

First published in 2003 by John Murray (Publishers)
A division of Hodder Headline

A CIP catalogue record for this title is available from the British
Library

ISBN 0-7195-6039 X

Typeset in Adobe Palatino 11/14 pt by
Servis Filmsetting Ltd, Manchester
Printed and bound in Great Britain by Clays Ltd, St Ives plc

John Murray (Publishers)
338 Euston Road
London
NW1 3BH

Contents

Contents

Acknowledgements

The advantage of writing for a number of publications, disparate but all committed to sparky writing and accurate information, is that I have had the chance to write for different readerships, and also for editors with differing views on what is important. It is a matter of pride to me that I am a hired pen and that my job is to give editors what they want, even when they are not always quite sure themselves. I am grateful to all those who have edited my columns over the years, at *The Spectator*, *Observer*, *Sunday Telegraph*, *Daily Telegraph*, *Independent* and *Independent Magazine*, both for giving me the opportunity to express my ideas and for trusting me to get on with it. I have been very lucky.

I warmly thank Michael Shaw and Jonathan Pegg at Curtis, Brown for their efforts on my behalf, and also the team at John Murray, in particular Caroline Knox, Caroline Westmore, Sam Evans, Helen Guthrie, Liz Robinson and Oula Jones. Working with them has been an entirely pleasurable experience. Thanks are also due to Timothy Jaques, who once again has illustrated my work so amusingly. Among his many talents is an ability to spell orchid names correctly and I am grateful to him for that.

Not much would be possible, however, without the efforts of Cynthia Ogilvie and Mick Clarke, whose continuing interest, commitment and determined hard work in the garden, add greatly to my pleasure in it all.

Introduction

In 1917, a tea rose was named after Lady Hillingdon, an avid gardener only remembered today for having confided to her diary that, when visited at night by her husband, she would lie back and think of England. The rose, a lovely apricot with purple leaves in spring which is still grown by gardeners, was described in a nurseryman's catalogue, with presumably unconscious irony, as 'Good in a bed, but better against a wall'. This has been a favourite silly joke of gardeners for nearly a century, and I am of the cast of mind to respect tradition. The first volume of my selected journalism, published by John Murray in 2001, was entitled *Good in a Bed*. This is the sequel. It follows the same format, with the difference that the former consisted entirely of articles reproduced from *The Spectator*, whereas this one also includes pieces written over some years for the *Observer*, *Sunday Telegraph*, *Daily Telegraph*, *Independent* and *Independent Magazine*.

In the course of compiling this volume, I have had the enjoyment of revisiting old haunts, pleasures and controversies. Journalism is ephemeral, by its very nature, but gardening is not. I hope that readers will stumble across pieces they enjoyed first time round or, more likely (since the vast majority of people read only one newspaper), something they have never seen before.

Of course, not all the articles have stood the test of time, and several have disqualified themselves on those grounds. Moreover, an otherwise promising article has occasionally had to be counted out because of some dreary and bureaucratic but necessary paragraph (concerning nurseries and plant prices, say) which has become quite pointless with the passing of the years. I have tended to choose, therefore, those pieces which do retain all or much of their relevance and are concerned with plants, gardens, the practicalities of gardening, garden and planting design, and with gardening friends and foes. I have also included a number of miscellaneous articles – on Chelsea Flower Show, plant hunting in Nepal and Millennial predictions, for example – which I hope might intrigue or amuse, even if they are not immediately useful. One of the great joys of writing about gardening is that it is possible to touch on aspects of human experience which do not seem, on the face of it, to have anything to do with the subject. Gardening is part of life, we cannot escape that. Gardeners exhibit all the strengths and frailties of other mortals, and provide a great source of fascination and amusement for anyone with eyes to see.

As with *Good in a Bed*, this is a book composed of short essays mostly around eight hundred words long. Oh, how often have I wished for more space in which to develop an idea, but on such occasions I try to remember Blaise Pascal's wise remark: '*Je n'ai fait celle-ci plus longue que parceque je n'ai pas eu le loisir de la faire plus courte* [I have made this letter longer than usual, because I lack the time to make it short]'. In any event, they are of a length which makes it possible to read one or two before falling asleep at night.

I find I have learned things from this book which I must once have known but have since quite forgotten. It was Reginald Farrer who in typically teasing way said of his magnum opus, *The English Rock Garden*: 'It contains at least a thousand times as much knowledge as I myself possess, or can ever hope to attain.' I know exactly what he means.

The articles are essentially as I wrote them originally, rather than as they appeared in print and, moreover, in all cases where it does not make a nonsense of them they have been edited for this book so that they read as if they were contemporary. For example, if I wrote in a 1993 article that some organisation had been founded ten years earlier, the ten years has been changed to twenty. This is because I wish the articles to retain their relevance, where possible.

It is a rather odd, though certainly not an unpleasant, exercise, revisiting twenty years' work. What surprises me is how quickly patterns emerge. I appear to have an interest bordering on obsession in the weather and in soils, but hedges, roses, fruit cages, apple trees, Leyland cypress, *Verbena bonariensis*, garden wildlife and groundsel seem also to bulk large in my life. I can only hope that they do so in your life, too.

1

People, Places and Events

Picture the scene, if you will. It was late April, we (that is, me, my husband and our Nepali guide, Gyanu) were sitting in the shade under an open thatched 'gazebo' at a makeshift trekker's camp, more than 2,000 metres above sea level, in the wooded foothills of the Himalayas, recovering from a morning's stiff uphill walk by drinking warm Coca-Cola out of glass bottles. We were on a day trek from the valley floor, some 1,200 metres below, on the lookout for flowers, and had already come across late blossoms of the stately, tree-like *Rhododendron arboreum*, the red-flowered rhododendron which is the national flower of Nepal. Gyanu was charming, friendly, a stupendous walker (as you might expect from a man brought up

5

in a village four days' march from the nearest bus stop), spoke good enough English to make, and appreciate, jokes in the language, and was knowledgeable about the fascinating and beautiful birds we could see and hear, not to mention the peaks of the massive, snow-covered Annapurna range, twenty miles away and 7,000 metres high. He did not appear, however, very interested in flowers.

So, as we rested, I got out my field guide to the flora of the Himalayas. Gyanu was intrigued, drew his chair closer, and together we pored over hundreds of photographs of Nepali native plants, from rhododendrons to magnolias, from primulas to corydalis, from arisaemas to tree-climbing orchids.There are nearly twice as many native Nepali plant species as the British Isles can boast, and they are mostly rather more showy.

As a result of this interlude, the afternoon went swimmingly. With a visual memory to match his capacity for gradient walking, Gyanu had me well beaten in the speed with which he could mark out interesting plants along the way, pointing out *Berberis aristata, Viburnum erubescens, Melastoma normale, Mazus surculosus* and a whole lot else which was flowering. With alacrity he picked leaves of trees for me, and waited patiently while I checked them in my book, or stopped to take photographs. He had a touching faith in my botanical expertise, for he was prepared to eat the sweet yellow berries of a blackberry-relative called *Rubus ellipticus.* In the pre-monsoon period, when the weather has become very hot and yet the rains have not properly begun, the range of flowers, especially on the floor of the woodland which we passed through, is probably not as wide as it might be in either March or June, and we were in central Nepal, too far west for many of the rhododendrons. But I had great fun identifying trees, such as a walnut-relative I had never heard of called *Engelhardia* as well as a number of handsome evergreen oak and pine species, from their leaves and needles.

Although I have often looked for wild flowers in Britain, I

have never had the chance to do so abroad, particularly not in a country famous for the richness and diversity of its flora. It is an instructive exercise. To begin with, you think that you will see masses of different species all in one place, when in fact you are likely to see groups of the same species together, with occasional singletons. Altitude, geographical location, soil, terrain, aspect, human activity and, of course, time of year make an impact on what you see, and field guides can only ever give an approximate idea of what you might find. Even though I had expected to have a fuller notebook by the end of the day, the excitement of seeing plants in the wild was intense.

The other most striking feature about the day was how often I was strongly reminded, as we walked through wooded gorges, up hills or along streams, of the better kind of mature woodland garden which can be found in Surrey or Sussex, Cornwall or Argyle. The difference was that British gardens would be more colourful, especially at this time of year. That is because they have been deliberately planted for maximum effect and maintained in such a way that every plant earns its space. I was forced to the conclusion that, despite the lack of majestic mountain background scenery, British gardeners over the last 150 years or so have succeeded in some ways in out-Himalaying the Himalayas. They have condensed a month's hard trek into an afternoon's stroll. Go to Nepal, if you can. If you cannot, a visit in May, when they look their best, to any one of the hundreds of fine woodland gardens open to the public in the British Isles is definitely the next best thing.

Independent

Left on Afghanistan's Plains   *3 November 2001*

I imagine that, until the troubles there, most of us would have had difficulty placing Afghanistan accurately on the world map and, even if we could, would have been tempted to dismiss it as a barren, desolate land. However, in 1913 C.M. Villiers Stuart wrote in his *Gardens of the Great Mughals*: 'Nowhere in the world, perhaps, is spring more wonderful than in the high tableland of Persia and the mountainous countries' (that is, Afghanistan and Turkey) 'lying east and west of it. Nowhere, certainly, are there such contrasts of climate: summer's heat and winter's cold alternately strip the country bare of colour, but spring pays for all; a brief spring – only a few weeks – into which is crowded all the flowering season of the year with a wealth of bloom hardly to be realised in more equable climates such as England and Japan, where the gardens flower on gaily for many months in succession.' It is true that when winter draws on the countryside must be bleak indeed, but a number of our finest spring-flowering bulbs come from Afghanistan, among other places, so perhaps we can have some faint inkling of what it must be like to be there in April and May.

Harsh winters with snow-melt in spring and dry, hot summers are the natural habitat for many bulbs, and it is not surprising that a number of beautiful tulip, crocus and Juno iris species have in the past been collected in Afghanistan, some of which – like *Crocus korolkowii* and *Tulipa orphanidea*, not to mention the spectacular crown imperials, *Fritillaria imperialis* – we grow in our gardens. What is more, there are also a number of perennials and shrubs in cultivation in Britain which come from this region, including the amazing foxtail lilies, *Eremurus robustus* (pink) and *E. stenophyllus* (golden-yellow), as well as pink-flowered *Phlomis cashmeriana* and the sweet, single-flowered, bright-yellow *Rosa ecae*. As for alpines, you would expect a good showing from such a mountainous country, and cushion-plants in particular, like *Dionysia* and *Acantholimon*, are well represented. Unfortunately, the grazing of animals means that the length of spring flowering of bulbs and shrubs can be truncated, as anything remotely palatable is soon eaten off.

There are plenty of cultivated plants as well, despite the cli-

matic extremes. Junipers, pomegranates, mulberries, pista-
chios and walnuts all grow in Afghanistan. It is easy to forget,
since the country has been in such turmoil for so long, that the
great sixteenth-century Mughal emperor and garden-maker
Babur laid out and improved many gardens around Kabul,
including the famous Garden of Fidelity in 1508. This wonderful garden was irrigated and divided into four sections by
water channels, and planted with sugar-cane, orange trees,
pomegranates and clover, as a painting and his memoirs
prove. Babur, whom we would call a passionate plantsman
(when he wasn't subjugating unruly Afghanis), also wrote in
1504 of finding thirty-two types of tulip in the foothills of the
Hindu Kush.

Although a number of intrepid Western plant hunters have
traversed this country over the last 150 years, no botanist, as
far as I can discover, has travelled through Afghanistan since
the Russian invasion in 1979. In the twenty years before that,
however, a time of relative calm, there were a number of extensive expeditions which succeeded in adding to the body of
knowledge now encapsulated in the recently-completed and
monumental *Flora Iranica*, overseen by Professor Karl Heinz
Rechinger in Vienna. Admiral Paul Furse and his wife Polly,
for example, crossed Persia (now Iran) and Afghanistan in
1964, and found several new species, including *Iris afghanica*
and *Fritillaria bucharica*, the latter quite widely grown in
gardens now. Dr Chris Grey-Wilson and Professor Tom Hewer
travelled far and wide in 1970, finding a new dionysia and
exploring the different habitats of a country which ranges in
altitude from 500 to 6,000 metres, and from desert in the north-
west to lush pasture on the northern slopes of the central
Hindu Kush. Other adventurous botanists included the
Swede, Professor Per Wendelbo, who named a new greeny-
brown figwort *Scrophularia landroveri*, after the form of trans-
port indispensable to the modern plant-hunter in Central Asia.

I thought about all this recently when I was planting

Eremurus robustus in the garden. This foxtail lily is often treated as a bulb and sold by bulb firms but is in fact a fleshy-rooted perennial which sends up a leafless spire of densely packed, star-shaped pink flowers with prominent stamens, in early summer. I had to go to some lengths to achieve the right conditions to grow it, for it thrives best in a free-draining but fertile sandy loam, in a sheltered place. It also needs (and that is in the lap of the gods) cold weather in winter to encourage it to flower.

Paul Furse wrote in 1964 about seeing masses of eight-foot spikes of this plant in the Hindu Kush, and of how 'The lorry drivers were fascinated with these and cut them to decorate their beautifully-painted machines, tying them to bumpers and wings and body till they looked like birthday-cake lorries with pink candles.' Let us hope that now, when the eremurus bloom, Afghanis will be in the mood to celebrate and festoon their lorries once more.

Independent

Concealing a Richer Dust   22 June 2002

Two weeks ago I went to Normandy in the company of my husband and his parents, to attend a ceremony of remembrance for D-Day veterans from my father-in-law's regiment at its memorial in Creully, liberated on 6 June 1944. It was a salutary experience for someone like me, born after the war, to have the opportunity – no, more than that: the privilege – of meeting a number of courteous, jokey and self-deprecating former soldiers who sometimes gave the impression they could not quite believe their luck in having survived to old age, when they had spent their youth in such extreme circumstances. I felt this especially in the British cemeteries we visited, where clean-carved headstones mark the buried remains of men who were far more than simply names to my father-in-law: his tank driver and co-driver, killed when the tank was shelled, as well as a number of brother officers who perished in the first furious days of the invasion.

One attitude common to the veterans I met was gratitude to the Commonwealth War Graves Commission for the care with which the British cemeteries are kept. There is a serene and homely appropriateness about these graveyard gardens – consisting as they do of rows of limestone or Botticino marble headstones, behind narrow rectilinear beds of border flowers, surrounded by closely mown, fine-textured lawns – which must be as comforting to old soldiers as the thought that these cemeteries will be looked after in perpetuity.

As early as 1916, the Assistant Director of the Royal Botanic Gardens at Kew was asked to make recommendations about the plants that should be grown, and Gertrude Jekyll was also consulted. They chose principally cottagey plants, which the troops would have known from home: in front of the headstones dwarf hardy perennials, alpines and bulbs, which incidentally help prevent rainwater and mud splashing them, and roses planted beside every other one, so that they can be alternated when replaced, minimising the risk of 'rose replant disease'. There can be as many as twenty different plant species or cultivars used in a border, repeated in phases down the row.

On a June day the borders make as pretty and floriferous a picture as you could hope for, the purple young leaves of the numerous floribunda roses chiming well with pinks, dark blue hardy salvias and bright blue flax. Every so often a border has been carved out behind the headstones as well as in front, so that taller delphiniums and the like serve to break up the 'sea of headstones' effect.

In the larger cemeteries there are also shrubberies, pergolas hung with scented climbers and specimen trees, now well grown after nearly sixty years. The sheltering hedges are of beech, hornbeam or yew, except in rural Normandy – as, for example, at the lovely little cemetery of Jerusalem on the

Bayeux/Tilly-sur-Seulles road, where the trimmed boundary hedge consists of native trees and shrubs, such as you will find in the *bocage*.

These days, to husband resources, the Commission's gardeners generally work in mobile teams, but the most pernickety observer could not complain about the standard of maintenance. I scarcely saw a weed anywhere in the sandy soil. Occasionally, flowers obscure the moving personal inscriptions which are carved near the base of many of the stones, but that only serves to intensify the sensation that these cemeteries are life-affirming gardens, rather than gloomy burial grounds. Buried here are not just 'the fallen', but so many individuals, each of whom left a home and family behind, and familiar flowers give eloquent expression to that.

Daily Telegraph

The Garden at Mount Stewart   23 June 1993

There is a garden in the British Isles of such exotic magnificence and scope as to make it, in my opinion, one of the great gardens of the world. It is beautifully set beside the sea and filled with rare and tender plants which grow like weeds, placed together by a sure, artistic hand. It is well-cared-for, open to the public every day in the season, and can accommodate any amount of visitors, for it extends to 80 acres. Yet, for all its many virtues, it is seen by fewer than 60,000 people a year – a quarter the number who crowd Sissinghurst's narrow paths each summer.

Its relative unpopularity seems quite inexplicable – unless you know that Mount Stewart lies 15 miles from Belfast. Then all becomes depressingly clear: Ulster has a small indigenous population and a tourist industry which accounts for only 2 per cent of the province's GDP. To all who know what a pleasure it is to travel around Northern Ireland, that seems an injustice.

Mount Stewart is almost in a class of its own, for it combines breadth of vision, plantsmanship and the benefits for growth of an extremely mild (though not entirely frost-free) and moist maritime climate. It was mainly laid out by Edith, wife of the seventh Marquess of Londonderry, who came to live here with her husband in 1921. She was already well-known as a political hostess who entertained memorably at Londonderry House in London and founded the Ark Club, but at Mount Stewart her energy and creativity found a very different outlet.

The garden is almost continental in its eclecticism. Even a simple catalogue of its component gardens will give some idea of the number of influences working on Lady Londonderry: the Italian Garden; the Sunk Garden; the Mairi Garden (named after her youngest daughter, who slept there as a baby in her pram); the Spanish Garden; the Peace Garden; the Lily Wood; the Shamrock Garden; the Memorial Glade; the Lake Walk; the Rhododendron Wood; and so on, and so forth. Yet, considering the scale, the scheme is impressively coherent.

Very large and formal parterre gardens to the west and south of the substantial Georgian mansion give way to more informal spaces and then flowery woodland. Not only is there something to see all the year, but a great deal of care was, and is, taken with the colour schemes. (The fact that Lady Londonderry's notebooks from the 1930s still exist has helped the National Trust, who took over the garden in 1955.)

Only in the Sunk Garden can the hand of a designer – in this case, Gertrude Jekyll – be discerned, and even so Lady Londonderry only accepted the design, not the planting plan.The personal nature of this immense garden is underlined by a jokiness which speaks of uncrushable self-confidence. This is exemplified by the famous Dodo Terrace, to one side of the parterre Italian Garden, which consists of a loggia and pillars topped by cement creatures, such as dodos, which represent members of the Ark Club who were given the names of animals.* There is also the Shamrock Garden, bounded by a yew hedge in the shape of a shamrock, with the Red Hand of Ulster in red begonias and a topiary Irish harp. Change of ownership and public access necessarily blur the individuality of any private garden, but they cannot erase the stamp of Lady Londonderry's personality at Mount Stewart.

For the plantsman, this garden offers a range of unusual and tender specimens he or she is unlikely to see outside Tresco or Inverewe. Many southern hemisphere genera such as *Eucalyptus, Olearia* and *Cordyline* are well represented, and in rude health. It was a particular pleasure to find the showy Chatham Island forget-me-not, *Myosotidium hortensia*, which only thrives where there is a salt tang in the air.

That many very keen garden visitors in Britain will never see Mount Stewart is not much short of a tragedy. For those who take the trouble – and, goodness knows, it is not difficult to reach for a generation bred to travel the world, much of it far, far more dangerous for the tourist than Northern Ireland – there is a real treat in store.

Sunday Telegraph

Boots' Millennium Sculpture Garden   24 June 2000

Everyone I know with a garden seems to have marked the end of the second millennium in some way: by installing a sundial or a gate, by laying out a new border, or by planting a specimen tree – in my case a small-leafed lime, which I have hopes will survive until the next millennium. Most of us have, of necessity, thought small. Not so Lord Blyth of Rowington, the Chairman of The Boots Company, whose idea it was in 1996 to develop a Millennium Sculpture Garden at the company's

* My grandfather, John Buchan, was, by coincidence, part of this club, and known as The Buck.

14

headquarters and industrial complex at Beeston on the edge of Nottingham.

Lord Blyth wished to transform a windswept and under-utilised fifteen-acre area in front of a very large pre-war, Modernist building (one of several for which this complex is famous), in order to improve the environment for the eight thousand and more employees who work there. Until this project got under way the site, which is the size of a large village, was entirely laid out on spacious but utilitarian lines, the 'landscaping' consisting mainly of lawns, with scattered trees and shrubs. Indeed, considering Boots' pre-occupation with promoting health and well-being, and its presence at Beeston since the late 1920s, it is perhaps surprising that so little had previously been done to landscape it imaginatively.

On one part of the site, at least, that omission has been grandly remedied. The Millennium Sculpture Garden consists of four parts: planted terraces in front and to one side of the romantically-named D31 amenities building (designed by Sir Henry John Tanner in 1937, and now housing the Boots Museum); a formal herb garden; and a level grass plain beyond which is a woodland of mainly native trees and shrubs. A number of monumental sculptures are disposed about the garden, acting as eye-catchers, as well as fountains in the formal gardens, and two original verses (by John Fairfax) carved in stone set on the terrace wall.

The garden's designer, Mark Lutyens, together with nine sculptors, an inscription carver, two furniture designers, a lighting specialist and a poet, were brought together by James Knox, of Art for Work, who since 1992 has commissioned contemporary works of art for The Boots Company. Knox has acted as patron, mentor, and link between the creative elements and the company's board. In the process of development Mark Lutyens worked closely with Boots' grounds and engineering departments, the former planting and maintaining the garden, the latter making much of the furniture, and helping set the sculptures in place.

The upper terrace is laid out as a seating area, with a line of clipped, evergreen privet trees (*Ligustrum lucidum*) to provide shade and vertical accent. Below the terrace wall is a broad promenade, with on one side a rose garden, shaded in summer by *Malus* 'Everest', and two seating areas under a light pergola of pleached plane trees. Topiary is a recurring theme, and foliage texture and shape seem more important than colour, with stands of *Acanthus spinosus*, *Sisyrinchium striatum* and phormiums prominent.

On the other side of the promenade is the box-edged herb garden, shaped like a goose-foot, a reference to the founder Jesse Boot's original herbal medicine shop in Goose Gate, Nottingham. There is a central handsome carved fountain, echoed by several witty semi-circular stainless steel benches, in pairs facing each other; these are open-slatted, allowing rosemary to grow through, which releases its scent when anyone sits down. They were designed by Lutyens, a great-great-nephew of Sir Edwin and inheritor of both his forebear's capacity to turn his hand to many kinds of design, and his attention to detail. The hard landscape, the benches, the 'book-end' wood and steel pergolas at each end of the upper terrace and even some of the garden's lights are his work.

Beyond the grass plain is the woodland, a 're-creation' of nearby Sherwood Forest (and including a clone from the Great Oak itself). It contains three thousand mainly native trees and woodland shrubs, underplanted with bluebells and other flowers, and, in summer at least, already effectively hides a car park. After only two years, the bird population has significantly increased here.

What is interesting about this garden is the way it implicitly rejects both what has gone before on the site, and contemporary preoccupations: it is neither 1930s 'Modernist' nor twenty-first-century 'minimalist'; the sculptures, though wonderfully imaginative, are essentially representational, not abstract; the benches and lighting are of industrial materials, sure, but traditional in their fitness for purpose; the planting is sophisticated, unified and lively, but its soft colours and emphasis on topiary are not modern; and enormous trouble has been taken to source truly native plants for the woodland, in an area hugely disturbed by Man.

A private patron has employed an Arts-and-Crafts-influenced landscape architect committed to hand-craftsmanship and the needs of people rather than machines, to create gardens which appeal to, rather than challenge and discomfort, the onlooker. In the context of a vast industrial complex, with a backdrop of towering chimneys, such respect for the garden's users verges on the heroic. The nearby buildings may have been designed by knighted architects of terrifying eminence, and be listed up to the hilt, but they still have the power to intimidate. The garden designer's achievement has been to place them in a humane setting. Small wonder that this garden has rapidly become a favourite place for recreation, and even for office meetings on fine days. Jesse Boot, a great Methodist philanthropist, would surely have approved.

Independent

A la recherche   *28 September 2002*

It is funny, as they say, how the years roll away. Sitting in the Jodrell Laboratory lecture theatre one Friday afternoon in September, watching prizes being given out to the students who had just completed the three-year Kew diploma course, I was tugged by memories of my own time as a student there, more than twenty years ago. In that hall I had listened to lectures on plant physiology, genetics, structural botany, landscape construction, and a whole host of other things designed to turn me into a rounded horticulturist. I admit I dozed peacefully through turf culture and machinery maintenance and puzzled over surveying and entomology, but I was gripped by ecology, systematic botany and amenity horticulture. In the same place I gave my first public lecture, on the history of topiary, to the quaintly-named Kew Mutual Improvement Society, an attentive but not uncritical audience. How lucky, I thought, I had been.

For once a 'Kewite', always a 'Kewite'. At the prizegiving the Director of the Royal Botanic Gardens, Professor Peter Crane, told the students they would always be welcome at Kew. And he meant it. You belong for life, just as much as if you had studied at an Oxbridge college, or joined the Brigade of Guards. You are in the gang, and an international one at that. Kewites are to be found all over the place – in tropical botanic gardens, in large country estates, in newspapers and television, in landscape design consultancies. It is, I cannot deny, an honour of which I am proud. In my line of work alone, Kew has nurtured Alan Titchmarsh, Dan Pearson, Tony Lord, Anne Swithinbank, Graham Rice and Matthew Biggs. I feel like a Halberdier in Evelyn Waugh's *Sword of Honour* trilogy: I never want to do anything that might dull the lustre of the name.

Many of the students, then as now, had changed career, and therein lies much of their success. The bright-eyed, self-assured, clever young people I saw receiving diplomas have drive and ambition, born of real enthusiasm for plants. Sarah Morgan, who graduated that day, told me that she had spent several years in the music promotion business before a love of plants nagged so insistently that she became a gardener and applied to study at Kew. For her, the place has a real romance. Which is just as well, since the pay is not princely – although, in the circumstances, reasonable, since students are paid even for the three months of the year when they come in from the gardens for study and lectures. I do remember, slightly ruefully, trying to live a social, woman-about-town London existence in the late 1970s on £29.50 a week.

There is one difference between then and now. The students

are adventurous, and helped to be so by the burgeoning number of travel bursaries available to them. One student is shortly embarking on her *second* visit to Bhutan, another studying the flora of St Vincent, a third grappling with terrestrial orchids in western Australia. As I watched them collect their cheques, I cannot deny I felt a pang of envy, and a keen sense of opportunities missed. Ah, well.

I reminisced with Sarah about life as a Kew gardener and student: the boiler-suits, the steel-toecapped boots, the dirty fingernails, the camaraderie among friends you will value all your life, the grinding boredom of cutting grass edges in the Arboretum, the terrifying but exhilarating Plant Idents. And we talked of what it was like to do weekend glasshouse duty in summer, which could mean being quite alone in Decimus Burton's remarkable Palm House, early on a sunny Saturday morning. 'Magic!' said Sarah. 'Magic!' I replied.

Daily Telegraph

Tales from the Chelsea Embankment   29 May 1994

Chelsea Flower Show is rather like Ratty's picnic in *The Wind in the Willows*. There are showgardensgardendesign plansherbaceousperennialscarpetbeddingtropicalrainforests floraldecorationsvegetableslawnmowersconservatories botanicalpaintingshandylittlegadgets . . . If, like Mole, you feel like crying 'O stop, stop, this is too much' I can only reply, 'Do you really think so? It is only what I always see on these yearly excursions', which is why the question invariably asked on our return home – 'Is Chelsea better than ever?' – is so difficult to answer. It is true that, each year, there are certain features which distinguish it from the one before, but any judgement of quality depends more on whether your feet hurt than on any objective measure. Chelsea is the apogee of national and international horticultural expertise, in its infinitely various forms. In the face of that, facile comparisons shrivel.

What I can say is that there seems to be a collective consciousness among Chelsea exhibitors. It is inconceivable that they have put their heads together beforehand, yet certain ideas and attitudes are prominent, especially in the show gardens. This year, the urge to look backwards was again strong, an impulse approved by the judges, who gave Gold Medals to the *Daily Telegraph* abbey garden (which celebrated the work of nineteenth-century gardening clerics), the French eighteenth-century garden sponsored by *Harper's & Queen*, and *You Magazine*'s derelict glasshouse from a Dorset estate.

It did seem as if children, once thought of as antipathetic to the successful garden, received more attention. The pupils of Littleham Primary School in Exmouth designed the *Daily Mirror* garden, those of Castle School, Thornbury helped with Leyhill Prison's garden, and the needs of children were the moving force behind the gold medal-winning 'Wind in the Willows' garden, sponsored by Wyevale. Here, my childhood companions Ratty and Mr Toad, decked out in various shades of *Alternanthera*, lounged by the side of a safe river bank.

Once again you could see clearly that, for professional garden designers, Chelsea provides the chance to create gardens which they normally only dream about, hedged around as they are, day to day, by the restrictions imposed on them by clients' purses and imaginations. But buried in the plump flesh of fantasy is a kernel of realism.

Moreover, there were similarities in colour schemes. The colours in many of the show gardens and also the Marquee nursery exhibits were purples, deep blues and greys. No self-respecting display was without the vinous foliage plant *Heuchera* 'Palace Purple', the rich purple-flowered ornamental onion *Allium aflatunense*, and the grey and purple *Lavandula stoechas*. Ten years ago, all was cream rhododendron and variegated hosta.

For some plants to become almost clichés at Chelsea seems strange, especially since the gardener's skill in playing the seasonal game increases the already almost infinite variety. When you can have crocuses and hybrid tea roses flowering simultaneously, the chains of time are loosened.

The rose's reward for allowing itself to be forced into growth is the launch of many new varieties at Chelsea, some weeks before their true season. I liked the look of 'White Cloud', a pillar climbing rose from John Mattock's nursery, with ivory white flowers in large trusses on thorny stems; it is scented, and supposed to repeat well. At the other end of the spectrum is the 1994 Rose of the Year, 'Festival', a patio rose with bright crimson semi-double flowers, silvery-white on the outside. David Austin can be depended upon to introduce a few of his 'English' roses each year: 'Molyneux', a clear bright yellow with ragged petal edges, reminiscent of the old *rugosa* 'Fimbriata', caught my eye. In the herbaceous perennial line, Bressingham Plants was offering a Jacob's ladder with brightly variegated leaves, called *Polemonium caeruleum* 'Brise d'Anjou'. It seems to me an excellent plant, but best grown for its foliage; the blue-mauve flowers add little to its attractions.

In the always interesting, if underrated, scientific section I found news of work being done by the University of Derby on preserving tiny pieces of plant meristem (growing points) in liquid nitrogen at minus 190°C, indefinitely. Despite the fervent prayers of Californians, this technique of 'cryo-preservation' (suspended animation to you and me) offers no hope for humans, but it has enormous potential for saving rarities in the more adaptable plant kingdom.

The innovation which most immediately caught my eye, however, was the solar-powered lawn mower shown by Husqvarna. For the livelong day, apparently, it will move over the ground on small wheels cutting the grass with very fine rotary blades. The idea is that you leave it to traverse your lawn at will all through the season. It sleeps only when you do.

Unfortunately this machine is not on sale until next year, so we will have to contain our souls in patience till then. It will also cost about £2,000, but who cares? If it really works, it will be, like Chelsea Flower Show itself, a fantasy come to life.*

Sunday Telegraph

The following article was published a matter of days before the extra-ordinarily dramatic and tragic events which shook the stability of the monarchy in Nepal, and put in doubt a great deal more than just its flower export industry.

Himalayan Tea and Sympathy   19 May 2001

So the Chelsea Flower Show is upon us again, and we journalists must polish up our superlatives and sharpen our noses for a good story. This year, however, I find my thoughts straying often to another flower show, which I visited in the last week of April: the three-day 1st International Floriculture Trade Fair, organised by the Floriculture Association of Nepal (FAN), at the Exhibition Centre in Kathmandu.

In some important respects, it was not unlike Chelsea. It was, for example, opened by royalty, in this case by Her Majesty Queen Aishwarya Rajya Laxmi Devi Shah, and she was welcomed by the Nepal Police, who presented a Royal Salute with a 'musical band'. Her Majesty also gave away the prizes. Present at the occasion, according to the English-language daily newspaper, *The Rising Nepal*, were a great number of business, diplomatic and political dignitaries, including the Minister for Forest and Soil Conservation (I wish Britain had one of those). Although I missed this opening, it sounded very much like the stately Royal procession around Chelsea Flower Show which

---

* There are now at least two robotic mowers on the market, but they need charging by battery. They cost less than £700 . . . and I am very tempted.

begins at 5 p.m. on the Monday of the show – except, that is, that the Kathmandu venue is more Birmingham NEC than Chelsea Hospital grounds. The exhibition centre is set in a park, but it is a large, concrete-floored, metal barn without too many trimmings, although it did boast an excellent café selling Tibetan *momos* and delicious Himalayan tea, sweetened with sugar and spiced with cardamom and cinnamon.

This is the sixth annual exposition but the first international one, since of the 37 nurseries and cut-flower concerns represented, 12 were from India and Sikkim. The nurseries mainly laid their wares out on the ground or on low tables. Many of the plants were in clear polythene soft pots, and were essentially the usual crowd which you will find throughout the subtropical and warm-temperate world: African marigolds, zinnias, geraniums, petunias, antirrhinums, carnations, verbenas. They were well grown in what looked very like garden soil. In larger pots, some of them terracotta, were dahlias, anthuriums, fuchsias, bougainvillaeas, cypripedium orchids, trachycarpus palms, Himalayan pines, and strelitzias. They almost glowed with health, underlining the stated belief of the President of FAN, Anap Rai, that Nepal is a favourable place for floriculture because of its geographical and climatic situation. You can say that again, Mr Rai. After all, Nepal has more than five thousand species of native flowering plant, of which 246 are endemic to Nepal and found nowhere else.

Where this show differed from Chelsea was in the lack of crowds. Here was a different Nepal from that of the noisy, dusty streets outside: well-dressed women in elegant saris were buying non-native plants in flower for their town gardens, just as we do. The atmosphere was neither hectic nor claustrophobic, but cheerful and purposeful, despite the mild gloom of the venue. A sign on the wall above the award-winning Kumari Nursery display read: 'Promote Greenery Someway? Greenery Promote Everyway!! Take care of a plant as your child.'

Although the crowd, such as it was, was intent on buying plants, the emphasis of the organisers was on the cut-flower industry, which is also based on non-native plants, principally gladioli, roses and carnations. This market has grown exponentially from a very low base in ten years. In 1992 there were 80 nurseries in Nepal; there are now 250, gladiolus production has gone up from 150 'sticks' to 6,000 a day, and the sales value of plants and cut flowers has increased seven-fold, to Rs 70 million (just over £650,000) in that time. The rose market, especially, is doing well. Strangely, orchid sales have not grown significantly. Orchids grow in the clefts of trees in the Kathmandu Valley and the jungles of Nepal, and are fed to cattle as fodder. They are a slow-growing nursery crop, however. Experts say that increasing the market requires a strategy; indeed, although there is some government aid for the floriculture industry, businessmen complain that it is bureaucratic, and more help is needed, especially in providing cold store and transportation facilities, if the export trade is to be encouraged.

As so many people discover, Chelsea Flower Show is the Platonic ideal of a flower show, unimprovable in any very noticeable way, certainly as far as the quality of plant cultivation and the sheer impact that flowers can have on a crowd are concerned. It is nearly a hundred years since the first Great Spring Show (held in a much smaller way in Temple Gardens), and the accumulated wisdom of that century will have been tapped to produce the exhibits. It occurred to me as I walked around the show in Kathmandu that the Nepali nurserymen might just benefit from dedicated, focused help and advice from those who show at Chelsea, especially those nurserymen skilled in the nurture and the display of sub-tropical plants, as well as from cut-flower exporters like the States of Jersey Department of Agriculture and Fisheries. What Nepal has, and we could help bridge, is not a skills or enthusiasm gap but an information and technology chasm.

Independent

Welsh Wizardry 21 August 1999

For those brave, determined souls who exhibit their vegetables in large county and national shows, August is the most exciting month of the year. By now, most vegetables grown by showmen are reaching impressive maturity. This is when living tableaux of glistening white leeks as thick as your wrist, globose onions, spotless potatoes, ruler-straight runner beans and impossibly long, but immaculate, parsnips and carrots are set up, impressing onlookers (suddenly and shamefully conscious of their own short, stringy beans and bolting lettuces at home) with the skill and the attention to detail, even wizardry, needed to bring humdrum edible plants to such perfection.

Generally the names of these wizard vegetable growers are unfamiliar to the rest of the gardening world, but there is one exception. Medwyn Williams is one of the most successful vegetable exhibitors of all time, whose column in the showman's newspaper, *Garden News*, has appeared weekly for the last fifteen years (quite an achievement in itself for a native Welsh-speaker who did not learn English until he was ten). His articles are required reading for hard-to-please exhibitors, small- and big-time, who are known to paste his articles in scrapbooks. His reputation is based partly on his success as a grower of exhibition vegetables, and partly on the truly monumental trade stands he stages at major shows, like Chelsea; these are ostensibly to advertise his specialist vegetable seed business, but also provide a formidable horticultural challenge – that of producing mature vegetables in a temperate climate by late May – for a man who needs challenges like the rest of us need oxygen.

Those who have seen his Chelsea exhibits would no doubt love to know how Medwyn can possible achieve about forty kinds of vegetable at their peak so early in the season. After a visit to his home in the Anglesey village of (deep breath) Llanfairpwllgwyngyllgogerycwyrndrobwllllantysiliogogogoch, I am convinced it is partly due to his capacity for keeping meticulous diaries over many years, but mostly to minute observation of the ways these plants grow, their requirements, and how they can be encouraged or restrained. He is lucky that he can rent glasshouse bench space from University College, Bangor, just across the Menai Straits, and friends and neighbours lend him ground; but a great deal is grown simply in his back garden.

Not surprisingly, Medwyn's father is also a very keen exhibitor, and has shown at the Anglesey County Show for 53 consecutive years. I was treated to an old Welsh saying, translated as: 'Where the hen scratches, the chickens will pick up the bits.' All his adult life, even while working as a civil engineer, Medwyn has found time to cultivate and to show, winning major prizes in Wales and England, including 'best collection, six kinds of vegetable' at five consecutive National Championships of the National Vegetable Society. Now 57, he is retired from the Highways Department and concentrates on showing, judging, and selling mail-order exhibition vegetable seeds, including a number of his own selections.

Medwyn's front garden is bright with summer flowers, for the vegetables are grown at the back of the house, on a south-facing slope, terraced to provide level ground. This area consists almost entirely of raised beds made with concrete blocks, and a number of small greenhouses. Glamorous, no, but highly efficient. In the onion house, for example, the enormous bulbs grow through a covering of black-and-white plastic mulch, black on the underside to suppress weeds, white on top to reflect sun onto the foliage. In another, leeks are planted between two barriers of stout canes which support the munificent foliage, while the 'barrels' are wrapped in black plastic damp-proofing to achieve that perfect Macleans whiteness. Peas are grown on cordons, with their tendrils carefully removed; French beans are planted in pots. Each plant receives individual, and regular, attention from Medwyn and his apprentice, Paul Owen.

Medwyn belies many of the widespread but erroneous beliefs about showmen. He is not interested in growing giant vegetables, unless size is accompanied by quality. His motto is: 'If you can't eat it, you shouldn't be showing it.' He is also happy to share any secrets he has, for he prefers to pit his skill against equals. He admires other competitors, if simply because they are the only ones who truly understand the nature, and burden, of the work. His attachment to fair play would put a prep-school cricket eleven to shame. Moreover, contrary to another popular myth, he brings a forward-thinking, scientific and ingenious approach to his craft, as he says other exhibitors do, using artificial lighting, undersoil heating, complex potting composts and fertiliser regimes, but very few pesticides. The old image of the cloth-capped allotmenteer is no longer very accurate, he maintains; he numbers women and professionals among his customers. 'There are a lot of thinking gardeners out there.'

His attributes have not gone unnoticed. He is a Royal Horticultural Society judge, and is presently engaged in helping to revise the RHS's *Show Handbook*. He agrees with me that criticism of some show schedules is justified, in particular of committees not responding enough to changes in vegetable growing and fashion, and thinks that the revision of the *Handbook* is timely.

Vegetable growing at this level is not just an arcane pastime for the truly committed, but has beneficial spin-offs for 'ordinary' gardeners like you and me. The breeding work done by commercial concerns and amateur gardeners alike has resulted in major advances in recent years. Who now could bother to grow 'Tender and True' parsnip and risk canker when they can choose the resistant 'Gladiator', which does as well in the kitchen as on the showbench? We have exhibitors like Medwyn to thank for showing us what is possible.

Daily Telegraph

Cultivating Holiness
30 September 2000

There is a proud tradition in this country, stretching back at least two centuries, of Anglican clergymen involving themselves seriously in the study of botany and horticulture. You only have to think of Canon Ellacombe of Bitton, after whose garden the snowdrop 'Bitton' is named; the Revd Samuel Reynolds Hole, Dean of Rochester and legendary rosarian; the Revd William Wilks, who bred the Shirley poppy; and the Revd J.H. Pemberton, who developed the strain of Hybrid Musk roses that includes 'Penelope' and 'Felicia'. We gardeners owe a debt to these men's intellectual rigour, inquiring minds, prodigious energy, and lively sense of the wonder of God's creation.

In our age, things are rather different. Clergymen have no curates to tend their flocks and no servants to tend their households, yet often have the care of several more parishes than their Victorian forebears, since the Church of England hierarchy sometimes appears to concern itself with saving money as much as souls. Yet here and there is a cleric who still holds a torch for horticultural and botanical excellence, to the greater glory of God. One of these is the Revd Mervyn Wilson, rector for the past twenty years of Bulwick in north-east Northamptonshire, and before that of a parish in Bermondsey. Despite busy and dedicated parish work, around a handsome rectory he has succeeded in developing a locally-renowned garden where he nurtures a keen interest in the cultivation of hardy fruits.

His acre-and-a-half country garden of great charm is planted, as Mervyn says, 'for beauty and utility', full of good plants, topiarised hedges, mature trees, and limestone walls, for which this part of Northamptonshire is noted and beyond which can be glimpsed fat, woolly sheep safely grazing. There is an extensive vegetable plot, but the garden's great glory is its fruit trees – apples, plums, pears, mulberries, even figs –

planted either as standards or against the walls. The varieties have been chosen to provide a continuous supply. The apples are grown on MM106 or M26 rootstocks, which Mervyn says means less work for him as most varieties thrive better than they do on more dwarfing rootstocks like M9 or M27 (they also look more in keeping with the setting). That said, the Rector is a punctilious pruner, to keep trees healthy and fruitful. Chickens peck among the windfalls, and hives of bees ensure good pollination in our cold East Midland springs, as well as plenty of honey.*

I spent a happy afternoon with Mervyn, picking his brains about the best fruit varieties for my own garden a few miles away. Fruit, especially apples and pears, can be particular about location, and it makes sense to plant those which are known to thrive locally. Although he is wary of being dogmatic about what does best, his own garden includes a mixture of old and newish apple varieties: 'Ashmead's Kernel' (raised about 1700), 'Suntan' (1956), 'Newton Wonder' (1870), 'Monarch' (1888), 'Pitmaston Pineapple' (1785), 'Duke of Devonshire' (1835), 'St Edmund's Pippin', 'Blenheim Orange' (1740). And, of course, our local apples: 'Barnack Beauty' (1840) and 'Lord Burghley' (1834), both raised near Stamford, as well as 'Wyken Pippin' from near Coventry.

I am not the first to ask Mervyn's impressively well-informed opinion, and I won't be the last. He is probably our county's foremost apple expert, who lectures locally, identifies fruit at organised regional Apple Days, and is trusted with the grafting of rare varieties from important old orchards. His background is both clerical and horticultural, for he is the son and grandson of clergymen while his uncle, Sir Chad Woodward, had an apple – 'Chad's Favourite' – named after him. Mervyn and his wife, Margaret, cultivated an allotment at Surrey Docks when living in Bermondsey, but it was when

* My husband owes his bees to the Revd Mervyn Wilson: see page 213.

they arrived at Bulwick that a large country garden really fired his interest and enthusiasm.

The garden is run on basic organic principles, though very occasionally Mervyn will use a fungicide to keep blight on wall-trained pears at bay. There is scab, brown rot and bitter pit, as you can imagine, but more than enough unblemished fruit is harvested to cook with, give away, and make into apple juice and cider.

He may have something of the other-worldly monk about him, with his wispy grey hair, kindly, humorous expression and thoughtful conversation, but he is also down-to-earth, as happy to discuss the reasons for decline in church attendances as the genealogy of the apple 'Pitmaston Pineapple'. To him, the garden is both a peaceful place of contemplation, which he is happy to share with others, and a busy, fruitful workplace. 'Land is also for the cultivation of Holiness.' He and Margaret offer the garden and house for Quiet Garden Ministry days, to give people the opportunity for prayer, silence, reflection, and the appreciation of beauty. Several times in the year the garden is open for charity under the National Gardens Scheme: with the Rector on hand, this is a good chance to tap into some pomological wisdom.

Independent

The Lure of High and Lonely Places   18 May 2000

The Alpine Garden Society dates from 1929, probably the high-water mark of interest in rock gardening in this country, and owes its foundation in large part to the influence of a man who died nine years earlier. Reginald Farrer was, quite simply, the most idiosyncratic, individual and naturally gifted garden writer, alpine plantsman and plant collector of the twentieth century.

Although born to relative ease as the son of a Yorkshire

landowner and Liberal MP in 1880, he had miseries heaped upon him from the start. He had a cleft palate, which required surgery, and a hare lip, so he never went to school, but was brought up by a doting, blinkered, churchy mother and an uncomprehending father at Ingleborough Hall in Clapham, Yorkshire, in the shadow of the limestone Ingleborough mountain. During his lonely childhood he became a proficient botanist, finding *Arenaria gothica* on the mountain-top, the first sighting of the Yorkshire sandwort there, and making his first rock garden when he was fourteen years old.

As a young man Reginald was short, fat, camp, waspish, egotistic and trouble-making, with a screechy voice and difficult manners. At Balliol, Oxford, he read Classics and was drawn to the brightest and most attractive of the pre-war Oxford generation, Raymond Asquith and Aubrey Herbert; his suffocating devotion to the careless Herbert (the so-called Man who was Greenmantle) caused him yet more misery. His conventional parents, who kept him short of money, failed to understand his yearning for the world's recognition, and their mutual incompatibility led to acrimonious rows and silences, made infinitely worse when he became a Buddhist after a spell in Ceylon in 1907. He wrote novels and plays which were less and less well-received, and the cause of great disappointment to him.

While he was at Oxford, however, Reginald founded an alpine nursery at his home at Ingleborough, and rapidly acquired a reputation for his knowledge and his ability to grow rock plants. He may have felt stifled and misunderstood at home, but at least he grew up understanding what limestone plants from high places required. In 1907 he published *My Rock Garden*, which was an immediate success and made his name. He had found his niche. It was followed by others, most notably the monumental *The English Rock Garden*, an encyclopaedia in two volumes, his magnum opus, still useful as a work of reference today. His style was overblown but winning, witty, wonderfully colourful and forthright. Here is his description of *Eritrichium nanum,* a high alpine forget-me-not: 'But the King of the Alps . . . should be adored not touched. He is so impossible of cultivation that to take him from his native crevices seems murder as clear as to bruise a butterfly in our hands – an act more certain to put the blue heavens (whence the plant has surely descended straight and undefiled upon our dusty earth) in a rage, than any number of robin redbreasts in cages.' Or this, of *Primula secundiflora:* 'the outside of the bell is of a waxen dulled flesh-colour, filmed with a strange powdery bloom, and suffused with lines and nerves and flush-ings of claret and deep rose, with blue mysteriously suggested over the whole, omnipresent as the faintest of tints, like a whiff of onion in a good salad.' He certainly influenced the way gar-deners have written ever since, in particular the attribution of human characteristics to plants, as in 'demanding', 'miffy', 'good-natured'.

Farrer had been a keen walker in the European Alps since his Oxford days, and was surprisingly hardy and tireless. Having set up a syndicate in which garden owners bought shares in return for seed, in early 1914 he set off for the Himalayas, to Kansu, the Chinese province nearest to Tibet. This trip led to some important introductions, notably *Viburnum farreri, Buddleja alternifolia, Potentilla fruticosa* and *Daphne tangutica,* and to one of his finest books, *On the Eaves of the World.* The next year he found *Gentiana farreri* in Tibet. He was at his best when in the high and lonely places. But it was all cut painfully short: in October 1920 he died in Burma of bronchial pneumo-nia, alone except for his faithful native servants.

Nicola Shulman's fascinating short biography of Reginald Farrer succeeds in revealing as much as is possible of a man whose copious diaries were cut up with scissors by his mother after his death. I could have wished for more about his travels, successful plant acquisitions and books, but *A Rage for Rock Gardening* (Short Books, 2000) is a miracle of conciseness, nevertheless, and has the great merit of introducing Farrer to a new generation of readers, just when the world might be in danger of forgetting him. If we value the flora of the high places – and the success of the Alpine Garden Society suggests that many gardeners do – that should never be allowed to happen.

Independent

2

Garden and Plant Design

The Best-laid Plans   *26 August 1990*

There can be few topics of conversation more suitable for inclusion in 'Great Bores of Today' than the laying-out of one's garden. I find that even my best friends would really rather pretend that they have not just had to pick their way over large holes dug in the ground and half a ton of brick-shaped pavers. They are terrified lest if they show, by one chance remark, any recognition that we are having work done, I will tell them *all* about it.

We have lived in the same cottage for more than ten years, the victims, if that is not too strong a word, of other people's ideas on garden design. Now we have finally girded our loins and set out on the fiendishly expensive business of undoing those other people's ideas and imposing our own in their stead. This work consists of building some pillars and putting up trellis between them, putting in new brick steps and paths to replace concrete paving slabs and grass slopes, and laying a south-facing terrace so that there is some hardstanding for pots and also somewhere to eat outside.

The biggest lesson I have learned is how difficult it is to take one's own excellent advice. The work has, not surprisingly, required the moving of plants which were in the way of building operations. If I had been bossing anyone else, I would have laid particular – to the point of pompous – emphasis on the importance of transplanting in the dormant season, or April at the latest. In reality I have dug them up when the builders have asked me to.

The reason for this fecklessness is not lack of knowledge about where the work was to be done (although in all jobs of this kind the best-laid plans have to be modified), it is psychological. In the spring it was hard to know exactly what would need to be moved, and there seemed no real urgency. As the summer wore on and the soil became progressively drier, the thought of moving anything, especially the large shrubs (even if one had anywhere much to put them), became increasingly unattractive.

'Heeling-in', unless it is done very thoroughly, leaves roots rather close to the surface of the soil. When finally pressed to transplant shrubs I dug big holes and watered the plants well in, but I am resigned to one or two failures. It was interesting how many old-established shrubs were clinging to the soil they had occupied for many years like a child's wobbly tooth, by one or two slender strands of root.

The other psychological effect of having a garden trodden over, however carefully, is that one ceases to be able to bring oneself to weed, spray, tie in, or do any other necessary jobs with the same fervour as usual. I had not properly realised before how feeling not quite in control has a most enervating effect on one's resolve.

Although my garden may have suffered, at least temporarily, watching the work proceed has been surprisingly enjoyable. This is particularly true of the terrace. We have chosen multi-coloured clay pavers as an alternative to paving slabs, because of their versatility and their suitability in this cottage-garden setting. They look almost as if they were old bricks which have been found lying about and used, as was often done in the past by cottagers. Although they are handmade and therefore satisfying in their variety, we have nevertheless decided to lay them on concrete, with mortar joints, so that there is no risk of the pedestrian precinct look which can happen when wire-cut pavers are butted together.

The pattern we have chosen to lay them in is the same as that used for the bottom terrace at Bodnant, the National Trust garden in the Conway valley in North Wales. It consists of a succession of large diamonds filled with central bricks placed at 45 degrees to the diamond. Not just 'Great Bores of Today' but 'Pseuds' Corner' as well.

Observer

A Change of Scene*   *30 January 1994*

Gardening when you have recently moved house is an odd experience. Or so I have found. It is almost as if the garden did not belong to me, but instead I am doing the work as a favour to the real owner. Because I have so far planted nothing but merely taken over the care of the plants already there, it is hard yet to feel much affection for them. They are still somebody else's babies.

* In the autumn of 1993, we moved six miles, in order to acquire a much larger garden.

Anyone in the same position will know what I mean. For a start, you scarcely know the garden, let alone its contents. You may well have seen it only in two or three fleeting, if appraising, glimpses several months earlier. You have a memory of cherry blossom or ripening apples, and a vague impression of a shrub border, perhaps, or a rockery.

If you are like me, the photographs you took when you first visited the house have proved helpful, but they only illustrate one moment, not a succession of moments.

As for the individual plants, they are a mystery. The name and flower colour of the tree paeony whose dead wood I have just removed in an attempt to do something both useful and harmless is quite unknown to me. No mental picture of its summer glory shields me from the biting wind. For all I know, it will turn out to be quite unsuitable for its place, and work done on it will have been wasted labour*.

After a few weeks or months, depending rather on the season of your moving, you probably feel that you must do something soon; for, like every other new owner, you have taken on a neglected garden. The process of buying and selling a house is usually so lengthy and taxing that sellers give up gardening some time before the removal van arrives, and new buyers are too preoccupied initially with wiring and redecoration, drains and neighbours, and deciding where to hang the pictures. The garden has had to come second. Once you have caught your breath, the flower beds will already be weedy, the roses in need of pruning, the climbers falling away from the walls.

That being the case, it may be consoling to know that you should neglect the garden for a while longer. Few articles of faith in the horticultural canon are so immutable as the one which says you should wait a year to 'see what comes up'. Only a fool or a rich man pulls everything out in the first season and starts again from scratch.

* For how it did turn out, see page 118.

If you are a creative gardener, you may find that the first year in a new garden is a frustrating time, so I suggest you dissipate your energies in keeping weeds down, tying those climbers to the walls, and taking photographs and notes as plants emerge.

Placing a bamboo cane next to a flowering plant, having affixed a label bearing its name, is the most useful task you can do. This exercise becomes even more valuable if you add the plant's colour, height, and season of flowering. These labels then become the basis of a reference system for future designs, since nobody wants to abandon healthy plants as a matter of course, just because they are in the wrong place or not one's own choice. Some labels have a ready-drilled hole through which a piece of string can be passed, otherwise cut a thin notch in the top of the cane and insert the label into it.

What if something flowers whose name you do not know? This happens to everybody, however knowledgeable they consider themselves. Fortunately, there are a number of helpful reference books filled with clear colour photographs. That said, and pride and natural curiosity apart, the name matters far less than its colour and season of interest, if you are to be moving or abandoning plants; it only becomes truly necessary if you wish to buy more of the same thing.

The real benefit of waiting a season before making wholesale changes lies elsewhere, however. Watching carefully through the garden's year should endear many of those presently unloved, because unfamiliar and unpaid-for, plants to you. Familiarity often breeds content.

Sunday Telegraph

Where Roses and White Lilies Grow   12 June 1994

I can only have been about five years old at the time, but I still remember my mother's shock. We were driving 'the pretty way' to the railway station, a country road under wooded chalk hills, when she braked hard as she came round a corner to avoid hitting a fat-bottomed baby crawling across the road. To the left was an open wicket gate in a thick hedge, beyond which ran a straight, steep path up to a farmworker's brick and flint semi-detached cottage. Near the door was parked a large pram, from which the baby had obviously climbed. I do not remember my mother carrying the baby up the path, nor its mother's horror, relief and self-justification but, so random is memory, I do recall the garden.

Recently, after an interval of more than thirty years, I drove past that same pair of cottages. The hedge dividing one garden from the other and from the road was gone, as were the rectangular beds with their flowers and fruit bushes on each side of the path; instead, there was a gravel apron, bounded halfway up the garden by a low semi-circular reconstituted-stone wall, which retained enough soil to grow a few alpines and small shrubs. The two cottages were obviously now one, and the owners had taken the opportunity to rid the garden of the 'tyranny' of straight lines. In the process, they must have buried good soil beneath the gravel – soil which would have been fed and cultivated for a century or more. It made me feel rather sad.

From the Middle Ages until the end of the nineteenth century, gardens, both in town and country, were important for cottagers' health, and in bad times even for their survival: they grew herbs, vegetables, fruits and a few easy-to-propagate herbaceous flowers, many of them selected forms of native plants. Layout was dictated by convenience and thrift, which meant straight lines of vegetables but hugger-mugger patches of profuse annuals and hardy perennials. My farmworker's garden had been part of that long tradition.

The true cottage garden – where you can still find it – has a *Lonicera nitida* or privet hedge surrounding two large beds intersected by narrow paths. These beds, filled with 'Maris Piper' potatoes, 'Scarlet Emperor' runner beans, 'Fillbasket' sprouts and 'The Leveller' gooseberries, are hemmed by one sort of gladiolus (propagated over the years from a single corm given by a neighbour), a variety of colourful old-fashioned floribunda roses grown from slips, a few white Madonna lilies, a bush or two of lavender, and masses of aubrietia and 'snow-in-summer'. There is a native honeysuckle round the door, lily-of-the-valley in the shade near the back door, a 'Doyenné du Comice' pear on the old privy wall, and a 'Bramley' apple and a 'Merryweather' damson marooned in the sea of earth of the chicken run.

That is not what most garden-owners want these days – now that we have so much more money and education. The true cottage garden, with its unco-ordinated plantings and emphasis on produce, would not give us the scope we want for making elegant and harmonious colour schemes, using the huge range of perennial plants now available to us. Yet we yearn to share its virtues of honest simplicity, which is why gardeners – from Gertrude Jekyll onwards – have developed a stylised, sophisticated version of the real, but not quite satisfactory, thing.

The 'cottage' gardens which are being made now often have tremendous charm; their owners use good forms of old cottage garden plants, especially herbaceous perennials, and plenty of attractive foliage, but steer well clear of makeweight shrubs and coloured conifers. Annuals mean *Phacelia campanularia* and lime-green *Nicotiana*, not pot marigolds and clarkia. It has become an all-year-round garden: in the true cottager's garden, winter colour consisted of blue-green 'January King' cabbages; in the 'cottage' garden there are the mixed colours of hellebores, hepaticas and *Galanthus elwesii*.

A great virtue of the modern 'cottage' garden is that it need not be confined to cottages in the country; you can make it anywhere without feeling that you are playing ducks and drakes with your surroundings, provided that your house is reasonably modest. After all, historically, townspeople cultivated cottage gardens long before villagers did. Moreover, cottage gardens are best made on a small, intimate scale, which suits modern gardeners just fine.

Not everyone will agree, but I believe that the 'cottage' garden should still retain its regularity, even its straight lines. Or perhaps I should say straightish, for no cottage path is ruler-straight, no cottage hedge is cut with a true 'batter'. Once you introduce curving borders, island beds and hidden corners, something of the artless simplicity is lost.

Nor must the cottage gardener use wall and paving materials unsympathetic to the house's architecture, however cheap and available these may be. More even than the curves, it was the uniform reconstituted 'stone' which destroyed the congruity, and thus the charm, of the farmworker's cottage garden on the pretty way to the railway station.

Sunday Telegraph

Context is All   27 July 2002

The *Shell Guide to Northamptonshire*, which was published in 1968, refers to our village as 'Pretty and picturesque with hollyhocks against the stone'. I am sure that the author would be pleased to know that the hollyhocks bloom still in July, pressed up against the stone walls in the village street, as if trying to escape from the fumes of traffic passing by.

I have purposely added to the numbers with seed-raised strains, planting them right up close to the lowish wall which separates our garden from the churchyard next door. I love the mixture of pastel and strong colours, and even the wrapped parcels of fallen flowers which dry to look like goose droppings. The hollyhock, for many as well as myself, is one symbol of enduring rural life.

Which, on the face of it, is strange, since hollyhocks are not truly native, *Alcea rosea* coming originally from Turkey in the sixteenth century, but their association over four centuries with

41

cottage gardening makes them seem that way. Others which arrived at about the same time include potatoes, tomatoes, crown imperials, and philadelphus. A whole lot more, like walnut, sweet chestnut and ground elder, came here with the Romans and so, strictly speaking, are not native either.

So how much time must elapse before we begin instinctively to treat a plant as at least an honorary native? In particular, what plants which have become common in the last twenty years will we ever accept as appropriate in the countryside? I do hope the yellow-leaved 'Castlewellan' Leyland cypress is not one of them.

There are two problems with × *Cupressocyparis leylandii*, bred a little over a hundred years ago. No native tree or shrub, even yew, has a leaf and stem configuration quite like it, so even when neatly trimmed (and a plant which can grow four feet a year does not stay neat for long) it always seems foreign. In towns or suburbs that does not matter so much, for a living, breathing hedge will always seem so much less alien than harsh paving and a mishmash of architectural styles. In rural areas, however, where native trees and shrubs are still common, it looks much more out of place. I am stuck, for the time being, with an inherited Leyland boundary hedge in my garden, and I dislike it more than I can say. But the yellow 'Castlewellan', which is spreading like a stain across rural areas, is far worse, for our native trees and shrubs are without exception cloaked in varying shades of green.

Whenever I bring up the subject of coloured-leafed trees and shrubs, and their undesirability in the country landscape (which is quite often, since I mind about it), I encounter two opposite responses. Some correspondents agree with me that there is a case for exercising restraint in rural situations because congruity, context and tradition are fragile, and easily destroyed. Others imply (they are mostly too polite to say anything rude outright) that I am arrogant, snobbish and dictatorial, and that the garden-owner has a perfect right to do absolutely and exactly what he or she likes, regardless of situations where their planting decisions may affect others, and regardless of what they consider to be subjective aesthetics. Well, I may be arrogant, snobbish and dictatorial, but I genuinely think my reaction has nothing to do with individual taste, and everything to do with a respect for context, and a sensitivity to the agonising fragility of traditional landscape. Were I to live to be four hundred, however, perhaps I might change my mind about yellow-leafed conifers. Perhaps.

Daily Telegraph

Living Skeletons   *15 September 2001*

I have been thinking a lot about hedges lately. This will not surprise you, since mid September is the moment usually suggested for planting hardy evergreen hedges, on lighter soils at least: after the ground has become softened by early autumn rains, one hopes, but before it becomes cold, inhospitable, and inimical to rapid root growth. However, it is not the cultivation of hedges which is preoccupying me but their remarkable contribution, often unsung, to the look of gardens.

Over the years, garden-makers have established beyond peradventure that the best way to make a garden look bigger is to divide it up. Nothing shrinks a garden so much as being able to take it all in at a glance. Hedges, tall or short depending on the space to be enclosed and the degree of privacy or mystery required, are the obvious answer where walls are too expensive or sympathetic materials to make them with are unavailable. There is a slightly yielding quality to the most militarily-trimmed hedge which makes it more *simpatico* than a wall of hard-edged, wire-cut modern bricks or reconstituted stone. Hedges can form the vital link between the stern geometric lines of a house and the easier, laxer, boundaries of a garden. And of course they make the best possible backcloth to colourful borders. In the words of the great garden designer Russell Page, 'Hedges will make the living green skeleton of the garden; the rigid framework which your planting will clothe with muscles and flesh.' Quite.

The almost unique versatility of the hedge as a garden arte-fact resides in the fact that individual plants are put so close together, at 45 cm or even less, that intricate curves are just as possible as dead-straight lines. Although there is symmetry inherent in using a number of identical individuals, asymmet-ric lengths of hedge can serve the modernist's turn just as well as symmetric ones can serve the formalist's.

Their contribution to atmosphere is, if anything, even more striking. A scarcely pruned hedgerow of native species – hawthorn, dog rose, sloe, wayfarer's tree, spindle, say – speaks as eloquently of a country garden as a dunnock or a field mouse; a close-clipped, yellow-leafed privet is a sure guide to a suburban one; a 'knot' made of dwarf box points to a self-consciously historical garden, while a neat rectangle of *Berberis thunbergii* 'Helmond Pillar' is an indicator of a contemporary or modernist one. By their hedges, ye shall know them.

With such versatility and flexibility on offer it seems churlish to complain – as so many people do – that Leyland cypress grows too fast, yew and holly too slowly, that privet is too common and box too prone to blight. For we are lucky to have the range we do to choose from. Think what it takes a hedge to survive ferocious annual or biennial pruning, not to mention the unhealthy and unnatural conditions inherent in so many plants being grown very close together. Hornbeam, beech, yew and cypress become mighty forest trees if left to themselves, yet they can be kept for many years at a child's height. Hornbeam and beech, though resolutely deciduous, can be persuaded to retain their dead leaves all winter if they are pruned in early summer. These are remarkable plants, and we should resist any tempta-tion to disregard them just because they are so amenable.

The result of a careless disregard is that we do not think it necessary to spend good money on acquiring top-rate plants, and we pay for that in the end. A hedge consists of a number of identical individuals, you hope; but in many cases that hope is only pious, for seedling hedging plants are everywhere in the trade, and seedlings may be sufficiently different from each other to ensure that your hedge never looks *quite* uniform. This matters most with evergreens, like yew or Leyland cypress. If I write with a certain bitterness it is because I have, in a moment of weakness and impecuniousness, bought seedling yews, and the hedging which is such an important aspect of my garden will always slightly pain me as a result. So, make stern enquiries of any nurseryman as to the provenance of his stock and, if he says they are seedlings, do at least pick out your own plants, to try to ensure reasonable uniformity. Vegetatively propagated stock will be substantially more expensive but it is worth it, believe me.

And prepare the ground well, with plenty of organic matter in the dug trench. You will be repaid if you do. Water well, too, after planting, and protect evergreen hedges from the worst effects of cold winter winds by rigging up windbreak netting. The more trouble you take, the less you will have to complain of slowness or disease in later years. Gardens, as well as gardeners, need healthy bones.

Independent

The Importance of Good Bone Structure 20 November 1999

There was a boy at my husband's school called 'Greasy'. I know nothing about him except what I have divined from his name, and from the fact that he once wrote these deathless words in a biology essay: 'Bones are to stop your arms floping into a blob.' As the leaves finally come off the trees and the herbaceous perennials in borders are cut back, many gardens are also in danger of floping into blobs. They need some bones to hold them up.

Good bone structure is as important in a garden as it is in a middle-aged woman when the flesh first begins to thin or sag. It can be made with what we call hard landscaping – that is, paving, walling, steps, trellis, fencing and arches – but also with most evergreens, especially the tight-knit clippable ones, and those relatively few deciduous shrubs and trees with dense branches and sturdy stems. Most deciduous plants, unfortunately, lose their shape when they lose their leaves, and are inclined to degenerate into airy twigginess or blobby ground-covering. And this dormant period lasts almost half the year. They are the flesh which sags, and we need now to think how to plan our gardens so that the bone structure can show through in winter.

I am afraid it means some appreciation of the virtues of geometry, another subject likely to have stumped 'Greasy'. Garden planning is at least partly about managing space, and that you do by defining it with, or carving it up into, geometric shapes. Straight lines, especially squares and rectangles, best create a formal effect, but for a semi-formal atmosphere curves, parabolas and circles can be employed as well, or instead. Both horizontal and vertical planes need to be considered. Vertical hard structures or strong plantings will give you light and shadow in winter sunshine, and their visual impact will be enhanced when their shapes are dusted in frost or light snow. The pattern remains throughout the winter, in fact the absence of summer flowers and other clutter brings it more starkly into relief; except when there is heavy snowfall, of course, in which case the pristine beauty of a blanket of snow more than compensates for any temporary loss of definition.

Hard landscaping is plainly important for creating the garden's skeleton; but so too are plants, especially hedging, which is capable of making almost any shape you like. This is particularly true if you use small plants, like dwarf box (such as *Buxus sempervirens* 'Suffruticosa' or *B. microphylla*) which have tiny leaves and can be planted very close together. It is no accident that dwarf box has, for centuries, been the preferred constituent of parterres and knot gardens where intricate shapes were realised on the ground for the benefit of people looking down on them from the upper storeys of the house.

For a taller hedge yew is desirable, except where the soil is badly drained or as a boundary hedge next to a field where there are livestock, for all parts of this plant, with the exception of the red 'arils' round the seeds, are poisonous. If you would prefer to use another conifer but are terrified, rightly, of Leyland cypress, I suggest you use either *Chamaecyparis lawsoniana* 'Green Hedger' or *Thuja plicata* 'Atrovirens'. Other good clippable evergreens are hollies (*Ilex*) and *Osmanthus delavayi*. As I never tire of pointing out, the only really important thing to remember when buying plants for hedging is that they should all be propagated vegetatively, so that they are identical. It is vital to ask before you buy.

Hedging need not necessarily be evergreen to retain its thick-knit structure in winter: some willows and bamboos make good barriers or space dividers, and hornbeam (*Carpinus betulus*) and beech (*Fagus sylvatica*) are also both sturdily structural; moreover, if you trim these hedges in summer, the brown dead leaves will not be shed in November but will endure on the twigs until the new ones emerge in April.

Structure can also be created in the garden using specimen evergreen trees and shrubs, although it is usually fatal to dot them about any old how: like a too-liberal use of exclamation marks on the page, this will be distracting and unilluminating. They must have a purpose – guarding each side of an entrance, ending a vista, or defining a space. The revival of interest in restrained topiary in recent years points to a greater understanding of its role in the winter garden, especially when plants are placed in pairs or as edging to paths and walkways.

Late November is an excellent time for planting deciduous hedging, but evergreens are best left until the spring; unless, that is, you can find them on offer in containers and can protect them adequately from desiccating winds with green, perforated polypropylene 'windbreak material', fixed firmly to posts, not only for the first winter but for the next as well. Otherwise, spend the time in November preparing the soil well by digging out a trench, filling it loosely with a mixture of soil and home-made compost or rotted manure, and leaving it to settle until April. This sort of garden planting is absorbing, fraught with tension (because it is so important to get the measuring right) and physically tiring. However, though you may flope into a blob at the end of it, your garden certainly won't.

Independent

Thinking Outside the Box 19 October 2002

Autumn has turned the leaves of wild elder bushes to yellow and mauve, and the haws and hips are bright red, so it is not surprising if I have hedges on my mind: the farm boundaries and hedgerows of the county where I live, of course, but their domesticated garden relations as well. Hedges are deeply embedded in the culture, traditions and history of Britain, more so than we probably imagine, and their popularity for garden use owes at least something to the power of folk memory. Hedges have for many centuries been symbols of ownership, privacy and security, all aspects of life which resonate profoundly with gardeners. Boundary hedges protect us from the world outside while stating categorically, if mutely, the extent of our control.

Hedges are more than symbols, however; they are powerful and flexible garden design tools, their versatility a challenge to our creativity and inventiveness. Because they consist of many identical (you hope) individuals, capable of being planted close together and usually growing at the same speed, they can be used to make a straight line, serpentine curves, or a circle. You cannot say that of a fence, while any wall that can do the same costs exponentially more. And, although there are plenty of ugly walling materials on the market, with the exception of the yellow-leafed conifers there is no such thing as an ugly shrub or tree species which is amenable to being clipped as a hedge. Yew, thuja, hawthorn, hornbeam, beech, hazel, black-thorn, field maple, box, holly, rose, potentilla, escallonia, photinia and pittosporum: all have their particular virtues, their champions, and their place.

The straight hedge is by far the most popular kind, of course, not only to define boundaries but also to make semi-opaque internal divisions in formal layouts. Low hedges can simply suggest areas of different use, say, in a *potager*, while solid 'buttresses' can divide colour sections in a long border. Taller hedges can be used to accentuate the force of perspective and appear to enlarge a garden if two, seemingly parallel, hedges are planted progressively closer together. A straight hedge can also be used to cast shadows, or even act as a linear sculpture. In the quad of St Catherine's College in Oxford, designed by the Danish modernist Arne Jacobsen, clipped hedges are interposed between brick walls of the same height, providing contrast of colour and texture within a strictly harmonious whole.

Serpentine hedges have the capacity to make a setting seem less formal, yet still provide symmetry. Circular hedges are used to great effect at, for example, Sissinghurst, where the so-called Rondel in the Rose Garden almost completely detaches one part of the garden from another, yet provides the meeting-place for four paths. Coincidentally, it also makes a striking architectural feature – because it is so thick, neatly clipped and symmetrical – when viewed from the top of the Tudor tower.

In my own garden, a curving path has been made much more inviting by the planting of a hornbeam hedge along one side of its length. This path begins at a gap in a wall, where the first four hornbeam plants will also provide a living arch in time. Arches tempt you to walk under them, encouraging you to move through a garden in a particular direction. They are easy to make using comparatively quick-growing species like hornbeam. You simply allow at least two stems, one on each side of the path, to grow on unchecked when the rest of the hedge is clipped; then attach them to a very simple, rigid wire framework in the shape of an upside-down U, until the stems have lignified sufficiently to stay there of their own accord.

Hedge plants' ability to sustain close clipping means that their shapes can vary in thickness, and they can also be topiarised, which essentially is making shapes with living plants, and is a tradition which goes back in this country to the Romans. There is substantial enthusiasm these days for 'cloud-hedges', informally-shaped, cushiony, evergreen hedges which appear to billow and roll. Anyone who knows Piet Oudolf's garden and nursery at Hummelo in eastern Holland will know what creative use he makes of cloud-hedges, and indeed many other kinds. There are pillars, arches, pathway boundaries and, most memorably, a succession of closely-planted yew hedges which seem, from a distance, to interlock; they are cut on straight lines but at different angles, first on one diagonal, then on the other, so that they appear to dip towards each other, and the urge to pass between them is almost irresistible. In a garden where deciduous, herbaceous perennials are such dominant components, these hedges provide all-important permanent structures, especially valuable in the winter. And they can do so in our gardens as well, if we are just prepared to think outside the box.

Independent Magazine

Shady Dealings
3 June 2000

I look forward all year to early June. Don't you? Much as I love the spring, especially in the countryside and the wilder shores of my garden, there is something very special about the first flush of shrub and climbing roses, the perfect early flowers of sweet peas, the confident spikes of delphiniums and lupins, the whole part-natural, part man-made splendour of it all.

For many people, however, June is not the time of unalloyed pleasure which it ought to be, or not if they have large trees and shrubs and tall hedges in their gardens. The leaves of deciduous plants are now fully developed and the shade cast by them has achieved its full measure. These leaves will gradually darken through the summer, but the damage is already done. Those happy, carefree days of spring, full of the colour of early flowers revelling in cool sunshine, are over. From now on, it will be a struggle for many understorey plants to do much more than survive in reduced light levels, under too much protection from refreshing summer rains, and in soil systematically robbed of moisture and nutrients by larger, more efficient life-forms.

So how best to plant these areas of summer shade to provide flowers from June onwards? The best course is to take care to choose species which, in their homeland, grow in similar conditions, and so have had millennia in which to evolve to take advantage of them. We call them, loosely, woodland plants. And, although many of them flower in late autumn, winter or spring, flourishing when the leaves are not on the trees, the list of summer-flowerers is longer than you might think. It is always worth checking the provenance of any plant you have bought, or might buy, in an encyclopaedia. For the truth is that background can matter as much to a plant as to a Labour Cabinet Minister or Oxbridge applicant.

Hostas, for example, come mostly from woods in Japan, while herbaceous *Geranium macrorrhizum* and *G. phaeum* grow in the woods and meadows of the Alps and eastern Europe. These are obvious choices for shady places, as are astilbes from Japan and China, but there are also lilies which will happily grow in part shade, such as *Lilium henryi*, *L. martagon* and *L.*

pyrenaicum. The plant enthusiasts among you might like to seek out *Anemonopsis macrophylla*, a woodland plant from Japan which has 75-cm tall nodding lilac flowers from July, and is rather a poppet.

Many plants will flower more generously in the sun, it is true, but will tolerate shade for part of the day and can be used to add some colour in out-of-the-way places. *Alchemilla mollis*, for example, will give a reasonable account of itself, as will border phlox, provided the soil is fertile and moist. Nor must we ignore many of the day-lilies (*Hemerocallis*), like the fabulous *H. citrina* with clear lemon-yellow trumpet flowers which breathe fragrance on July evenings.

This year, gardeners with shady places to clothe are luckier than usual. So much rain in April and late May means that understorey plants will manage better than usual, for longer, in a moist soil. Even so, there will probably come a point in July or August when leaves will curl, flop, and droop, flowers will run to seed, and there will be an atmosphere of quiet desperation about the place, like the Happy Hour in a singles bar.

There are a number of stratagems to head off this undesirable state of affairs. Having chosen carefully, you can also improve growing conditions. There is no doubt that plants will tolerate shade more easily if they can take up sufficient moisture, especially in hot weather; indeed, there are some which will actively thrive in shade, but only if the soil stays damp in summer. Digging in home-made compost or other organic matter before planting and spreading a thick layer of composted bark, home-made leaf mould or spent mushroom compost around the plants makes a noticeable difference. (Take care with mushroom compost, incidentally, if you have an acid soil and want to grow acid-loving plants, like astilbes; it contains calcium carbonate – to help whiten the mushrooms – and will raise the pH of the soil temporarily.) You could also consider raising the crown of any overshadowing tree by removing the lower branches, and thereby lightening the gloom. All these are ways of making conditions more bearable for plants in summer, and preventing the formation of no-go areas at the border.

Independent

Taking the Waiting out of Wanting   23 June 2001

I do not normally cast myself in the role of Cassandra, I can assure you. I hate people warning me of future potential problems when the sun is shining so high in the sky, metaphorically speaking, so I try not to inflict downbeat prognostications on others. Nevertheless (ah, you knew there would be a 'nevertheless'), as we pass the longest day and gardens are looking their most alluring and floriferous, I feel the need to issue a mild warning: that this is one of the most critical moments in the year for planning future plantings.

Before you snort, and stomp off into the garden to do something really enjoyable, like picking roses for the house, you might like to reflect a moment on whether there is truly nothing, even at this moment of lush growth and generous flowering, that might be improved. Are all the beds and borders filled, but not overfilled, with plants which you like, and which contribute fully to a pleasing, attractive whole, creating just the atmosphere you wish to promote?

This is an exceptional year for wholehearted flowering, thanks to the extraordinarily wet autumn and winter, and frost-free spring. Most gardens probably look as good at the moment (provided the monumental weeds have been vanquished) as they ever do. This will be small consolation to you if your ground floor flooded last November, of course, but is good news for the rest of us. And yet, and yet . . . most of us know, deep down, that we could achieve more.

I am not suggesting you do anything very arduous. Far from it. One of the most useful tasks at the moment is to take photographs of the garden, using one of those perfectly ordinary cameras capable of imprinting the date on the photograph. If you build up a little portfolio of shots, all dated, then a number of difficulties, clashes or gaps will soon make themselves apparent. The true root of what is presently a vague disquiet may become plain. A few notes, along the lines of 'too much blue', 'nasty combination of pinks', 'gap after alliums go over', will clarify thoughts without seeming too burdensome a task for a summer's day.

I am not stating the blindingly obvious, strangely. Indeed, it is counter-instinctive. Late June is when you are supposed to bask in what you have achieved, not worry about what you have not. However, if you want to improve on what you have, you need to think about ordering plants from specialist nurseries now. This is true especially of roses, the rarest of which always sell out quickly (and nurseries work on a first-come, first-served basis, as you would probably expect), as well as irises, even though the former are not actually sent out until November, and the latter in August and September.

Certain sorts of bulbs, in particular autumn crocuses (like *Crocus speciosus*), colchicums, sternbergias and prepared hyacinths, also need to be ordered now or soon. Specialist bulb nurseries, like Broadleigh Gardens, for example, have a separate dispatch date for these bulbs in late August or early September, to ensure they are planted early, leaving the bulk of the spring-flowering bulbs to be sent out from mid September to mid November. Crocuses and colchicums planted in early September will flower in October, for the bulbs already have formed flower buds inside. 'Prepared' hyacinths which are to be forced will provide flowers at Christmas if planted in bowls at the same time.

Not everyone wants to order from specialist nurseries, of course; in which case they should haunt garden centres instead. There is no doubt that most gardeners find it easiest to plant their garden successfully if they buy plants when they are flowering, or at least at their most rudely healthy. There is no shame in this, for not everyone is gifted with an accurate colour memory, and the photographs in books can mislead. Most people do not want to buy roses, for example, when they are just three sticks in a pot. Buying plants now has the advantage of taking the waiting out of wanting (so important to our generation) and, provided we do not give in to impulse as a matter of course but have some kind of plan of what we want, it has some benefits. Late June is still not too late to plant containerised plants, provided the soil is prepared well beforehand with organic matter and watered, the top of the soil mulched, and the roots watered regularly in dry weather. Otherwise, you run the risk of the plants dying in double quick time. I mean it. It is true. But the trouble with being a Cassandra, of course, is that you are destined never to be believed.

Independent

Sunset Boulevard *30 October 1999*

For a short period of my life, in the early 1980s, I designed other people's gardens. It was an instructive experience, although not one I should necessarily like to repeat. The fact that I did it for only a short time was not – I insist – from a lack of knowledge, aptitude, or expertise, but rather from a faulty personality. I just did not have the necessary character either to withstand the ill-tempered sniping between married clients who could not agree with each other and wanted me to act as referee, or to charge anyone the proper rate for the job, at a time before it was generally appreciated how expensive the business was if done properly.

I wish, however, that, while I was doing it, I had been given a pound for every time a client said to me 'I like all flower colours – except orange, of course.' Why 'of course'? I could not understand this strange antipathy towards the colour orange then, and I do not understand it now.

Recently I visited Sissinghurst Castle in Kent, the National Trust garden developed by Vita Sackville-West and her husband, Harold Nicolson, from 1930. It was the day before it closed for the winter. The garden generally had a *fin de saison* (or perhaps, since it was 1999, *fin de siècle* would be a more appropriate expression?) look about it, as you would expect in mid October, although it is always a pleasure to be there. However, I knew that even at that time of year there would be something sufficiently thrilling in the South Cottage garden to stiffen the sinews and summon up the blood, and I was not disappointed. This is a comparatively small but always densely planted part of the garden, where the colour scheme has for many years been predominantly yellow, orange and scarlet. As Vita Sackville-West described it in her column in the *Observer* in 1955: '. . . a muddle of flowers, but all of them in the range of colours you might find in a sunset'.

The first object that strikes the eye in this garden is the enormous round copper tub in the centre. When I saw it, it was planted with the half-hardy, small, lax, shrubby *Mimulus aurantiacus* var. *puniceus* (what we used to call *M. glutinosus*). 'Aurantiacus' means orange and 'puniceus' means scarlet, so its flower-colour can be imagined; personally, I find it reminds me in depth and tone of an ever-so-slightly sucked orange Smartie. These flowers are set off well by dark green, narrow, sticky leaves, but even better by the verdigris patina of the tub.

Close by were a couple of other orange scorchers: the half-hardy annual *Tithonia rotundifolia* 'Torch', a plant closely related to the zinnia and with the same demand for hot dry summers, and the very unusual half-hardy sub-shrub *Leonotis leonurus* or lion's ear, which looks like a healthy, vigorous, bright-orange-flowered bergamot. The garden fizzed with vigour and life. Despite the lateness of the season (and the fact that there had been two slight frosts that week) the dahlias were still in full flight, in particular a short one with purple foliage and orange single flowers called 'East Court'. This is not widely available but in a sense that does not matter, for there are other similar ones to be found in dahlia catalogues.

Of course these orange flowers were not set in isolation but among scarlet-flowered cannas, yellow *Bidens*, the deep scarlet rose 'Dusky Maiden', dusty-red *Arctotis* 'Flame' and other plants at the same end of the colour spectrum, and with comparable strength of colour. Orange flowers need a context, it is true, but that is easy enough to give them. The deep bottle-green of a yew hedge is an excellent foil, as are the many purple-leafed shrubs and plants currently so much in vogue, especially those like *Cotinus* 'Grace' whose leaves turn from purple to scarlet in late autumn.

In my own garden, I am presently enjoying the long-lasting burnt-orange flowers of *Chrysanthemum* 'Cottage Apricot'. 'Apricot' is a common euphemism for 'orange', I find, for nurserymen know how chary gardeners are of that word. I used to call this plant 'warm apricot' too, but I really think that bronzey-orange is more exact. Whatever it is, it works if planted in conjunction with violet-blue asters such as 'Barr's Blue', and the angular sprays of lilac-purple *Verbena bonariensis.* I do not want pastel colours or subtle effects at this time of year, when I have to view the garden through a mist of drizzle or in a restless wind. I want plants that rage against the dying of the light.

Of course there are instances when orange can be too bossy, too dominant, too keen to show up the timidity of other flower colours, and there are also times in the season, such as mid-summer, when blue-reds rather than yellow-reds seem to fit one's mood more exactly. But in autumn, when the leaves on trees and shrubs are showing how beautiful orange can be when blended and melded with scarlet and yellow, it seems only right to mirror the effect closer to earth.

Independent

Let It Be
1 April 2000

Contrary to the wishes of many gardening commentators (and I reluctantly count myself among them), there are plenty of people who are quite content with their gardens as they are, and have little desire to change them. It is true they may enjoy items in the media describing new, original or wacky ideas in garden design, and they may be curious to catch a glimpse of new plants, but that does not mean that they have the slightest intention of trying out either novel plants or a new layout in their own gardens, conscious as they are that any improvement in look may be illusory, or may not justify the effort involved or the long wait for maturity.

Who can blame them? These gardeners may well have made their gardens years ago, but they still feel an intense thrill each spring as the same, much-loved plants emerge in the same place and go on to flower in – more or less – the same order. These gardeners can even rely on weeds for continuity: hairy bitter cress and groundsel in the vanguard, followed by goosegrass and speedwell, then nettles, and finally bindweed bringing up the rear. In a fast-moving, uncertain world there is a lot to be said for staying put, and letting your garden do the same. The following remarks are therefore addressed to all those discerning readers who are at this moment making a garden which, once done, they hope will stay done.

They, and I, appreciate that this can never be entirely possible, of course. Planting a garden is not like decorating the sitting-room. The biggest obstacle is the dynamic of plant growth; all vegetable matter changes in the course of the year, and that change often includes expansion. Nevertheless, it is possible to concentrate your attention on those plants which do their changing slowly, even imperceptibly, while avoiding plants which die out suddenly or prematurely, those which grow very fast and don't know when to stop, and those which need a lot of fussing over each year.

Among the attention seekers you have to place Leyland cypress very high on the list. A hedge of this plant won't do with just one trim a year like yew or beech: it has to have two, if not three. It is doubly damned in this context by there being no upper limit to that growth. Other offenders include privet, periwinkle (both *Vinca major* and *V. minor*), certain bamboos and grasses, Chinese lanterns (*Physalis alkekengi*) and Virginia creeper (*Parthenocissus*). But in this class you can also include annuals and biennials, in fact all bedding plants which require you to replant your borders, or part of them, twice a year. And vegetables are a no-no, unless you think only in terms of perennials such as asparagus, and globe and Jerusalem artichokes.

Instead, I suggest you concentrate on slower-growing yet handsome and tidy evergreens, such as yew, osmanthus, hollies and many viburnums, together with dwarf or slow-growing conifers. Choose also perennials without a reputation for rampageousness, such as pulmonarias and most herbaceous geraniums (though avoid *Geranium* 'Wargrave Pink'), and all those which actively dislike being bothered and disturbed, like platycodon and dictamnus.

Almost as infuriating to gardeners determined to be contented with their lot are those plants which die out suddenly, leaving gaping holes in otherwise perfect schemes. Particular offenders are fast-growing, slightly tender shrubs such as ceanothus, abutilon, and cistus. None of these make old bones, so I should avoid using too many of them.

At the other end of the scale there are tough, hardy plants which, once in, will go on doing their stuff until Hell freezes or the garden is sold off as a building plot, whichever is the sooner. Flowering bulbs, especially small ones, spring immediately to mind. Remnants of Victorian gardens still exist where snowdrops, aconites, *Crocus tommasinianus*, and Madonna lilies (*Lilium candidum*) still bloom each year when all around is ruinous. And there are plenty of shrubs which, provided they are pruned occasionally, will last pretty well for ever. Who ever saw a forsythia or philadelphus die of old age?

I have to admit that, although I sympathise with all those who wish to make their garden, then leave it be, I am constitutionally unsuited to doing the same myself. It seems to me that it is possible to create very nice gardens this way, but I could never quite make the sacrifice of growing dwarf conifers. And, truthfully, I believe that there are times when even the most settled of us feel the need for a little excitement in our lives. I find that excitement at this time of year by sowing ephemeral, but really charming, hardy annuals. Sorry.

Independent

3

Practicalities

When the Living is Easy 29 June 2002

A light and not unpleasant melancholy, like a brief, thin
summer rain, descends upon me when the longest day is past.
I would never go so far as to say that the best was over for
another year, but I do mourn the slow recession of the light
and, with it, the opportunity to be working in the garden on
summer evenings.

I am sure, indeed I know, I am not alone. The first thing that
many people do on arriving home on a June evening, after
greeting the wife, the children and the dog (although not necessarily in that order), is to step outside to see what might have
unfolded its petals that day, and to sniff the mock-orange-
scented air. I know, because people tell me so. And can there be

any greater restorative, any more soothing balm to the savage breast?

For just as many people, I guess, early summer weekday evenings are the only times they have for garden work apart from the weekends, which the world will insist on cramming full of perfectly pleasant but time-consuming Speech Days, sporting events, al fresco lunches, and interminable weddings. So, however tired the legs are after a rush hour of strap-hanging, however painful the head after a boiling hot traffic jam, it is out into the garden after supper, to see what can be achieved in the couple of hours before the light fades.

Two blessed hours, not for energetic weeding, for that is too tiring, but for essential, enjoyable little jobs like thinning carrots, tying in the shoots of rampant clematis, sowing seed of biennials in a nursery bed, picking strawberries or flowers for the house, and removing the sideshoots from sweet peas. These are all things which are easily forgotten during periods of macro-gardening (which means weeding and mowing, mostly) on a Sunday afternoon, and they are noiseless occupations, far removed from the whirr and growl of shredder and mower. No one wishes to disturb their neighbours' peace – nor yet their own.

Two hours, too, when thoughts can break free from all the frustrations and anxieties of working life, when both triumphs and disasters can be seen for the imposters they are, when the thrush sings in a tall thuja, collar doves coo softly in the apple trees, and the colour bleaches slowly out of the roses. Tuesday evenings are my favourite, because that is bell-ringing night in our nearest town, and from the tallest steeple in the county the immemorial strains of 'Bob Doubles' drift across the streets and fields towards me.

And I do believe that those hours spent at midsummer – finishing any left-over planting, weeding among seedlings, quietly observing plants, noting good colour combinations, pouncing on incipient pests – can make the difference between gardening success and failure for a season. There are even a couple of jobs which it is absolutely crucial to do at this moment. One is summer pruning of pears and apples grown in 'restricted' forms (that is, espalier, cordon, fan and pyramid), which needs to be done when this year's shoots have become woody at the base, shown by the darkening green of the leaves, which usually happens in late June or early July. The other early July job is sowing Oriental brassicas, for they are shockers for bolting if sown before the longest day. I shall be outside in the evenings next week. Will you?

Daily Telegraph

A Rare Treat   25 May 2002

Last week we should have been in Greece, walking in mountains and looking at wild flowers. We booked the holiday in January, and since then I have been studying maps and botanical field guides so that we might squeeze every moment of pleasure out of a precious short week. For twenty years I have wanted to visit the Mediterranean at this time of year, and it looked like I had finally made it.

In the end, we didn't go. My husband had not recovered from an illness in time, so we cancelled the holiday. I suppressed imaginings of rocky hillsides bright with purple *Iris attica*, yellow *Ophrys lutea* or white *Cistus salvifolius*, and planned a week of solid gardening instead.

As events turned out, it was the best thing that could possibly have happened. This May has been quite trying for conscientious gardeners, for the combination of moist soil and higher-than-average temperatures has encouraged extravagant growth. I had been metaphorically wringing my hands before our projected departure about the staking, tying and mowing desperately needed, not to mention keeping the kitchen garden weeded and putting straw round the strawberries. Now, there was nothing to stop me doing something constructive about it. Even for me, an uninterrupted week in the garden is a rare treat. And so it transpired that I passed some of the most pleasant gardening hours since the days when I was a paid professional gardener and felt that I had all the time in the world to do 'a proper job'.

Most gardeners, let us face it, must snatch some pretty unforgiving minutes for gardening. Tasks are often skimped or abandoned as impractical from lack of time or opportunity, not from necessity. Last week, on the other hand, I had the luxury of attending minutely to the young espalier-trained pear trees growing against walls. The first tier only has been trained so far. The lengthening shoots suitable for the next tier needed to be carefully tied with raffia to short canes, angled at 45 degrees, which would support them until the autumn, when growth has slowed and they could be lowered to the horizontal. It was painstaking, patient and utterly absorbing work, carried out with the sun on my back and the sound of a distant cuckoo in my ear. I could not have been happier or counted myself more fortunate if I had been sitting in a taverna looking out towards a caerulean sea. What is more, I had been saved from the disappointment that inevitably attends travelling, according to Alain de Botton, as a result of having to take me and my hand-wringing along.

Needless to say, I did not achieve everything I planned at the beginning of the week. Nevertheless, by the end the balance in the garden had altered, shifting decisively back my way, so that equilibrium has been at least temporarily restored. I look with pleasure at what is flowering or soon to flower, and am no longer fatally distracted by imperfections. That change alone has been as good as any rest.

It was the reserves of patience I discovered in myself that was the best feature, confirming my belief that (to misquote Janis Joplin) patience is just another word for nothing else to do. All too rarely, I realise, do I say to myself: 'This job takes as long as it takes.' Yet therein lies the deepest satisfaction. Even the rough, tough jobs acquired a certain serenity in this unusual frame of mind. I might be strimming docks of Herculean proportions, but the work could be done at a measured pace. I could stop when I liked, to listen to the thrush or watch a charm of goldfinches rise up in a flutter from a patch of groundsel. Best of all, wherever I was in the garden, I had the time to look, really look, at my plants.

Daily Telegraph

Cut off their Heads!   *13 July 2002*

Gardening is full of myths. One of the more enduring is that dead-heading is what delicately-nurtured females did in the garden in the old days to give themselves some vaguely useful occupation when they wanted to be outside in the summer. I blame those post-war drawing-room comedies, when the likes of Celia Johnson would enter through the French windows, trug basket and secateurs in hand – for how could any horticultural task be taken seriously when done by a woman in a floaty dress and straw hat?

Yet, for me, dead-heading is one of the most important ways of spending time in the summer. I do it almost in my sleep. A walk to the kitchen garden or compost heaps, which leads past a mixed border, is a stuttering progress as I nip off a dying head here and there, stuffing the browning debris in whatever pocket is available. I have been known to scatter decaying petals along the pew when reaching for my collection in church, but I cannot change my ways.

Nor do I want to, truthfully. I confess I wish to trigger a hormonal chain reaction in plants by removing their seed-bearing organs. That is because plants which flower early in the summer, in particular, have an enormous and, for us, satisfactory impulse (I won't say *com*pulsion, because it would look as if a plant thought about it) to produce more flowers to compensate for those abruptly lost.

In this garden, herbaceous geraniums, delphiniums, garden pinks, lupins, phlox, all throw up more flowers if punctiliously dead-headed, while it is an obvious impetus to repeat-flowering roses to settle on the task of making more flowers. It is also the only way of keeping the really promiscuous seeders like *Alchemilla mollis* in check.

With many plants, such as rhododendrons, it is a simple matter of snapping off the seed-heads, but I find the neatest way with roses is to cut a few inches of stem to above the first leaf. I never remove any leaves with the stem, as used to be advised, for the plant needs all the healthy leaves it has, especially considering how many succumb to blackspot in the course of the average summer. If I am pushed for time, I just snap them off where they would naturally drop if left to themselves, about an inch below the flower-head.

The difficulty with all dead-heading is deciding whether to sacrifice those few flowers which are left when most are going over, or to return in a week's time for the stragglers. Personally, with the exception of penstemons and repeat-flowering roses I go for all or nothing, for generally only those people with relatively small gardens can realistically contemplate daily passes.

If I did not dead-head, when would I ever really touch my plants, except by accident when weeding, or in a once-a year-prune? Last week I cut every flowering head from a carpet of *Stachys byzantina* 'Primrose Heron', as they are rather coarse and floppy and I grow this plant for the yellow cast to its felted silver leaves. It was an intensely sensual experience, for 'lamb's ears' are as soft as a Labrador puppy's, and I really cannot think of higher praise than that.

So dead-heading is the most tactile of occupations, teaching me aspects of my plants which would be hidden from me otherwise. Plants reveal their distinctive personalities partly through their texture, after all, and I cannot possibly discern that fully with my hands in my pockets.

Daily Telegraph

'Tis an Unweeded Garden that Grows to Seed 19 June 1999

If I ever feel real self-doubt in the garden, May and June is when it clutches me by the throat. This season has seen my confidence dribble away like water through sand, for I am forced to admit that, if there is a boss in the garden, it ain't necessarily always me. In my established flower borders, at least, the weeds have got the better of me.

Keeping on top of weeds is as much a matter of personality as circumstance. Successfully ridding your borders of the ones that matter while ignoring those which don't depends on courage, ruthlessness and realism quite as much as time, energy or expertise. No one has enough time to weed their garden properly (by which we mean completely) if it is anything larger than a pocket-handkerchief, so the most successful gardeners are those who know when and where to strike, and do so with conviction; in particular, they make it a high priority in spring. I must reluctantly distance myself from their number this year, for though I know what to do, I have not always done it.

The weather has not helped. The last nine months have been comparatively wet and mild, conspiring to produce a crop of weeds this summer of quite gargantuan proportions, and limiting the opportunities for doing something about them. But that is no reason for giving up.

Anyone who is serious about weeding effectively needs to know the difference between a perennial and an annual weed. Many annual weeds can be left (provided that they are not visually intrusive) at least until they flower; the exceptions being those sneaky little ones like shepherd's purse, hairy bitter cress and groundsel which flower and seed several times through the season and, in mild years, all year round. But goosegrass, annual grasses, speedwell and sowthistle only require attention when they are about to set seed, or if they become infested with aphids and other insects which also threaten cultivated plants.

Even if you do not know their names, you can tell they are annual because they have only rudimentary root systems. The roots of perennials are more extensive and can be a good means of identification: perennial nettles have stringy yellow roots; ground elder has fat, white, shallow roots; couch grass, thin pointed runners with very sharp points; bindweed, thin, solid, creamy white roots.

Some people use a garden fork for digging up these weeds, but I prefer to get down on my knees, on a foam mat, and use a sturdy hand fork. That way I can burrow under shrubs and roses more easily. I put the roots of perennials in a separate bucket, for they must be burnt, or bagged up and thrown away. Putting them in the compost bin is the equivalent of deliberately sowing tares among wheat, for one day soon they will end up back in the borders again.

Old gardeners will shake their heads and tell you that perennial weeds can grow from tiny portions of roots, and that you can never rid your soil of them entirely. Frequent, consistent attacks, however, undoubtedly weaken them substantially. My greatest bugbear, bindweed, can be eliminated entirely in time, provided you don't object to using weedkiller. You place bamboo canes in the soil next to bindweed when it first appears in mid spring. Then, when it has obligingly climbed up the stems, and before it flaunts its beautiful but insolent white trumpets at you, use an old paint brush to lightly coat each leaf with diluted glyphosate, a systemic herbicide which kills roots as well as leaves.

Mercifully, the present weed surge is a temporary phenomenon, which is just as well or I might be tempted to shoot myself. By mid-July plant growth is almost visibly slowing, and there is a chance (provided the soil is not rock-solid by then) to get topside of the weeds, as we say round here. And each July is so pleasant in the garden that it brings on a blessed amnesia. Until next year. My resolution must surely be to set aside a small portion of every day next March and April to weed, weed, weed. It will make all the difference to my self-esteem. What about you?

Independent

A Darned Long Row to Hoe   30 June 2001

'Keep pushing your hoe through' was an eminently practical and common command when I was a student gardener at Kew in the late 1970s, especially from the man who organised and marked the vegetable plots which were entrusted to our imperfect care in the first year of our training. This phrase became an ironic greeting between students (we were an unsophisticated lot), thanks to its faint suggestiveness. The phrase jangled in my head during the many hours I spent trying to outdo the efforts of my contemporaries in the creation of an allotment of neat orderliness and high productivity. For I was as fiercely competitive as the rest, and knew perfectly well how heavily weighted the marking would be in favour of those plots which were weed-free on the day randomly chosen for adjudication.

In due season I harvested quite heroic quantities of kohl rabi and beetroot, summer cabbage and cauliflower, which I with difficulty offloaded on my richer, more blasé, non-gardening London friends. Only the sweet corn (which they might have been grateful for) failed to mature, ravaged unceremoniously by rats which scurried up at night from the River Thames nearby.

I have no doubt that the success we enjoyed depended as

much on that hoe-pushing as on the monumental quantities of manure, produced by Metropolitan Police horses, which was dug in each winter. We were taught that we should skim the sharpened Dutch hoe over the surface of the soil as lightly as a swallow skimming a pool, so that the tops of the weeds would fall and shrivel quickly to pale ghosts in the sunshine. The Dutch hoe was never meant to sort out perennial weeds, except in as much as the regular removal of green leaf growth would dampen their enthusiasm: it was, *par excellence*, for defeating annual, seed-raised weeds which compete with such vim and vigour for any nutrients and moisture in a plant's rhizosphere. We were also taught to hoe methodically to and fro, even where we could not see any tell-tale disorderly green growth, on the grounds that any germinated weed, however tiny, would soon make its presence felt. This was a counsel of per-fection, to be sure, but it haunts me to this day, so that hoeing is not the relaxed, agreeable, brain-idling occupation it should be, but a ferociously purposeful task.

I was an enthusiastic hoer in those days, for I had learned early. The sound of the clash and clink of forged steel on stone accompanied my childhood, for my mother would hoe her large rose beds on many afternoons in summer. In the 1960s rose beds usually only contained roses, so there were expanses of brown earth between in which to scuffle and shuffle. Because offering to help gave me her undivided attention (I come from a very large family), I could hoe with some skill long before I could name the weeds I cut down with such energy.

Of course, in the intervening twenty years since I left Kew, much has changed. Some people no longer grow their vege-tables in the straight rows for which the Dutch hoe, with its small head and long handle, is so eminently suited; or they grow them in narrow raised beds, where a short-handled onion hoe is often more useful. Many other gardeners are punctilious about laying down mulches to suppress annual weeds and avoid the use of the hoe; 'mulch' was a word that I do not ever remember hearing when I was a child, and certainly I never saw anyone use such a thing. These days, even among those who do not always get round to spreading mulches, there is a widespread belief that the hoe is an offensive weapon which removes just the kind of seedlings it might be interesting to keep.

All this I know, but I still feel that there are one or two places in many gardens where a deftly-brandished hoe is just the ticket: where drought-loving plants are grown in gravel rather than soil; in borders where half-hardy annuals predominate; between permanent fruit bushes, and in conventionally-organised vegetable gardens. The hoe not only breaks up and aerates soil after heavy rain but can be used in summer to provide a dry surface, to prevent further evaporation into the atmosphere from below in the soil.

Moreover, if you cannot get on with the Dutch hoe, there are two other kinds which can be wielded even more precisely, the 'swoe' and the 'winged weeder'. The 'swoe' has a bent neck and a thin stainless steel blade, making it look rather like a lightweight golf club, and it is excellent for getting at weeds close to plants. The 'winged weeder' is triangular in shape and can be both pushed and pulled.

What do I use? Well, as was probably just, I inherited the forged-steel, small-headed, wooden-handled, worm-ridden hoe which my mother used all those summer afternoons long ago, and I use that. I think I should be sorry if I could not give way to sentiment from time to time, even in the furiously practical matter of hoeing weeds in the garden.

Independent

Small Is Beautiful   *18 May 2002*

'A garden should be rather small, Or you will have no fun at all' is a rhyme which strikes a chord with me. Nine years ago we chose to move from a house with a small, manageable garden to what might be aptly called 'a challenge'. Why do gardening commentators talk about those with 'only' small gardens? What about those of us with 'only' large gardens? At this time of year, we are the ones to be pitied, patronised, even laughed at, for our foolishness in taking on such a commitment.

As an ex-small gardener (by acreage fractions rather than physique) I know that no task ever takes very long or is very hard. Nothing is completely exhausting, bank- or back-breaking, or daunting. There is even a whole race of plants which might have been deliberately designed for small gardens – namely, alpines and rock plants, an enormous number of which can be crammed into a confined spot, and which never look so good in the wide open spaces of the large garden.

The main thing the small gardener lacks (although I admit that it is a lot) is choice in larger plants, and variety generally. The frustration of not being able to grow certain apparently indispensable trees, shrubs and climbers is intense at times – and was admittedly a factor in our move – although the large gardener cannot find the right conditions for everything he or she wants, either. There are also the understandable frustrations of having no space to put up mini-goalposts, no feeling that you can really get right away from your neighbours, however nice they are. Only these drawbacks prevent the small gardener's happiness from being complete, I should have thought.

An account of a typical mid May in this garden might help reconcile small gardeners to their lot. This month is less the season of birdsong and fresh flowers than of non-stop fire-fighting. When I used to put my feet up on the terrace on a sunny day, now I am thrashing through the rankest weeds behind a wheeled petrol-driven strimmer, the sweat standing out in beads on my forehead, cursing every time I catch the trunk of a carefully nurtured tree or wear out or snap the plastic cord, which I know will require a fifty-yard tramp back to the toolshed for another.

I am beset by the constant feeling that I should be somewhere else, doing something else. There is little time for admiring handiwork or sniffing the flowers; little time for social life or reading novels, come to that. Any task I attempt – from pricking out seedlings to weeding the fruit cage – takes most of the afternoon. Some jobs, such as painting the fence, require a week's holiday to complete, and so are studiously avoided. Although I have, if I am spared, another thirty years of gardening in me, I worry fitfully at this time of most vigorous growth about how I shall manage as I get older. Many of my design aims centre on planting trees and shrubs that can grow into a 'wild' woodland, and borders near the house which are tenanted with properly vigorous yet well-behaved plants, against the day when I can no longer bend to weed, or be bothered to prune.

I don't worry often, though. Mostly, I am too preoccupied with what I should be doing now to bother about the future. And, to tell the truth, stemming the tide of docks and nettles in the wilder parts is only half the story, for there are some lovely jobs as well. Who does not find pleasure, on a sunlit evening, in sowing vegetable and hardy biennial seeds, thinning lettuces, hoeing carefully between the rows, nipping out the sideshoots of tomatoes grown in the greenhouse? Or digging up and heeling in spent tulips, collecting the seed of winter aconites and snowdrops, taking leaf cuttings of streptocarpus, moving half-hardy annuals in and out of protection to harden them off, tying in the stems of sweet peas, staking perennials, or checking the roses for incipient blackspot? Now I think of it, these are all tasks that small gardeners can enjoy just as much. Lucky things.

Daily Telegraph

The Cutting Edge   *19 April 1997*

Like it or not, there are basic differences between the sexes. Apart from the obvious ones (women cannot remember football results for longer than it takes to cross the kitchen and silence James Alexander Gordon; men believe that a shopping list is just a first draft, open to adventurous revision), there is also a marked gender divide in gardening. For so many men, and so few women, gardening has always meant 'lawning'.

For many decades, the care of the lawn excused men from doing much else in the garden. So exigent were its demands that nothing more could be expected of a busy man. And, to tell the truth, we women were happy to leave them to it. After all, lawn maintenance meant grappling with mowing machines of obscure design and obscurer operation, impossible to start and even harder to stop, which seemed to us noisy, dangerous and polluting; machines which had minuscule grass boxes needing repeated emptying onto mounds of clippings which heated and festered into a black goo; machines which required frequent bouts of tinkering, a full complement of spanners, and a broad agricultural vocabulary.

That was just the mowing. Care of lawns also seemed to entail a dreary succession of other tasks, such as 'spiking' and 'scarifying', feeding and weedkilling, which were hard but not interesting labour, and were especially onerous at just those times of the year (spring and autumn) when we had more than enough to do elsewhere.

Over the last few years, however, something of a revolution has taken place in the world of the green sward. Most marked is the way that the rotary-bladed mower has largely eclipsed the cylinder mower as the machine for general use. Sixty per cent of mowers sold now are rotary machines. The 'finish' these produce is not so good as that of a cylinder-bladed mower, because it is impossible to cut so low, and the coarser types of grasses flourish at the expense of the finer; but we have learned to live with the compromise because these machines are lighter and easier to manoeuvre, and the whole business takes a great deal less time.

Lawn mower engines such as the almost ubiquitous Briggs and Stratton start without brute force, and even sometimes at the first pull or turn of the switch. Many machines now run on unleaded petrol. Those people who don't want to wake the neighbouring dead, and have a small lawn, can use an electri-cally-powered machine which affords much the same sensa-tion as vacuuming the sitting-room carpet. Small rotary machines can be fitted with plastic blades, which will cut down the risk of toe amputation. Some are available with back-rollers, to provide that much-loved stripey effect once the sole province of the cylinder mower. You can now buy larger mowers, both 'ride-on' and 'walk power', whose blades cut the grass up so small that it need not be collected in a box and dumped but can be left on the lawn; the clippings will eventu-ally degrade and help feed the lawn and, in the meantime, are too small to be easily and annoyingly tracked into the house. Should there still be cuttings to be dumped somewhere, there is a product ('Biotal Garotta') which will rot them into usable compost. Grass seed mixtures are available which grow com-paratively slowly, thus lengthening the intervals between mowing.

There is a substantial range of dedicated products for feeding, weeding or moss-killing (and sometimes all three simultaneously), and inexpensive hoppers on wheels, called lawn spreaders, which will distribute these reasonably evenly. Those concerned that nitrogen in spring fertilisers leaches too easily from the soil can, these days, buy slow-release nitroge-nous fertilisers instead.

No longer need the lawn be aerated by laborious spiking with an ordinary garden fork, for you can hire small spiking machines or even buy spikes to attach to shoes. Nor need you even consider the shoulder-breaking task of raking the 'thatch' (dead grass) with a spring-tined rake, for there are power rakers for sale, or hire, which make short work of this.

The lawn, the last bastion of male supremacy and arcane expertise in the garden, has fallen, thanks in part to manufacturers' cool-headed assessment of the importance of women as consumers of garden products. We can now stand shoulder to shoulder with our menfolk, sharing, on equal terms, all aspects of lawn maintenance. Around the country, women will greet this news with the same unbridled enthusiasm they feel when they hear the words 'And now for the complete classified results.'

The Spectator

Right Ho, Aunts!   27 January 1990

It was 'one of those medium-sized houses with a goodish bit of very tidy garden and a . . . shrubbery that looked as if it had just come back from the dry cleaner.' Bertie Wooster had a keen eye for a garden, even when in the soup. These days, although he would find plenty of shrubberies belonging to the sort of house where (as he rightly deduced) somebody's aunt lived, they would not look as if they had been to the hairdresser, let alone the dry cleaner.

At first sight, the reason for this seems simply that aunts (a sorority to which I am proud to belong) now have great difficulty finding the sort of labour prepared to spend its days groping among the dusty deutzias to pull out couch and stinging nettles, or prune Portugal laurels into tight balls with secateurs and saw.

However, just as important is the influence, since Bertie's day, of a school of opinion which believes that a great deal of pruning of established shrubs is unnecessary, and even wrong if it runs counter to their natural habit and beauty. (Indeed, this idea was advocated by William Robinson as long ago as 1870:

76

but aunts are not noted for being quick off the mark.) The min-imalist approach to pruning finds a ready echo in many gar-deners' breasts because it gives intellectual support to natural diffidence or indolence. In many auntly gardens, shrubs are only touched if they are obviously dying from lack of light or their branches threaten to remove an eye; shrub borders full of exotic escallonias, berberises and viburnums resemble nothing so much as native woodland brakes.

I should be the last person to advocate a wholehearted return to the Woosterian experience, for I rebel against really tidy and clean gardens. What is more, too close or inexpert pruning can, paradoxically, inhibit flowering on those shrubs which go in for it. Even in my not-so-distant childhood, it was still the delight (or duty) of the jobbing gardener to trim round the edge of a shrub, regardless of the plant's habit or, even more important, whether it flowered on the 'old' wood or the 'new'. The old wood in the centre was left alone, while the newer, more vigor-ous growths found their way onto the bonfire. As this pruning was usually done in late winter or early spring, the chances were that only the buddlejas, which flower on wood made in the current year, flourished. The rest lost all their flower buds except those too high for the gardener to be bothered to reach. The ground beneath was left as brown and bare as a ploughed field.

There is a middle way, however. I freely admit that many of the shrubs encountered in gardens (and here I leave aside all hedges, wall shrubs and climbers, which obviously need some attention) do not need any pruning at all, except the occasional trimming out of dead, diseased or very old wood, and possi-bly the tipping-back of long shoots if they block the path or give the shrub an oddly asymmetrical look.

That said, more radical pruning is sometimes necessary or advisable. In the next month or so, for example, late-summer-flowering shrubs such as *Caryopteris* × *clandonensis*, *Spiraea* × *bumalda*, *Tamarix pentandra*, buddlejas and *Hydrangea paniculata*

'Grandiflora', all of which flower on new wood, should have last year's growths cut back almost to their bases, so that the new wood can grow freely. So should those shrubs grown for their decorative winter bark, like *Cornus alba* 'Sibirica'. It is less important to prune winter and spring flowerers such as forsythia, which flower on last season's wood; when young and unformed these should have such shoots removed after they have done their stuff but, once established, may be left alone. Any shrub which has grown very dense and is not flowering profusely can be thinned; the sensible modern practice (except with brooms, which hate this treatment) is to remove a few branches right back into the bush, cutting them flush with a main stem.

The idea is to cultivate shrubs which have the 'natural' form, but Nature improved by a certain artfulness. In this way a straggly, unkempt youth should soon give way to a more solid and dignified, yet prolific, maturity. Aunts, whether they are gardeners or not, are sure to approve.

The Spectator

The Art of the Possible   *23 November 2002*

Pruning. Why do I love it so much? It is surprisingly exhilarating to remove dead rose stems and crossing apple boughs, fell the tall stems of buddleja and cut out fruited blackcurrant stems, in the process releasing the energy of a plant to achieve its optimum potential. Exhilarating, too, to prune for aesthetic effect, with espaliered pears or wall-trained roses. And, what is more, there is scarcely a moment in the year when I cannot justify being out in the garden somewhere cutting bits off something. In February it is clematis and buddleja, in March winter jasmine, in April *Rubus cockburnianus*, in May forsythia, in June kolkwitzia, in July deciduous hedges, in August wisteria, in September rambling roses, in October climbing roses, in

November apple and pear trees, in December English roses. Sometimes I think that psychological forces are at work here, an urge to simplify my life through simplifying my shrubs. Or not.

In any event, and for whatever reason, neither rain nor sun, wind nor hail, sleet nor frost, can separate me from the deciduous trees in the paddock in early winter. Sure, I know that 'the books' tell you not to prune in frosty weather, but it has to be most unusually harsh in November and December to damage hardy deciduous plants which are in the process of becoming as dormant as hedgehogs. So last week, when nearly two inches of rain had fallen and I would have been a fool to go messing around in the borders, I laced up my boots, crushed a hat on my head, pulled on my gloves, took Grecian saw and secateurs in hand, and went out into the paddock. Here there are a couple of hundred ten-year-old trees planted in grass, with plenty of low shoots which need removing to make mowing around the trees easier, and to encourage the sap to travel quickly upwards in late winter and early spring.

I chose this moment, just when the leaves have fallen, for a long time ago I learned my lesson about making a tree bleed. It was an *Acer griseum*, the pride of my collection of Asian maples. One year it needed a few low branches removed, and I picked mid February for the job. I knew at once that it was a mistake. The first cut caused clear sap to well up from the severed stem like an unshed tear before trembling and slipping down the sides of the branch. Horrified, I ran indoors for a rag with which to staunch the bleeding. Within minutes it was soaked. I was distraught. It was like watching one of my own limbs bleed. Eventually the haemorrhaging slowed and stopped, and the tree was not noticeably weakened, but it was a nasty moment

At this time of year I try to find time for those deciduous shrubs which I failed to get to earlier on. We are told 'in books' that you should prune early-summer-flowerers, like philadelphus, weigela, deutzia and lilac, after flowering, and so you should. In a perfect world. But my kind of pruning is designed principally to cut out the very oldest wood ('keep your shrubs young', a wise gardening friend used to tell me) as well as those stems which have flowered. The idea is to retain the shrub's natural shape as much as possible, not trim it into a tight ball as was once the fashion, and which effectively destroys many of the developing flower buds for next season. If I had only one shrub, a philadelphus, in the garden, it would be pruned in late July, but there is too much else which clamours for attention at that time. After all, gardening, as much as politics, is the art of the possible. Although they don't tell you that 'in books'.

Daily Telegraph

Keeping Up Standards   17 March 2001

The world is divided into those people who think 'standard' roses are just the ticket for lining a path or creating height in a flower bed, and those who think that there is barely ever any justification for them. Being somewhat cross-grained by nature, I find myself in the latter group. I am far from against the idea of making shrubs into 'half-standards' (that is, with three to four feet of clear stem below the head of foliage and flower), but somehow the rose, with its dreary leafless twigginess in winter, its capacity for suckering and its potentially large and heavy blooms in summer, seems one of the worst candidates of all for such treatment.

Because they are so obviously the result of artifice and control, standard roses look particularly unsuitable in rural situations. I remember how I instinctively disliked the way they were used to flank the path through the churchyard to our country church when I was still a child, and long before I had considered the matter rationally. Those roses never

flowered very freely and always looked angular and uncom-
fortable, leaning on their stakes, like old men leaning heavily
on sticks.

Yet if you talk of 'standards', most people think in terms of
roses, and roses alone.The idea almost certainly originated in
France in the last-but-one century. Not only were the French
mad keen breeders of roses in those days (think of all those
lovely roses with names like 'Madame Alfred Carrière' and
'Souvenir du Dr Jamain'), but they were also pruners, clippers
and trimmers of great skill and ingenuity. Dusty, knobbly-
stemmed standard roses are still very much a feature of French
parks today.

The only circumstances in which I think their use truly justified is where they give height to a rose garden, or where they are
grown in containers. In both these instances the 'weeping' standard is for me the most successful type, when either a climbing
rose such as 'François Juranville' or a ground-covering rose like
'White Flower Carpet' is employed. Then, especially if they are
grown as a matching pair, to flank a door or gate, rose standards
can look quite handsome. And, of course, if grown in pots they
can be moved somewhere inconspicuous when they are not
flowering.

There are other plants, however, which I think much better
suited to this pruning regime. Fuchsias, for example, with their
flaky cinnamon bark and their dense flush of leaves, make
wonderful standards, not only because the sight is so redolent
of crumbly wooden glasshouses in old gardens but because, in
due season, they are covered in a massed *frou-frou* of pink and
white ballet-dancer flowers which look more in scale than the
enormous rose blooms which result from hard pruning.

As well as fuchsias, pelargoniums and marguerites are also
suitable for growing as standards, and are no more difficult to
tackle. With all these, it is a matter of taking a rooted cutting
in spring and letting one stem grow up strongly and well-
supported, pinching out the top when it has attained the

required height, removing sideshoots lower down the stem, and feeding and potting on regularly to ensure vigorous growth. The following year, the mophead is encouraged into a good shape by the pinching-out (cutting-back) of long sideshoots.

Also surprisingly ornamental is the gooseberry 'standard', which makes a suitable centrepiece to a decorative vegetable bed, giving much-needed height among essentially spreading plants. Gooseberries come into fresh green leaf very early, which is an advantage; but, more important, the fruits are much less of a problem to pick, and the plants to prune, because the thorns are more easily avoided. The newish dessert variety 'Rokula', which has a somewhat pendulous habit, is especially suitable for this treatment. I have seen, already trained as standards, not only this gooseberry and the culinary gooseberry 'Invicta' but also a redcurrant, and a blackcurrant called 'Titania'. All these can be grown in large pots, too.

Perhaps the choicest shrub of all to be trained as a half-standard is the wisteria. It does not seem possible that you can keep such a superhumanly vigorous plant within such bounds, but you can, by developing a clear stem to about four feet, staking it well, and pruning back the long laterals in July or August and February, just as you would a wisteria planted against a pergola or house wall. Again, wisteria can be bought already trained.

Cultivating plants in this way is not difficult, but it requires good, consistent husbandry: you must be prepared to prune and pinch out attentively, and ruthlessly; and to stake and support the plant throughout its existence. It would seem that, as with so much in life, it is a matter of keeping up standards.

Independent

Reverting to Type   7 April 2001

In the general run of things I am a pacific soul, far more anxious for a quiet life than to court controversy or disagreement. But in the spring, when the leaves are still young and fresh on the trees, I find myself becoming almost cross about a feature of gardening which mainly passes other people by. It is the very fact that it passes them by that makes me stroppy. I refer to the surprising number of variegated trees and shrubs in street, park and garden which are left untended after branches have reverted to green. Yes, I thought you would wonder what all the fuss was about.

I am not sure quite why I care so much, since I think variegation often overdone in gardens anyway. Variegated plants undoubtedly have their place (provided that they are not set adjacent to native plantings in the countryside, that is), but if everything is striped, splashed, spattered or otherwise parti-coloured one can soon tire of so much bright perkiness, and long instead for some ordinary, honest-to-goodness, plain green foliage. I think I must mind about reverted shoots and branches because it shows a carelessness for the welfare of individual plants. After all, if a gardener has bothered to pay a premium price for a plant which often grows more slowly than its green-leafed counterparts, burns up more readily in summer sunshine, and which is more likely to suffer harm from pest damage, then it is a pity, it seems to me, not to get the full value from what it *does* offer.

Reversion is such a common occurrence because variegation in plants is usually unstable. Variegation arises sometimes as a result of virus, but most often because some of the cells in a plant have mutated, forming what is known as a 'periclinal chimera'. 'Chimera' is a word we are likely to know from our school days as a mythical fire-eating monster, part lion, part goat, part serpent, which was killed by Bellerophon; we may perhaps also use it to mean a wild fancy. In the botanical world, however, it refers to a plant which has tissues of one genetic type surrounding the tissues of another. As a result, the plant either has leaf margins which differ in colour from the green centres, or vice versa. These contrasting colours are usually white or yellow, but can sometimes be pink, mauve or silver.

Nurserymen and growers love variegated plants. And who can blame them, for they are ideal for promoting the plant-buying proclivities of a susceptible public. Variegations arise from time to time as 'sports' from green-leafed plants and they can be easily propagated by vegetative means such as cuttings. The vast majority of new plants launched in the last few years have been variegated-leafed forms of established garden plants (when they have not been yellow-leafed varieties, that is). Think of *Polemonium* 'Brise d'Anjou' and *Ceanothus* 'Zanzibar', for example. The result is that there are more and more plants, especially shrubs, which need attention if a shoot reverts.

The trouble is that, if left unattended for any length of time, the totally green-leafed shoots which have arisen will flourish mightily at the expense of those which are variegated. That is because the chlorophyll which is such an important agent in photosynthesis is present in greater concentration in leaves which are all green, so these grow more strongly. Common reverters include members of the elaeagnus family, all the variegated- and golden-leafed forms of *Spiraea japonica*, like 'Anthony Waterer' and 'Goldflame', *Philadelphus coronarius* 'Variegata', the variegated box elder *Acer negundo* 'Variegata', and the variegated Norway maple, *Acer platanoides* 'Drummondii'. The latter is often grown as a park or street tree and it is not uncommon to see one with reverted branches, for local authorities do not appear to be any more on the *qui vive* to prevent this from happening than private gardeners.

Mostly, removing the reverted shoot is not a long or difficult job, and when gardens are sodden with late-autumn rain it is at least a task which can be carried out to ease frustration at not being able to get on elsewhere. All that is needed in most instances, is a pair of sharp secateurs or loppers, although acer branches may need sawing off. It is important to cut any reverted shoot back as close as possible to the stem from which it arose, or you risk the same thing happening again very quickly.

All this thought of reversion sent me out into the garden to check on those variegated shrubs which I do grow. I have discovered a green shoot emanating from *Elaeagnus pungens* 'Maculata' and will remove it shortly. In that way, I should avoid drawing down any wrath on my own head.

Independent

White or Black? 6 April 2002

Nothing about horticulture both irritates and soothes so much as its deep conservatism. Gardeners and nurserymen, aided and abetted by manufacturers and gardening commentators, still pursue some gardening practices more suited to Gosford Park in its heyday than to modern, modestly-sized and modestly-funded gardens. Take just one example: round, terracotta-coloured plastic plant pots are widely used, for no better reason than that they 'resemble' the clay pots they finally replaced (which, being hand-thrown, had to be round); yet this prevents the efficient use of precious space in tens of thousands of small greenhouses and cold frames. Square pots are easier to line out, stack and pack, yet not every commercial grower uses them even now. And, while on the subject of pots, why are they not white, rather than terracotta or black?

It has been known for twenty years (though not by me, I confess) that white pots have two distinct advantages over black ones for cultivating any vigorous plant which stays more than a few months in a pot before being sold, such as many perennials, shrubs and, most especially, trees. Black absorbs heat while white reflects it, so roots in white pots are less likely to be scorched and damaged in hot weather. Moreover, roots naturally (by the forces of negative phototropism and geotropism, for those who have found it impossible to forget their school botany, however hard they have tried) grow away from light, and obey the pull of gravity. In white pots, which allow a small amount of light through, roots grow straight downwards and do not impede each other; in black pots they grow to the edge and race round like motorbikes on the Wall of Death. This is especially serious for trees if they stay in the same-sized pot for more than a year, as 'secondary thickening' occurs to roots just as it does to trunks and stems.

Anyone who has carried home from the garden centre a six-foot-tall ornamental 'standard' tree may have discovered, on planting it, that it has 'girdled' roots. Even if you take care to pull the roots apart there is a chance that, when you take away the tree's supporting stake a couple of years hence, it will blow over. After planting, the knots of roots only very slowly and imperfectly push outwards into the surrounding soil, and may never recover enough to anchor the tree sufficiently. Growth may be stunted, vigour undermined, and the tree could even eventually die. I know from experience that a number of trees I have planted out of containers have not established as quickly or thrived as vigorously as I thought they should. (Incidentally, in case you are wondering, bare-rooted trees sent out by nurseries in winter have their own inherent problems; in particular, the propensity to die if their roots are allowed to dry out before planting.)

Needless to say, the superiority of white pots over black never struck me as it should until I came across someone with an enthusiasm for them amounting almost to messianic fervour – Mike Glover of Barcham Trees, an enormous wholesale nursery outside Ely in Cambridgeshire which grows a wide range of trees for 'amenity' (that is, public space) planting. What he said made immediate sense. Indeed, to me as a gardener it was a revelation as profound as, say, the first dawning realisation by a rugby coach that not all eight forwards need be committed to every ruck.

For the last ten years Barcham Trees has plumped exclusively for growing 'standard', 'multi-stemmed' and 'semi-mature' trees, up to a substantial 30 cm in girth, in white pots. These days the pots are made of a permeable polyweave material, which allows in some light, and also oxygen to promote fibrous root growth. The stock certainly looks very well. The trees for the recently-planted Jubilee Avenue of sweet chestnuts (*Castanea sativa*) in Hyde Park were supplied by this nursery, as are the trees for BBC Television's *Ground Force*.

So why it is that white flexible pots are not seen everywhere, if they are such an obvious improvement on black rigid ones? After all, raw plastic is a dull grey, so a dye has to be added to it in any case. Mike Glover says that rigid containers, of whatever colour, are easier to pot mechanically on nurseries, although his company has managed to develop a machine which can deal with flexible ones. We agreed that the answer probably lies in the look of them. Growers presumably think customers will object to shiny white containers that glisten disconcertingly in the sunshine, then turn grubby brown as time wears on. If that is really so, then we cannot complain if our trees refuse to thrive, or even peg out on us ten or twenty years down the line.

The Spectator

Name-Dropping   *14 August 1999*

One of the more unfortunate consequences of being a professional gardener, particularly one partly trained in a botanical institution, is that I must always know the name of a plant. It is a wretched compulsion, but one I am now probably too old to overcome. Although I am deeply envious of those who neither know nor care what their plants are called and only say airily when one asks, which one does, 'Oh, my neighbour gave me that whatjermacallit; pretty, isn't it?', I know that I cannot properly concentrate on its attributes, or study it closely, until I know its name.

My psyche was kinked long ago by the terrors of weekly Plant Identification Tests, so that even now I approach a plant which looks at a distance unfamiliar with eyes cast to the ground, searching for the label which will tell me what it is. In my youth this propensity was also a kind of scalp-hunting, I suppose, but it became an ingrained habit which I make only sporadic attempts to break. My excuse is that, as a journalist, I cannot write about plants if I cannot name them, but that is convenient *ex post facto* reasoning.

Sometimes, these days, I am painfully thwarted. Many owners of open gardens no longer label their plants, either because it is too time-consuming and expensive to do so or because the tags are so regularly stolen, usually by people who have already appropriated cuttings and who would like to keep a record of what they have pinched. Some owners think that, aesthetically, it is better not to turn their garden into a plant cemetery with so many mini-headstones, and I can see their point, although anyone who has ever tried to get hold of a plant they have seen on a garden visit will know the acute frustration of not being able to discover what it was.

Most normal people are not too bothered about labelling in their own garden. But I am condemned by circumstance to a lifetime of labelling, if only because my memory now would make a sieve look impenetrable. Over the years I have tried many kinds of label and marker, but rarely found them satisfactory. The problem lies in an unholy alliance between birds, the weather and the soil. The birds pull out the labels, and the rain mixed with splashed soil washes off the marking. The most widely available labels are made of white plastic, but neither soft lead pencil nor 'permanent' waterproof marker will last forever on them. Before the name has become engraved, like Calais, on my heart, there will be nothing left on the label but an indecipherable blur. Spitting on them and rubbing just makes it worse, in case you wondered.

I must have tried most methods of marking labels in my time, the most laborious being the etching of a black-veneered label with a thin metal stylus. So time-consuming was the process that even I had managed to learn the name by the time I had finished marking it on the label.

Moreover, any label made of plastic will degrade and break in time, and the flexible ones sent out by nursery growers, on rose bushes, for example, break off infuriatingly two years down the road, leaving only part of the name intact. I am left wondering whether a label with the legend *Rosa* 'The P—' refers to 'The Pilgrim', 'The Prince', 'The Prioress', or 'The Painter'.

I think, however, I have finally found the answer, thanks to Mary Keen, who suggested I write names on small black labels with a Pilot Silver Marker (Very Fine Point). Both tag and name appear to last an impressively long time and, because black absorbs rather than reflects light, the label is easier on the eye than white plastic. Moreover, as the silver marking appears to be long-lasting and waterproof, the labels can be almost completely buried in the ground, and only referred to if necessary.

For roses, which require something rather larger, I have invested in satisfyingly heavy zinc labels from Wartnaby Gardens. They can be written on with a soft lead pencil or an acid marking ink which Wartnaby also sell, but are old-fashioned enough for people to think that they look decorative.

Of course, another solution would be not to label my plants at all, but instead write their names in a loose-leaf folder divided into sections according to garden location and accompanied by the simple plans for plantings I drew up in the first place, and ones showing any major alterations since. In this way I could avoid the risk of turning the garden into a graveyard. Even more important, however, I need not even attempt to straighten out my psyche.

The Spectator

The Salt of the Earth   *14 August 1999*

Those who may be reading this on the beach somewhere far away from the cares of home and garden, in Europe at least, have probably cursed the seaweed that snatches at swimmers' legs or its fetid smell that catches in the throat as they lie on the sand. If you are a gardener, no doubt you have wondered how an extract from such horrible stuff can be every gardener's friend, the darling of the organic garden movement, and sold in most garden centres.

Long before the first garden centre was a twinkle in a nurseryman's eyes, seaweed was laboriously raked off beaches by gardeners and dug into the soil, both to help condition it and to aid plant growth. But for landlubbers seaweed has, for fifty years, come conveniently packaged as a concentrated liquid, although also in meal and 'calcified' forms.

Although we usually call liquid seaweed extract a 'foliar feed' or fertiliser, in fact it is a 'bio-stimulant', as Maxicrop International discovered when, in 1987, it began funding a variety of projects in British universities and research stations; the objective was to achieve scientific credibility for a product it had been selling to farmers and gardeners since 1952. In the process, it has been established that the nutrient and trace element content of seaweed extract is very small (although artificial fertilisers can be added to it); its active ingredients are mostly betaines, which are amino acids, as well as carbohydrates and sugars. These ingredients, the evidence suggests, promote the manufacture of the green photosynthesising pigment chlorophyll; in hardy plants they also slightly increase tolerance to frost and other environmental stresses such as drought; they enhance a plant's defence system, thus mitigating the effects of pest and disease assault; they encourage beneficial microbes in the soil and suppress some harmful soil fungi; they promote root growth and therefore nutrient uptake; they have even been found to improve seed germination. Is there no end to seaweed's virtues?

Apparently not, for seaweed is also a sustainable, renewable, natural resource, there is masses of it (and how!), and it not only demonstrably helps grow good plants but also appears to lessen the need for pesticides without itself being one. It also reinforces the advisability of feeding the soil, rather than the plant, which is something of an article of faith with organic growers.

A number of seaweed species are used by manufacturers around the world, but Maxicrop puts its faith in a brown seaweed called *Ascophyllum nodosum*, or knotted wrack, which grows round British shores but is in fact harvested in the clean, cold waters off Norway, north of the Arctic Circle. It is collected by fishermen who cut it on a four-year rotation, so that colonies can regenerate. This wrack is dried locally, made into meal, then sent to a factory in Corby, Northamptonshire where it is hydrolysed, a process which breaks down the cells, releasing their contents and making the well-known strong-smelling, brown, viscous liquid concentrate. Once diluted, it can be used as a soil drench when transplanting young plants or sprayed onto the leaves of more mature ones. The company recommend applications 'little and often'. Because it is a bio-stimulant rather than a fertiliser it is applied in highly diluted form, which is good news for us poor gardeners.

Seaweed extract is available either pure or with a variety of inorganic fertiliser additives, such as sequestered iron for acid-loving plants, and potash for tomatoes. These formulations have their uses but are not, of course, an option for the purist organic gardener. However, 'greens' need have no fears about dried seaweed meal, which can be used to boost a flagging compost heap and is credited with soil-conditioning properties, or about 'calcified' seaweed, made from a coral-like red seaweed, which is high in calcium and magnesium and is rec-ommended both for making acid soils more alkaline and for improving the structure of heavy clay ones.

For me, the great charm of the pure seaweed extract is that you can put it on at any time in the growing season. It can be watered even onto very dry soil, because there is no danger of it scorching roots. So if, on your return from holiday, you dis-cover your garden full of lacklustre plants, then you could do worse than bring something of the seaside back to the garden.

Independent

I Want To Be Alone   *13 November 1994*

November, as I may perhaps have implied before, is not a very promising month for the active gardener. Morning frosts slow up progress outside; night creeps on all too quickly. Weeding can be wet, digging can be difficult, planting can be a problem.

But enter a greenhouse, even if only gently heated, and its dry warmth and unique, and certainly not unpleasant, mingled smell of dead leaves, potting compost and garden twine are immediately cheering. It is a refuge from the stormy blast, not to mention the importunate demands of home and family; it offers you a respectable excuse to be alone, à la Garbo. You are quite safe; no one will follow you there, in case they are asked to weed under the staging or clean the glass with disin-fectant.

The greenhouse also offers the opportunity for innocent pot-tering and dreaming, not to mention equally innocent acts of propagation, which are best carried out there, now that potting sheds are a thing of the past.

You may say that the cool greenhouse has had its day, since we now have the modern conservatory, attached to the house and seemingly combining the best aspects of greenhouse and sunny sitting-room. For many people, the conservatory has solved the conundrum of how to add living space to the house for both humans and plants. The difference between the conservatory, as we now use the phrase, and the greenhouse is that the former is for people as much as, if not more than, for plants, whereas greenhouses are definitely for plants but will accommodate people – especially those who crave a little solitude. If you have never grown anything under cover before, a small greenhouse is the better, and cheaper, way to begin.

Before you put pen to paper to tell me what a wonderful environment you have created in your conservatory, for nurturing both plants and people, think back to what careful pains you took to deal with all those vexed questions concerning aspect, shading, ventilation, heating, security, not to mention pest and disease control and how to keep the place tidy. Not every conservatory is as well thought out and accoutred as yours, I feel sure.

In the greenhouse, which though often decorative is first and foremost a utilitarian structure, these circles are much more easily squared. As for plants, the only ones which are better accommodated in a conservatory than in a greenhouse are climbers which need a solid wall for their support. In the perfect world, therefore, you really need both.

What makes the free-standing greenhouse such an excellent place for growing plants is that the light is evenly distributed. That affects the quality of flower, and eliminates the drawn look which can occur in lean-to structures. My ideal greenhouse, which I will buy one day when my ship comes in, would have automatic vent openers, thermostatically controlled electric heating, automatic external roller blinds, a separate heated propagator, a capillary matting watering system; it would be big enough for me to landscape it 'naturalistically' or, at the very least, it would contain a number of staging levels, so that it could work for display as well as utility.

That is the ideal, but there are ways around the problem

caused by the non-appearance of ships. If you cannot make the greenhouse truly decorative (and the cheaper and smaller they are, the harder it is to do so), you can bring plants into the house once they begin to flower or look their best, rather than leaving them in the greenhouse to do their stuff. Heating is optional: a 'cold' greenhouse is really a large and better-insulated cold frame, eminently suited for a whole range of hardy plants and bulbs which will flower earlier and more cleanly for a little protection. The judicious use of bubble poly-thene attached to the glazing bars (though not masking the vents) helps keep out the worst weather in cold houses and saves money in cool ones.

Those of you who own a greenhouse which you keep just frost-free do not need me to sing its praises, but it is possible that you do not use it to the full. Are you, for example, presently engaged in potting-up lily-of-the-valley roots to provide early scented flowers in the house, or planting winter lettuce seedlings in the growing bags left after the tomatoes have finished, I wonder? This is the time to be potting-up (or -on) amaryllis bulbs, autumn-struck cuttings of tender plants like fuchsias and pelargoniums, sweet pea seedlings, and hardy winter-flowering plants such as Christmas roses (*Helleborus niger*) and polyanthus, which often get splashed and mangled in the open garden. November is the time for bringing in tender plants (fuchsias, dahlias, pelargoniums, begonias) which will lie doggo in the winter, so can be put under the staging in trays of dry peat or peat substitute.

Most importantly, it is the time to be enjoying the flowers of zygocactus, browallia, kalanchöe, nerine, saintpaulia, large-flowered chrysanthemums and perpetual-flowering carna-tions. Creating colour and scent in the darker days is, after all, one of the best reasons for gardening under glass – whatever kind of structure you choose.

Sunday Telegraph

4

Plants from Seed

A Small Success   7 October 2000

I do not boast about the conditions in my garden, in the general way. Which is just as well, since I don't have much to boast about. I live in a part of the East Midlands which I love dearly but which is prone to cold and dry springs and indifferent but droughty summers, and I garden on a soil which is nowhere near the deep, well-drained but moisture-retentive loam of my dreams and is in places as unforgiving as a slighted lover. Because I insist on retaining the pleasant rural view beyond the boundary, the garden is exposed to witheringly cold winds for half the year. Despite the care taken over them, plants do not grow conspicuously quickly or well here. There is every possibility that my garden is even less favoured than yours, and that may be saying a lot.

Just occasionally, though, something really works in the garden, sufficiently well for me to want to tell everybody about it. This particular small triumph concerns the temporary planting of half-hardy annuals in a bed under a two-foot-high wall and bounded by the paving of the terrace, exposed to what sun there is, and in a soil which is lighter and more free-draining than the rest of the garden. This bed is easily seen from many windows of the house, so it was crying out in June for something interesting to tide it over the summer, before its permanent planting this autumn and next spring. In the event, and quite beyond modest expectations, the scheme was tasteful without being dull, harmonious without being clichéd, and the plants billowed, flowed and rolled in a most satisfying way.

It was not really planned. By chance, a seed-sowing orgy in late February had resulted in far too many young plants of *Petunia* 'Prism Sunshine', together with masses of two newly-introduced half-hardy annuals, both from Suttons Seeds: *Ageratum* 'Red Sea' F1 and *Verbena* 'Serenity Mixed'. *Petunia grandiflora* 'Prism Sunshine' has soft lemon-yellow single trumpet flowers, produced prolifically over a long season, on 30 cm-tall plants. *Ageratum* 'Red Sea' is taller, at 50 cm, than most of its relations, with the usual tiny powder-puff flowers, but they are deep wine-red in bud, strong lavender when open, and almost purple as they fade. *Verbena* 'Serenity Mixed' produces delicate-looking, ferny-leaved plants up to 40 cm, with masses of clustered heads of pastel flowers.

The petunia seed was bought to provide plants for containers, but the last two were impulse buys, ordered because they sounded interesting but only suitable, I thought, for trialling in the first year in a spare plot of ground. If that worked, and I liked them, I would include them in a planting scheme for the following year. However, finding myself unexpectedly with a large area of ground – roughly ten square metres – to cover, I decided to take a chance and plant all the spare petunias with the ageratum and verbena, and give this low, rather delicate planting solidity and background with a few modestly-sized white argyranthemums, together with trailing blue *Convolvulus sabatius* and, another trailing plant, *Helichrysum petiolare* 'Limelight' with felty yellow-green leaves on long stems, and little or no flower.

The scheme was a bit of a gamble: I knew 'Prism Sunshine' to be a charming and reasonably weather-resilient pale yellow petunia, but I was a little mistrustful of the verbena, as mixtures have a way of being less harmonious than the catalogue picture would allow, while for all I knew the ageratum could have turned out to be carmine, rather than 'burgundy' as advertised.

I need not have worried. The ageratums were surprisingly pretty and harmonised beautifully with the verbenas, which really were pastel, without being wishy-washy. There were mauves, purples, pinks, and white among them, but because they were all at the blue end of the spectrum there was sweet harmony. As this verbena has been principally developed to trail from hanging baskets and containers, it covers the ground as well as the leafier, beefier petunias, if not better. And both ageratum and verbena flower their heads off for four solid months. Only last week did a mighty battering of rain and wind finally send them into retreat. What is more, *mirabile dictu*, cuttings taken in early September are already rooted and potted up in the greenhouse. Next spring I shall take more cuttings from these cuttings and fill the whole garden with pastel verbenas and 'floss flowers'.

It is true I cannot take all the credit for the success of this scheme, because it was partly accidental. But then, I cannot take the credit for the accidental virtues of my children either, yet that doesn't stop me boasting about them. Until my next conspicuous failure, therefore, I shall bask in the pleasant glow of this small success.

Independent

Gardening with Tears   18 August 2001

We all have our own ideas about what constitutes a thing of
beauty. It may be the opalescent lustre on a sea shell, or the
curve of a child's eyelash, or even the bowling action of Glenn
McGrath. For me, it is the flower of the Shirley poppy.

Recently, I went to a press day at a large seed firm's trial
grounds. It was a very pleasant occasion, and proved a good
opportunity for talking to marketing managers and production experts about new varieties and breeding programmes,
seed mixtures and commercial considerations, public taste and
private passions. Lunch was laid on, and my mood was
mellow as we fanned out across the trial grounds during an
afternoon of rainstorms.

Seed trial grounds consist of flat expanses of grass striped by
long rectangular flower beds full of strong colour in blocks,
like a child-giant's patchwork blanket. This effect is created by
the rows and rows of flowers raised from seed – both those
which the seedsmen already sell to gardeners through their
mail-order catalogues, and those called 'experimental', which
they are testing, both for appeal and uniformity, before offering them to the public.

Although I am naturally weepy and revel in a good blub, I
do not, in the general run of things, cry while at work, especially when I have just enjoyed a satisfactory lunch. However,
there was a moment as I stood beside the ranks of African
marigolds (*Tagetes erecta*) when I could cheerfully have wept. I
was beset with the thought that plant breeders should have
spent so much time, effort and money on developing something so demonstrably ugly and inelegant (if rainproof), as the
African marigold, neither easy to fit into a scheme nor capable
of producing pleasure on its own. The double flowers look like
butter-yellow or orange sponges transfixed to the top of truncated stems and surrounded by coarse, spikily pinnate leaves.
Just as there is no word in the English language which rhymes

with 'orange', so there is no word which could possibly describe the colour of 'Inca Orange'.

You cannot blame the seedsmen for growing these top-heavy oddities. As I was told with a rueful laugh more than once during the visit, the 'bottom line' generally rules what is grown. If there were no substantial market for African marigolds, they would not appear in catalogues. I do not know whether that says more about our aesthetic sense or our herd instinct.

So when I stumbled across a pathetic little row of Shirley poppies long past their best, I felt like an ancient but faithful churchgoer finally vouchsafed a heavenly vision, for in those few, frail, bedraggled flowers was a glimpse of the eternal. To say that they have 'tissue-paper' petals is to pay a great compliment to tissue paper, which is thick and coarse in comparison. Nothing else gets even close, however, to conjuring up the image created by those crumpled, folded petals. But it is the colours – the pale pink of a dawn sky, the blue-grey of a wood pigeon's wing, the crimson of fresh-spilt blood, the dusty pink of raspberry fool – that so enchant.

The Shirley poppy, of which there are several strains on the market, was first selected from the common scarlet corn poppy, *Papaver rhoeas*, by the Revd William Wilks, rector of Shirley in Surrey, a nineteenth-century gardening clergyman who, among other things, helped rescue the Royal Horticultural Society from oblivion, and is commemorated in the name of the cooking apple 'Revd. W. Wilks'. The original Shirley poppies, single and double, come in colours from white to crimson, scarlet, and dull orange, and there are picotees as well.

Later, just after the Second World War, the artist Sir Cedric Morris also selected good colour variants of cornfield poppies found while out walking in the fields near his home in Suffolk, and was responsible for developing the strain called *Papaver rhoeas* 'Fairy Wings' (also found in seed catalogues under the name 'Mother of Pearl'). As his friend and protégée Beth

Chatto puts it: 'Over more than thirty years, I watched Cedric developing this enchanting introduction, weeding out the scarlet poppies, [and] encouraging the purplish-grey tones, hoping one day a blue form might evolve.' There is no blue form, unfortunately, but the soft colours are all lovely.

As I stood in the trials field I thought of the patch of Shirley poppies at home, which have been flowering in their delicate and refined way under an elderly, crooked 'King of the Pippins' apple tree since May from a sowing made on Valentine's Day, and which are only now in August beginning to lose ground. After such a long season, when they have often seemed the best thing in the garden, the gradual fade-out of these flowers feels particularly poignant, somehow. Gulp.

The Spectator

Nature Imitating Art for a Change   *21 September 2002*

At first, I thought the unusually hot early September sun must have gone to my head. I certainly could not quite believe the evidence of my eyes. I was sitting in the kitchen drinking tea and looking out onto the terrace at a planting of *Verbena bonariensis* and *Nicotiana langsdorffii* – a very pleasing and deliberate mix of pinkish-purple and yellow-green flowers, though I say so who shouldn't – when a brimstone butterfly settled on the verbena and started to suck nectar from the long flower tubes. The palest lime green colour of the brimstone's underwings was the exact match of the nicotiana's flowers, and chimed just as beautifully with the purple of the verbena. It was the finest (well, to be truthful, probably the only) example I have ever seen in my garden of Nature imitating Art, and I was quite transfixed.

When I sowed this tobacco plant in spring, intending to put it close by a clump of self-seeded *Verbena bonariensis*, brimstone butterflies were very far from my mind. We don't see them very often in the garden, in any event, since there is not a great deal of buckthorn in the nearest hedgerows, and that is the one food their fussy caterpillars will deign to eat. We glimpse one or two adults in the spring, but then nothing until their progeny have matured in late summer. I doubt, however, whether I shall ever look at *Nicotiana langsdorffii* or *Verbena bonariensis* again without thinking of butterflies.

Nicotiana langsdorffii is one of those plants which deserves its present high reputation. It is easy to grow, for a start. On 19 March we sowed seed bought from Chiltern Seeds and it germinated two weeks later; we pricked out masses into modules on 16 April and they were flowering within a month of being planted out in early June. The greenish-yellow colour of the panicles of drooping bells, held on rangy, sticky, fishing-rod stems up to three feet tall, is a marvellous foil for purples and mauves but chimes also with *Hemerocallis citrina*, *Alchemilla mollis* and *Ruta graveolens* early in the summer and, later on, with the sky-blue of *Salvia patens* 'Cambridge Blue', the steel-blue leaves of the grass *Helictotrichon sempervirens*, and the deep yellow of *Bidens* 'Golden Goddess'. If you bother to lift up one of the upturned trumpet bells and look inside, you will see that the pollen is, intriguingly, blue. The strangest feature of this Brazilian member of the tobacco family, however, is that the flowers do not smell, day or night.

Although I grow *Nicotiana langsdorffii* for its capacity to fill spaces with a colour rarely found outside the tobacco family (except, of course, it now occurs to me, in *Zinnia* 'Green Envy', although that has a very different habit of growth), I am also acutely aware, as the wife of a new and very curious beekeeper, that these tubular bells are intensely attractive to honey bees, as well as to a whole lot of different solitary bees.

I suppose I could say, at my most pompous, that *Nicotiana langsdorffii* is the Platonic ideal of a summer annual: it has a long flowering season from midsummer to mid autumn; is very attractive to insects; adds an important ingredient to the garden's palette of colours, fitting in to a great variety of planting schemes; the seed can be gathered (sorry, Chiltern Seeds) and will come true, as it is a species; and, by virtue of its inherently ephemeral nature in this climate, it will change the aspect of a border for a growing season, yet we can say goodbye to it at the first frosts. You could not ask for much more of a tender annual than that.

Daily Telegraph

Purpletop Patches

10 November 2001

Is there no end to the virtuosity, star quality and sheer staying power of *Verbena bonariensis*? I ask this question purely rhetorically, by the way, for this slightly tender perennial, known colloquially as 'purpletop', is a real winner, and one on which most people are happy to lavish praise. Whenever I visit gardens between July and November, I can depend on at some point having an uncontroversially favourable discussion with the owners on the merits of this plant. And yet, ten years ago we had hardly heard of it.

The credit for popularising it must go to Christopher Lloyd of Great Dixter, who in articles and television interviews opened our eyes to its virtues, in particular the way that you can see through its airy, branching stems to plants beyond, thus enabling the gardener to put it near the front of borders and break up the too-predictable 'small at the front, tall at the back' way of planting perennials. It is also one of the best companions for 'English' roses because its colour harmonises well with all those pinks and whites, and its habit does not obscure, or fight with, that of the shrubs.

It is this semi-transparency which so endears it to us. Earlier in the year, one of my most satisfying plantings resulted from placing this verbena in front of a fat-bellied Cretan terracotta *pithoi* which stands in a narrow bed on the terrace. The slight obscuring of the pot only served to draw the eye inexorably to it. Now that I have removed the verbena, the naked pot has lost something of its allure. The slight veiling was so much more sexy, somehow, like a diaphanous stole draped over the shoulders of an odalisque.

This paragon of the summer and autumn garden has other attributes, however. It is tall, up to 1.5 m, yet its thin, square, wiry, sandpapery stems and sparse side-shoots are sturdy and do not need staking. There are few leaves, except at the base, for this is a clump-forming perennial. Those further up are opposite each other and clasp the stems; they are lance-shaped and covered in the same wiry hairs which give the stems their sandpaper feel. The flowers are scented, lavender-purple and tubular, and held in reddish-purple clusters about 5 cm across which endure after the flowers have set seed, turning gradually to brown. These tubular flowers are an irresistible draw to butterflies. In the late summer and autumn border of oranges, russets, deep reds, blues and mauves they are surprisingly *simpatico*, partly because of the red in the calyces and partly because of the comparatively delicate nature of each flowerhead, such a contrast to dahlias, chrysanthemums and asters.

This year, I sowed Thompson and Morgan seed on 13 February in gentle heat, pricked out the seedlings on 2 March, put the plants out in a sunny spot on 22 May, and they were flowering by mid July. As I write, on the fifth day of November, there are still plenty of flowers on the long stems. In late September I cut down a couple of plants, dug them up, potted them, and put them in the cold greenhouse. They have already made extensive sideshoots, so there will be plenty of cuttings material in the spring, if I need it. I shall hope to preserve those growing in the warmest spots outside, by cutting the stems down and mulching round the bases to protect them from winter cold. I have also collected some of the lettuce-like seed by tapping the spent flower heads, but in well-drained places this verbena will certainly self-seed.

And in that lies the vaguest, most tentative criticism which it is possible to level against this plant – namely, that it can seed too freely if it likes your soil, and the winters are mild. I am told that you must not willingly propagate this South American plant in Australia, as its prolific nature threatens to make it a bad agricultural weed there. (Poor Australia, for ever at the mercy of involuntary imperialism on the part of other people's wildlife.) Nevertheless, back here, its lack of true winter hardiness means that it is unlikely to do the same thing, and in the garden it is easy enough to weed it out where you really don't want it.

Brilliant as it undoubtedly is, *Verbena bonariensis* is not the only vervain worth growing in the garden. There are a number of excellent tender perennials such as 'Sissinghurst' (magenta-pink), 'Claret' (deep red), 'Lawrence Johnston' (scarlet), 'Silver Anne' (pink fading to silver-white) and the 'Tapien' series, which have a trailing habit. These will grace containers or can be used in bedding schemes and are as easy as anything to strike in August or September from cuttings, which is as well, for they will not come true from seed. Also very popular for bedding are the forms of *Verbena* × *hybrida*, such as 'Peaches and Cream', 'Crown Jewels' or 'Showtime'. They have the great merit of having single flowers, so all are attractive to butterflies. With the seed catalogues arriving by every post, this is definitely the moment for ordering a little star quality.

Independent

Electrifying Nasturtiums   26 May 2001

Everyone knows *Tropaeolum majus*, although no one calls it that. The common name is 'nasturtium', a corruption of a Latin phrase meaning 'having a pungent taste', and it has been a colourful feature of cottage gardens for hundreds of years, since its introduction from South America at the end of the sixteenth century. The popularity of nasturtiums has been due to their ease of cultivation, the fact that the petals, seeds, buds and leaves are edible (if peppery, especially when uncooked), and the flowering is bright and long-lasting. They were once also considered interesting curiosities, because it was thought that the leaves and flowers gave off sparks of electricity.

This is one of those plants about which pseudo-sophisticated gardeners are snootily dismissive and ultra-sophisticated gardeners, perhaps in compensation, a shade over-enthusiastic. It is hard to get it quite right. In my opinion, nasturtiums do have a place in the garden, but it is important to know what effect you want to make before letting them loose, for they are not really like anything else to be found in the summer garden, and they will not give of their best in all situations.

The broad, open trumpet flowers are about 5 cm across, with long curving spurs at the back, and they come in a range of colours that includes pink, yellow, orange, mahogany, and bright scarlet-red. The round leaves of most are fresh green, although there is also a much less vigorous variegated variety called 'Alaska' which has pale green, marbled and speckled foliage. (Surprisingly for a variegated plant, it comes true from seed.) Nasturtiums can be dwarf and bushy, in which case they grow 20 to 25 cm tall, semi-trailing, when they grow to about 40 cm, or trailing, when they can grow to 2.5 metres or more. A modern improvement on the old varieties is the spurless 'Whirlybird' series, which has yellow or red single flowers held well above the foliage. Lately some old varieties have come back into fashion, notably 'Empress of India', which has deep red flowers against attractive dark blue-green leaves, and the rather tender, double-flowered, orange-scarlet 'Hermine Grasshof', which has to be propagated – although this is easy enough – by stem-tip cuttings because it does not set seed. It is these last two which have caught the imagination of the sophisticates, especially for growing in ornamental kitchen gardens (*potagers*), for even if not a single petal is ever picked for a salad or an omelette (and it is not thought wise to eat a great deal of nasturtium at once), this hardy annual will associate with pretty well every herb you can think of.

Nasturtiums grow best in a moisture-retentive but well-drained soil, in sunshine. They absolutely don't want a rich soil, or they will grow leaves at the expense of flowers. The seeds are so big that they can be sown individually where you want them to flower, in late spring or even as late as early summer, should you want something to sow directly in the place where spring bedding has been. Alternatively, they can be sown in small pots or plug trays in the cold greenhouse in spring, and planted out after they have been hardened off. Their great enemy is the blackfly, which can sap their vigour considerably, and looks horrible. At the first sign, spray them with a contact pesticide recommended for vegetables, such as horticultural soap, just in case you fancy eating the flowers. Some gardeners deliberately plant a few nasturtiums parallel to a row of broad beans to attract the blackfly away from the beans.

The dwarf, bushy varieties can be grown in containers or as an edging at the front of flower borders. The semi-trailing, slightly taller 'Gleam' nasturtiums are very striking if planted to trail down a sunny bank. The very tall, trailing varieties can be encouraged to clamber up pergolas or over arches, and look especially attractive in a kitchen garden setting. They will happily, for example, clamber up a tripod of runner beans, without materially affecting the size of the bean crop. As the colours are so bright, they associate well with the purple foliage of, say, *Sambucus nigra* 'Guincho Purple' and the bronze of *Ferula communis* 'Purpurea', as well as deep blue summer flowers such as those of *Salvia guaranitica* 'Black and Blue'. So, if you are tired of pastel shades and in tune with the bold colour school of garden planting at present in the ascendancy, you might give nasturtiums a try. The effect could be electric.

Independent

Biennial Bother
13 May 2000

It is easy to see why God should have created annuals as well as perennials, but it is more of a mystery to me why the Almighty bothered with biennials. A biennial – a plant which makes leaf growth in the first year after germinating, usually in the shape of a basal rosette, then 'runs up' to flower in the second, sets seed and dies – seems neither fish nor fowl, somehow.

Don't get me wrong; I have nothing against biennials as garden plants. Far from it. There are a number of very attractive biennials which will grace any garden. It is just that I find it a puzzle why some plants should be capable of lasting over the winter, yet go on to die after one seed-bearing. If you can survive one winter, why not several?

Many gardeners scarcely give biennials a thought, I suspect, until the day that the parsley, left in the ground over winter, suddenly (or so it seems) produces a tall stem of cow-parsley-type flowers, while the leaves coarsen dramatically, making them wellnigh useless for the kitchen. It is enough to make anyone cross. You feel that it should have either died out in autumn like a proper annual, or carried on forever like a real perennial, instead of beguiling you into thinking that you could get away without sowing any more seed of it.

There are not, in truth, very many true biennials in gardens, but gardeners, being pragmatists, call anything which is sown one year and flowers and is pulled up the next a 'biennial'. They apply the term to monocarpic, short-lived perennials, which die after setting seed, even though that seeding may not happen until the third year or even later. And even some true perennials treated in the same way, such as sweet williams, are always known as biennials. It is not exactly a neat and tidy situation.

We consider 'biennials' (whatever they truly are) to be, together with tulips and other bulbs, the bulwarks of spring and early summer bedding schemes or border gap filling. Wallflowers (*Cheiranthus*), double daisies (*Bellis*), Canterbury bells (*Campanula × media*), forget-me-not (*Myosotis*), pansies, violas and sweet Williams (*Dianthus × barbatus*) are the best-known for this purpose. Seed needs to be sown in early summer either in a nursery bed or in pots, then transplanted or pricked out after germination, and the plants put in their flowering positions by the end of October.

Late May to mid July is usually the time advocated for sowing biennials if you are to get good sturdy plants to put out in the borders in late September and October, while the soil is still warm. Violas and pansies can be left until July. In really cold, windy areas, delay sowing any of them until July, so that plants are shorter and more likely to withstand winter gales.

Sow the seed thinly in rows in a sheltered, not too sunny place, where you won't accidentally disturb them, and keep the soil moist by consistent gentle watering. The rows should be labelled and sufficiently far apart for you to push a hoe through and keep the weeds down satisfactorily. Alternatively, very small seed such as that of bellis and forget-me-not can be sown in pots or seed trays, which you put in the cold frame and shade from hot sun.

As soon as outside-sown seedlings are large enough to handle, gently fork them up and replant at a greater distance, to grow on. This is so important; if you do not, you will get masses of spindly little plants which will be grudging about flowering the following spring.

There are a number of other biennials which are either too tall for this purpose or too slow to flower, but can still find a place as summer border fillers: the mullein, *Verbascum bombyciferum*, the foxglove, *Digitalis purpurea* 'Excelsior Strain' (wonderful in moderation among, for example, old-fashioned roses), the variegated tree mallow, *Lavatera arborea* 'Variegata', honesty, *Lunaria annua*, and even, if you are brave or foolhardy, the enormous and extremely prickly Scotch thistle, *Onopordon acanthium*. Angelica is also biennial.

As far as gardeners are concerned, it is less important to know whether a plant is a biennial or short-lived perennial than to know whether it may die out after flowering. If you don't know this, you run the risk of unwittingly creating troublesome gaps in your borders. I am thinking particularly of the Himalayan blue poppies, like *Meconopsis betonicifolia* and *M. integrifolia*, together with *Hedysarum coronarium*, French honeysuckle, *Papaver nudicaule* (Iceland poppy), and *Hesperis matronalis* (sweet rocket). These are all plants which we assume are proper perennials, probably because they are usually found for sale in pots. But they have a disconcerting propensity to die out (especially if the conditions don't quite suit them), so make sure you take the seed when it ripens in autumn and sow it immediately in pots in a cold frame (in the case of sweet rocket and Iceland poppy, sow *in situ* in spring), so that you have new young plants to put out the following year. You can never have enough of these plants, in my opinion, so should any of the parents survive, you will have cause to celebrate.

Independent

Perennial Pleasures   5 January 2001

It is possible that, over the Christmas and New Year holidays, you may manage to creep away somewhere quiet to study the seed catalogues which come through the post in such an avalanche in November. I hope so, for it can prove a potent antidote to the noise and kitchen grind of the festive season. (I write as a reasonably typical female who, by the day after Boxing Day, could cheerfully throttle Delia for her upbeat comments on home-made sausage rolls and *crème-de-menthe* jellies). It is also possible that you will already have read more than one gardening article about the novelties on offer among annuals and vegetables. All well and good, but there is more to the seed catalogues than bedding and eating. In particular, most seed catalogues (with the exception of real vegetable specialists like Marshall's) offer a wide choice of hardy perennials as well. These are easy to miss among all the publicity afforded to highly-bred F1 annuals, yet the seed is cheaper to buy and can often be sown later in the season, when the helter-skelter spring rush is over. And, once planted, they stay planted. Being perennial, unless your wants are really out of the ordinary, they do not have to be sown every year.

As we all know, if we collect seed of cultivated varieties of perennials in the garden there is a good chance that the seedlings will not all come 'true', that is, be identical to the parents. This is because they are of hybrid origin. But there are plenty of species perennials, as opposed to hybrids, which deserve a place in the garden and, even if sown in gentle heat in a windowsill propagator, will still be cheaper to acquire than a plant bought in a pot. Sowing seed will almost always ensure you get more than just one plant, which is handy if you are a forward-thinking gardener, keen to grow good masses of a particular perennial for 'prairie' effect, or if you just have a lot of space in your garden to fill.

In fact, you will discover plenty of perennial cultivars listed in catalogues. This is because seed companies often do careful selecting, so that some will in fact come true, or as true as makes little difference. Granted, seed firms will sometimes, in an excess of enthusiasm, give a cultivar name to what is simply a good form of the species, but there is no harm done by that. Most of us, most of the time, do not get too hung up on a name, and are happy to leave botany to botanists.

In deference to the modern gardener's supposed impatience, and unwillingness to have any gratification deferred, plant breeders have worked hard in recent years to develop

hardy perennials which will flower in their first year. They may
not flower very freely, but there will be something to show for
the effort and, in the second year, they will really put on a good
show. *Coreopsis* 'Early Sunrise' comes to mind, as does
Gaillardia grandiflora 'Goblin', *Achillea* 'Summer Pastels', and
the modern hollyhock strains. The catalogue issued by Mr
Fothergill's Seeds, for example, makes a point of highlighting
those perennials which, if sown early in the year, at the same
time as half-hardy annuals, will flower their first summer. Mr
Fothergill's also carries a range of what the company call
'Gardeners Store' perennials – that is, collections of seed of five
species from a garden-worthy perennial genus. These make up
in interest what the name lacks in an apostrophe. These selections include hardy geraniums, salvias, campanulas, and
pompon aquilegias.

Thompson and Morgan have *Lupin* 'Tutti Frutti', a mixture
of bi-coloured flowers on tall, sturdy flower spikes, which the
company says will flower in the first year yet with the quality
of 'expensive cuttings-raised plants'. They also have a form of
the meadow cranesbill, *Geranium pratense*, called 'Purple
Haze', which they promise has bronze-purple foliage, deepest
in tone if the plant is grown in shade. If the leaves come properly up to expectation, these should provide a strong harmony
with the mauve-blue flowers.

If you really want to delve among the nooks and crannies,
however, may I suggest you send for a catalogue from Chiltern
Seeds, which is always the last seedsman's catalogue to arrive
here (usually just before Christmas), but the most expectantly
awaited. Among their items is a woody-based perennial for the
connoisseur, *Salvia lavandulifolia* or 'Spanish sage'. This has a
rangy habit, narrow, whitish-grey downy leaves and short
midsummer spikes of violet-blue flowers. Its great glory is its
foliage rather than its flowers; this salvia is evergreen, and a
group of plants will lighten a well-drained sunny border as
well as artemisia or santolina. True, it is quite widely available

in nurseries, but at less than the price of a packet of seed? I
think not.

Independent

Sowing the Seeds of Success   21 December 2002

I once worked under a wonderful head gardener of the old
school, called Mr Clayton, who maintained that he always
drew up his seed order on Boxing Day, one of the few days in
the year when he was at leisure. I have never forgotten this,
principally because it seemed almost unbelievable (even
though I knew him to be a man of probity) that anyone could
find the time and peace to settle down with the mail-order catalogues the day after Christmas. Since there was never a
moment for solitude, let alone calm activity, on Boxing Day in
our house, I found it in me to envy him.

I don't suppose that I shall do my list this Boxing Day either,
but I may – perhaps when I am walking the dogs – at least
reflect on what it is that I want to achieve next year, and so
make my list rather shorter and more realistic when the
moment comes to ordering the seed. It is all too easy to become
carried away, as the many reproachful seed packets left for
more than a year in the seedbox remind me. In the past, my
eyes have simply been too big for my garden, or the time I have
for it.

Seed-sowing is a deeply satisfying, almost hypnotic, activity
which removes me completely from the hurly-burly – since no
one in the family ever makes the journey to the greenhouse to
find out what I am up to. It is also, thanks to improved techniques of storage and packaging and, therefore, germination,
usually very successful. But with the exception of large seed,
which can be sown individually into small pots or modular
trays and planted outside from there, most seedlings need to
be pricked out into modules or trays, and then often potted on

as well, and all that is very time- and space-consuming, especially with half-hardy annuals which must be sown in late
winter or early spring. Realistically, to justify sowing half-
hardy annuals you need more than just a few patio containers
to fill. Small-garden gardeners are better off buying plug
plants, which only need to be potted up once, and which can
also be ordered from the seed catalogues.

Perennials are another matter. Money spent on perennial
seed is rarely wasted, since the resulting plants usually become
permanent additions to the garden. Confusion sometimes
arises, however, because slightly tender or short-lived perennials are often referred to (understandably) in seed catalogues
as half-hardy annuals. For example, although I write this on a
desperately rainy day in December, I can still see *Rudbeckia
hirta* 'Indian Summer', called a half-hardy annual, making a
brave show in the border nearest the house. I fully expect, as it
is actually a short-lived perennial, that it will come again next
year. And I am grateful for that. Resolutely tender perennial
plants, like begonia, which we have to treat as half-hardy
annuals in Britain, have to look pretty good in the catalogues
if they are to find a place in my order.

As for the kitchen garden, it is tempting to buy the seed of
every type of vegetable you are prepared to eat – but unless
you have conscientious gardening help or a lot of time on your
hands, much of that seed will never get sown, while some may
be sown but never efficiently harvested. Sticking to vegetables
such as *mange-tout*, French beans, courgettes, tomatoes, and
saladings, which must be imported at most times of the year or
which make you cross at their cost in the supermarket, makes
more sense than condemning yourself to a summer battling
with carrot root fly or potato blight.

One of the problems with seeds is how many you get in a
packet. With the exception of F1 hybrid seed, which is sold in
very small quantities because the breeding has to be done in
a controlled environment, most packets contain enormous

numbers of seed. There were 325 of them in the packet of *Rudbeckia* 'Indian Summer' (I didn't count, but took Mr Fothergill's word for it). In theory, I could give spare seed to my garden-minded neighbours. In practice, it lies about in the greenhouse in an open packet, drying out and losing viability, until I get round to throwing it away. I would rather not dwell on all that garden promise sacrificed.

There is another very contemporary complication: the internet. Mr Clayton only chose from Suttons or Thompson and Morgan, as I recall; now, gardeners can find their way onto the websites of hundreds of suppliers, large and small, both at home and abroad. But in the same way that the huge choice in a modern supermarket can make you feel deathly tired, so trawling dozens of websites for the seed of particular plants is very hard work. I am certain Mr Clayton would have thought it a shocking waste of his precious time off.

Independent Magazine

5

Herbaceous Perennials

Foliage Foils   *16 March 2002*

It's that moment again, that blessed, magical, unrepeatable, fleeting moment in the year when the herbaceous perennials have begun to show themselves above ground once more, and the world feels new-minted and full of promise. The tough-leaved bergenias, hellebores, celandines and other winter-flowering perennials have played their part, and now is the time for fleshier, more fragile foliage, coloured that peculiarly fresh emerald-green straight from a child's paintbox. This is the colour of delphiniums, of Madonna lilies and deciduous ferns. It is also the colour of young nettles and groundsel, but let that pass.

There are plenty of new leaves which are not bright green, in fact, but which take on particular spring tints: there is the burnished bronze-red of the young shoots of *Euphorbia griffithii*, the coral-red tones of *Epimedium* × *rubrum*, the purple of the young leaves and stems of *Artemisia lactiflora* 'Guizhou', the clean silver-and-green variegations of pulmonarias and *Brunnera macrophylla* 'Hadspen Cream', the deep rhubarb-red of the Molly the Witch peony (*Paeonia mlokosewitchii*) which unfurls to glaucous blue-green. Every morning reveals some new shoot or leaf to marvel over. The backcloth to centre-stage daffodils and early tulips is woven out of a hundred foliage textures.

In garden centres everywhere there are pots in plenty, filled with the foliage of perennials of every hue. The label may illustrate the flower, but the evidence of the foliage is there before your eyes. Although I doubt the wisdom of impulse-buying as a way of planting a whole garden, I can see clearly enough that plants 'in the flesh' reveal much that no label or picture in a book ever could. In any event, the spring leaf colours of many perennials last as long as, if not longer than, the flowers, so there is good reason to choose many plants for their foliage alone.

Now, for example, is an excellent moment to study the relative merits of different herbaceous euphorbias. You cannot tell habit or flower conformation from a plant in a pot, but you can see how deep purple-red are the leaves and stems of *Euphorbia dulcis* 'Chameleon', how pink the stems of *E. sikkimensis*, how coppery-red those of *E. griffithii* 'Fireglow'. The evergreens, too, such as *E. martinii* and *E. amygdaloides* 'Rubra', are developing new shoots of deep, deep crimson.

Dicentras or 'bleeding hearts' must sell themselves in spring, for they die down long before summer is out. In harsh springs the young shoots are easily frosted, but in sheltered gardens they are a joy in March, when their neat fern-like leaves emerge and in April and May when they flower. The pink bleeding heart, *Dicentra spectabilis*, is the most commonly found, having red-flushed leaves which turn green as the stems age. These leaves are finely cut into lobes and make an attractive dome before the charming pink hearts, with white petals protruding, appear along arching stems. Some prefer the smaller *Dicentra formosa*, with even more finely-cut leaves and masses of flowers, but I would not be without either. There are also plenty of worthwhile garden varieties, like 'Stuart Boothman' which has blue-grey leaves.

Dicentras do fine in the shade of deciduous trees, provided the place is sheltered, and this will also suit *Brunnera macrophylla* 'Hadspen Cream', with striking heart-shaped leaves which are cream on the margins and associate so happily with the blue forget-me-not flowers in spring. 'Langtrees' has creamy spots rather than leaf edges, and 'Variegata' has white variegations.

For many people, spring has not sprung until the emergence of the conical spikes of hostas, the family *par excellence* for foliage colours and variegations. Epimediums, on the other hand, are near as dammit evergreen, yet in spring new leaves emerge, fresh green but often marvellously tinted in red, pink and copper. They are better seen if the old leaves are cut back in late winter. The leaves (strictly speaking, leaflets) of epimediums are mostly oval or heart-shaped and often ser-rated, and cover the ground quite well. Epimediums flower early, with star-shaped flowers which are often half-hidden by the leaves, although *E.* × *versicolor* 'Sulphureum', for example, holds them above the leaves. These are pale yellow, with very long spurs which give them the look of mini-columbines.

As spring merges into summer, much of the early leaf and stem colour of herbaceous perennials fades, especially during flowering, and greens become darker and more sober. In the case of some, however, such as epimediums and hostas, changes occur once more in autumn. But right now we have more than enough to relish, before it is gone.

Independent

The Oldest hath borne Most 27 May 2000

The oldest plant in my garden is hardly what you might expect. It is not a venerable, crooked oak or scruffy, stag-headed ash, but a centenarian tree peony which is not a tree at all but a four-foot-tall deciduous shrub. How do I know its age? Because the previous owner of our house, a woman of impeccable character, told me that when she and her husband bought the house more than thirty-five years ago, an old woman from the next village maintained that this plant was already at least seventy years old.

This sounds like one of those curiously fascinating stories which you read occasionally in the Letters page of *The Times*: 'Dear Sir, it might interest you to know that my great-uncle had a schoolfriend whose father, as a small boy, was tipped a gold sovereign by the Duke of Wellington. I remain, as ever, etc.' My letter would read: 'Dear Sir, it may interest you to know that I have a peony in my garden which witnessed the celebrations for the Diamond Jubilee of Her Majesty, Queen Victoria. I remain, as ever, etc.'

There is something rather marvellous about a plant which has seen so many seasons, bowed its head under so many gales, opened its flowers to so many uncertainly sunny May days, in peace and war, in want and plenty, indifferent to the many changes of occupier in the cottage in whose front garden it resides. It is also a fine plant in itself, in some years producing twenty or so enormous (20 cm diameter) double pale pink flowers, deep carmine at their bases, these flowers made up of masses of gorgeous, uneven, ruffled petals. They unfold from blue-green round buds above lobed glaucous leaves. The rounded shrub grows in a moisture-retaining soil in semi-shade, in the lee of a lowish stone wall over which the topmost flowers can sometimes be glimpsed from the road. This position means that it is well sheltered from cold winds and, worse, early spring frosts which would damage the young leaves. The flowers, which last for three weeks in May, are, despite their size and complexity, reasonably rain-proof. I trim the dead wood from this shrub from time to time, but otherwise do absolutely nothing to it, not even offering a scatter of bonemeal in spring. But then, peonies are famous for their tolerance of neglect, and their longevity; indeed, the herbaceous varieties, forms of *Paeonia lactiflora*, which are what we normally mean when we talk of garden peonies, positively resent being bothered, and can sulk and refuse to flower for a year or two after being transplanted.

I strongly suspect that my tree peony is a form of the so-called Moutan (hybrids of *P. suffruticosa*) from China, introduced to Europe in the mid nineteenth century. It is impossible to identify the varietal name for sure because the plant is so old, but it answers pretty well to the description of a cultivar called 'Duchesse de Morny', bred in France well over a hundred years ago, and not now offered by any British nursery.

Having been thoroughly eclipsed by the herbaceous varieties of peony since the beginning of the twentieth century, the tree peony is presently enjoying something of a revival, thanks to interest from nurserymen both in the United States and in Britain. New tree peonies have been arriving seemingly by every post since the early 1990s when China came out of its shell. Unlike the old Chinese peonies, these new varieties hold their flower heads up quite well, rather than burying them among the foliage. In this regard they resemble more closely the Japanese tree peonies, although the Japanese tend to have narrower, more elongated leaflets, are likely to be single or only semi-double in flower, and are less vigorous in habit. Both types are available from specialist nurseries such as Kelways, Phedar Nursery, and Claire Austin Hardy Plants.

Whether in transliterated Chinese or in English, Chinese tree peonies have glorious if fanciful names, such as 'Wu Long

Peng Sheng' ('Black Dragon Holds a Splendid Flower') and 'Qing Long Wo Mo Chi' ('Green Dragon Lying on a Chinese Inkstone'). It is worth growing them for their names alone, although I would urge you to try to remember them to hand on to your successors, if you sell your house and garden. These shrubs do not come cheap, because they are difficult and slow to propagate as a rule. Newly-introduced varieties from Kelways, for example, range from four to twenty times the cost of a well-grown hosta. However, that is hardly very much to pay, surely, for three weeks' floral pleasure every spring for the next hundred years.

Independent

The Lure of the Oriental   29 May 1999

I wonder how many other people notice the strange dearth of Oriental poppies at Chelsea Flower Show most years. With a few honourable exceptions they are conspicuous by their absence.

You may wonder why this should strike me so forcibly, since there is variety enough there for the most avid eye or sophisticated palate. Quite simply, it seems to me so strange that there should be daffodils, delphiniums, even dahlias and chrysanthemums, all of which are either forced on or held back in order to flower in Chelsea week, but very few varieties of *Papaver orientale*, which are actually flowering in gardens in late May.

Perhaps it is because gardeners are rather ambivalent about these plants; you need to have an exuberant spirit, and a bit of space, to see the point of them. But what else in late spring has such big, blowsy, almost tarty flowers, with their come-hither petals like wrinkled coloured tissue paper. These flowers do not bloom for more than a few weeks, but by golly, they make an impact when they are out. You cannot miss those six-inch-diameter, single, cupped flowers once they have broken free from their hairy, egg-shaped buds. They usually have black blotches in the centre and a fat boss of black anthers; if the stems are not staked in the spring they curl upwards like the branches of a candelabra. The leaves are large, deeply cut and intensely hairy, and help to make a dense, domey clump, which should also ideally be staked, for the leaf stalks fall flat on their backs after heavy rain.

I am sure that not everyone will agree, but it seems to me a great virtue of these leaves that they die down soon after flowering: this means that they will tolerate being mown over in midsummer, and are therefore suitable for growing in a flowering 'meadow'. In a border, of course, this dying-down may be a mixed blessing, for a gap opens up in July, but by then other large perennials will be pressing for space anyway. This plant is not for the tidy-minded gardener, certainly, but will reward the adventurous one.

The best-coloured poppy, I believe, is one called *Papaver orientale* 'Patty's Plum', which has deep and bloomy purple-red flowers; it looks superb combined with purple-leaved heucheras, the pink cow parsley (*Chaerophyllum hirsutum* 'Roseum'), glaucous-leaved hostas and deep-red astrantias. Its only real fault is that the flowers quickly fade to brown.

Although 'Patty's Plum' is the pick of the crop, I also rate highly 'Cedric Morris' (what its raiser called 'knicker pink'), 'Mrs Perry' (pale pink), 'Black and White' and 'Effendi' (very big salmon-pink flowers). There are more than sixty cultivated varieties to choose from, but they are not all worth having and it is best to see them in flower before parting with money. For they will be with you for life.

It is as well to know that Oriental poppies are one of those perennials which you can propagate by root cuttings. If you can get them to replicate themselves by sticking a piece of root in a pot or seed tray in the winter time, it is obvious that they can do the job perfectly well on their own. It is almost impossible to eradicate one of these plants, once you have it in the borders, and they are capable of creeping about, as well. My *bête-noire* is the orange 'Marcus Perry' (or it may be 'Allegro': they are very similar), which has flowers as bright, glowing and obvious as a Belisha beacon. You may well know the one I mean, for it seems a more or less obligatory denizen of old-established gardens. It was in the garden when we came and, try as I may, I cannot get rid of it.

I have even contemplated spot-weedkilling this orange poppy with a systemic herbicide which will kill the roots as well. But as it is my almost unbroken intention never to use weedkillers in the border, I have just resolved to make a virtue out of a necessity, and hedge it round with aggressively purple-flowered plants like *Allium* 'Purple Sensation', or even purple-foliage shrubs like *Cotinus* 'Grace' or *Berberis thunbergii* 'Atropurpurea', as well as the simultaneously-flowering *Geranium* 'Johnson's Blue'. That should take just enough of the sting out of the orange to create a sumptuous effect. The sort of effect which would look just terrific at Chelsea.

Independent

Fatal Amnesia   *12 August 2000*

In the world of gardening, sins of omission weigh more heavily on the soul than those of commission. For every plant I have pruned when I should have left it alone, there are ten others which I have failed to deal with properly in due season. The flesh is willing, but the memory is weak. My main border is presently suffering from the effects of a bout of amnesia earlier in the year, when I twice left undone those things which I ought to have done to an herbaceous clematis called *Clematis* × *jouiniana* 'Praecox'.

As a general rule, we think of clematis as deciduous climbers, not herbaceous perennials, but there are a number, of which *C.* × *jouiniana* is one, that have no tendrils, so cannot climb. This one grows to roughly a metre tall, has large three-lobed, serrated, matt bottle-green leaves growing from the axils of long shoots, from which also arise long-stalked clusters of small, faintly-scented, pale-blue tubular flowers consisting of four reflexed petals and lots of lemon-yellow stamens in the middle. The flowers are charming and produced in consider-able profusion for at least three months from midsummer to early autumn. This is an excellent plant for a mixed border, provided that two things are done to it. The first is to cut all the stems back either to the ground-sprawling woody framework which this plant is inclined to make, or even to ground level itself, towards the end of the dormant season; the second is to pinch back the vigorous new shoots in April, to encourage the production of sideshoots and, thus, a relatively compact plant. This is especially important in a wet spring, when leaf and shoot growth can be prodigious on a plant that revels in a damp soil.

Neither of these tasks did I perform, and the price has been paid by a number of the clematis' neighbours in the border, despite my staking it in May to try to make it grow up, rather than along. They have had the indignity of being jostled, pushed, and rapidly smothered. Although I spent some time last week cutting back all the clematis' long shoots, and losing masses of flower as a result, a nearby strobilanthes is still in a sulk, and a sturdy English rose, 'Charlotte', looks as pum-melled and battered as if she had just endured a rush-hour journey on the Northern Line.

My clematis and the closely-related, darker-blue *C.* × *hera-cleifolia* 'Wyevale' are the most vigorous of herbaceous clema-tis, it is true, but all of them grow well. The most choice are the forms of *Clematis integrifolia,* which have smaller, daintier leaves, a more naturally upright growth (60 to 90 cm), and nodding bell flowers composed of four twisted petals and cream stamens, in a number of very attractive colours, depending on the variety. The usual one has violet-blue flowers, but 'Rosea', for example, is bright pink, while 'Alba' is white and 'Hendersonii' has larger flowers than the type. Other herbaceous clematis to look out for include 'Alionushka', which won a Certificate of Merit from the British Clematis Society in 1998, with twisted pink, pendulous flowers and a 1.8 metre-tall habit. My favourite is *Clematis* × *durandii*, with saucer-shaped flowers of deep indigo, deeply-veined petals, and central bosses of golden stamens. This plant is what is confusingly called 'semi-herbaceous'; what is meant is that it is sufficiently tall to be used as a wall shrub. All herbaceous clematis need careful staking in spring, with either brushwood or metal stakes (I use Y-Stakes), which are soon hidden by the burgeoning foliage.

I would genuinely hate to give you the impression that these herbaceous clematis are troublesome, for they are not: pruning them is a pleasant pastime; they do not get 'wilt', which is a major boon; provided that the soil is in good heart and is mulched well (I *did* remember to do that at least in spring) they are reliable and profuse flowerers; they associate very well with herbaceous hardy perennials at their end of the colour spectrum, especially phloxes and *Aster* × *frikartii* 'Mönch', and are very useful as an understorey to the globe thistle, *Echinops bannaticus* 'Taplow Blue', which has rather bare lower stems by this point in the summer. *Clematis* × *jouiniana* and *C.* × *heracleifolia* can also be used to sprawl over old tree stumps or unsightly low features like manhole covers, or just employed as weed-suppressing ground cover in the wilder garden, where no harm will result if the shoots are not pinched back in spring. I think I'll move mine in the autumn – if I can remember.

Independent

Grassy Grace

Grace, especially grace under pressure, is a virtue we value just as much in plants as in people. At this time of year, with the winds beginning to pick up speed, the garden can seem a restless place as branches and foliage are tossed and bent this way and that. Not all of this activity is graceful, indeed it can be downright clumsy, but almost all the perennial 'ornamental' grasses, especially those which flower in late summer and autumn, are so configured that they seem never anything but fluid and sleek in their movements.

This is one of the reasons why we like them so much, I suppose. Even on still days the leaves of *Stipa tenuissima* will dip their arching tips, while the inflorescences of *S. calamagrostis* nod slightly, as if to an unregarded acquaintance. Still or restless, *Miscanthus sinensis* 'Silberfeder' draws the eye across the garden, especially when September sunlight falls on the silvery panicles of 'flowers', while the steel-blue foliage of *Helictotrichon sempervirens* contrasts most agreeably with the lime-green flowers of *Nicotiana langsdorffii*, and the yellow variegations of *Miscanthus sinensis* 'Zebrinus' (intriguingly) remain even as the foliage colour loses definition with age. There is never a dull moment in a garden where grasses are cherished.

The innate grace of grasses is the reason why they can be so effective in plantings, their airy-fairiness being often in such stark contrast to the bold, large-leaved aggression of late-flowering globe artichokes, angelica or echinops. What is more, they have the great virtue that, practically without exception, they die almost as gracefully as they have lived. They range in size from tiny little clumps for the front of the border or a patio pocket to 3.5-metre-tall Pampas grasses, but even when very tall several are still useful for small spaces: *Panicum virgatum*, for example, which is tall (2 metres) yet upright in habit, and delicate and airy in inflorescence, is invaluable if you are trying to avoid clumpy, midget plantings composed entirely of what the catalogues call, euphemistically, 'compact' plants.

Ornamental grasses chime beautifully with contemporary ideas about how we should lay out our gardens – away from the stiff and controlled towards laxer, wilder, more 'natural' plantings. You do not have to embrace completely the 'new perennial planting' philosophy, which originated on the Continent, to see how grasses can help counteract the artificiality of many border designs.

Moreover, grasses make up such a huge family of plants that there are sensible choices for most kinds of soils and situations. There are some which enjoy a rich, fertile, well-drained soil (such as *Miscanthus*), while others positively revel in the droughty conditions of a gravel garden (for example *Festuca glauca*). Summer-flowering *Milium effusum* grows best in semi-shade, while *Carex elata* 'Aurea' is for the waterside. No family of plants ever becomes really popular in gardens unless most of its members are relatively easy and amenable.

Most late summer- or autumn-flowering grasses are best planted in late spring, just as they are coming into growth, for they are at risk, in heavy soils in particular, if planted in autumn and left to languish through the winter. But they can be ordered in autumn from one of the many nurseries which make a speciality of them, to be delivered when the time is right. They are also popular garden centre plants at that time of year, particularly when the new growth begins and there is something to see.

Once you have unpacked them, or brought them home, take care with the planting, preparing the soil well first, digging generous planting holes and then planting them at the same level as they were in their pots, watering in well and mulching to preserve moisture. Grasses of the same species or cultivar should be planted at roughly the same distance as the height to which they will grow, information as to which is usually to be found on the label, but can otherwise be gleaned from any reference encyclopedia. Once they are established, and have flowered, their stems should be cut down in winter time unless they are evergreen, in which case they are simply tidied up, where necessary, in the spring.

Independent Magazine

Où sont les gelées d'antan? 4 December 1999

'Where are the snows (and frosts) of yesteryear?' As the evidence piles up that our climate is beginning to change, gardeners don't know whether to laugh or cry. On the one hand, they can see all the delicious possibilities of growing hitherto tender plants out of doors, without the expense or fuss of protecting them under glass in winter; on the other, they fear the effect on traditional, favourite plants of droughty, blazingly hot summers and wetter, warmer, windier winters, without long spells of cold to kill off pernicious pests or the chance to experience the beauty of frost or light snow on grass and leaf. After one such warm autumn, I am perilously close to tears.

I only have to think of ornamental grasses for my lip to tremble, for mounded clumps of arching, strappy leaves, pierced by tall stems of feathery heads, are just asking to be silvered by glistening frost. Yet here in Northamptonshire, at least, any frost there has been this autumn has melted away in a matter of hours, and we have seen no snow at all.

Except when touched by rime, grasses have an understated beauty, as if they were young girls at their first dance who had lived sheltered lives and never been told how lovely they were. They don't so much grab the limelight as back into it, when the stage has emptied of more confident performers. If herbaceous, they display subtle but alluring autumn colours of buff, brown, orange, bronze, or even red; if evergreen, they provide a kind of fluid structure, a yielding geometry to the winter border, not always very sturdy or dense, but nevertheless distinct.

Ornamental grasses are, therefore, just the ticket if you are trying to escape the tyranny of traditional border planting, those uneven-numbered clumps of perennials, tall at the back, short at the front. I use the evergreen (well, everorange-bronze) *Chionochloa rubra*, for example, as a *leitmotif* to run in a (densely-planted) curving, rippling stream through two borders separated from each other by a broad flight of steps. This *leitmotif* may not be exactly Wagnerian in scale and intensity, but it is pleasing and unifying none the less.

Deciduous grasses which have leaves that are coloured or variegated through the summer often retain some of that variegation even when the colour is bleaching out of the leaves in autumn. *Miscanthus sinensis* 'Zebrinus', for example, which has horizontal banding (hence its common name of zebra grass), does not lose that banding completely even when the green pigment disintegrates.

There are also a number of grasses which lend themselves to having their stems cut in late autumn and hung up to dry for indoor decoration. Pampas grasses (*Cortaderia selloana*, *C. selloana* 'Sunningdale' and the dwarf form 'Pumila') are only the best-known of these, for the many cultivars of *Miscanthus sinensis* – 'Silberfeder', 'Malepartus' and 'Kleine Fontane', for example – are also suitable, as is the mosquito grass, *Bouteloua gracilis*.

Grasses are categorised, by experts, as either 'cool-season' (like *Calamagrostis*, *Deschampsia* and *Molinia*) or 'warm-season' plants (for example, *Panicum*, *Miscanthus*, *Chionochloa*, *Cortaderia*). In layman's terms, the former come into growth in late winter or early spring, like hardy perennials, and can be treated in the same way, amenable to being planted out of containers in autumn or spring. They flower in spring or summer and are pretty hardy. The latter come into growth in early summer, flower in late summer and often retain their seed-heads for months. Many are not as hardy as 'cool-season' grasses. It is important that they are not planted until they begin to make growth. These are, principally, the grasses of choice for impact in the winter garden, so that is an excellent time to think about what you want, and where and how to order them. Grasses rarely give much clue to their appeal when seen in pots in garden centres, so I suggest you get hold of a catalogue from a specialist nursery, to learn something of the plants you want to buy, and order them in December for late spring delivery.

The time to appreciate grasses in winter is before the New Year, I always feel. Once the year has turned, those which have been left uncut to decorate the winter garden can begin to look distinctly tatty. Wet and windy weather, particularly, will take its toll on them, savaging the seedheads and bending the stems in half. If the climatologists have predicted right, that process may happen even earlier in future. Oh dear, pass the Kleenex.

Independent

Mind the August Gap   5 August 2000

From time to time people moan about the 'May gap' in borders, after the spring bulbs and shrubs have finished flowering but before the roses hit their stride. However, for some strange reason less is said about an early August gap, even though in my opinion it is worse, because the leaves of perennials no longer have the fresh crispness of new banknotes to make up for their lack of flowers. Perhaps our creative energies are exhausted by the end of July, and we find it convenient to forget that there are still several weeks to go before the huge tribe of autumn daisies turns the borders to rich purple and gold.

If you are at home rather than away in early August you might find it an instructive exercise to wander along your flower beds and count the number of perennials flowering in them. It is possible that you will be unpleasantly surprised. I imagine there will be those imposing thugs *Echinops*, *Macleaya* and *Acanthus*, as well as achilleas and penstemons in quantity, the last of the day lilies and the first of the crocosmias and Japanese anemones. If you like collecting plants, there may be *Campanula pyramidalis*, *Veronicastrum virginicum* and *Strobilanthes atropurpurea*. There will be the unimpressive tail-end of many summer-flowerers such as herbaceous geraniums. That is neither a very long nor an especially distinguished list, let's face it. Wait a minute, you say – there is a clump of something over there, with eye-wateringly bright carmine flowers on the top of miserable, wilting, foliage. Ah, yes: let us not forget the border phloxes.

The cultivated varieties of *Phlox paniculata* do not have an enviable reputation with discerning gardeners, which is actually a little unfair. They mostly grow to about 75 cm, although a few are as tall as a metre, and have a number of sturdy, bolt-upright stems, on the tops of which appear domed or flattish heads of single, deliciously and strongly scented flowers in a number of colours from white through the pinks to blue (well, violet-blue) and even orange. True, there are some electrifyingly carmine varieties such as 'Starfire' (a mystifying name, if ever there was one) which, when placed indiscriminately with golden heleniums, say, are enough to make you want to go and lie down in a darkened room, but there are many less startling varieties which can be a positive asset in the border.

Border phloxes are not delicate and refined in looks or demeanour, granted, but they are solid citizens, making dense clumps or even drifts if planted generously. They are never going to be the principal dancers on the garden stage, or even the *corps de ballet*, but they can be used as the townspeople and peasants, to make the scene look crowded and colourful. To do that properly, however, they have to be well looked after. You cannot just plonk phloxes in the ground and forget them, as we are all inclined to do. They are plants from open woodland and riversides in the eastern United States, and they need a well-nourished and moisture-retentive soil; their roots hate to be dry in summer, and are very prone to develop powdery mildew in those circumstances, especially if they are confined in an airless spot – say, close to a wall or hedge.

What is more, in old-established gardens where they have grown for many years, or into which they have been introduced as divisions from kind neighbours, they may well play host to stem eelworm. Eelworms, or nematodes to give them their scientific generic name, are microscopic creatures which, in the case of phlox, live in the stems and foliage, and do most obvious damage when the plant is growing strongly in summer. In a bad attack the stems swell markedly, and the leaves are conspicuously narrower and twisted. If you suspect a problem with phlox eelworm, don't split up plants every fourth spring or autumn, as the books tell you to do, but propagate them instead from root cuttings taken in the dormant season, as is the nurseryman's custom, and burn or bin affected stems and foliage. Buy new plants from reputable sources and don't, whatever you do, plant phlox in the same spot again.

As for the mildew, this can be mitigated by watering well round the roots in August, preferably with a liquid feed, taking care not to splash the leaves. This is usually the month when our soils are at their driest, and in drought plants suffer from starvation as well as thirst, because nutrients have to be dissolved in water to be absorbed by roots. Indeed, most August-flowering perennials, especially those with large expanses of leaf, will benefit from feeding now. So this month, if you have an opportunity to sit in a deckchair with a glass of something refreshing at hand, spare a few minutes first to refresh the perennials around you and, in particular, those poor, maligned phlox.

Independent

Visible Assets

What is with this word 'architectural', used so liberally to describe any plant with bold, individualistic foliage or rigid and angular form? Globe artichokes, agaves, eryngiums, onopordons, euphorbias, dahlias, cannas, bamboos, ferns, yuccas, bananas, palms and Pampas grass have all acquired this epithet; indeed, it seems to have become attached to any plant whose habit is not obviously yielding or formless. An adjective derived from the noun meaning 'the art or science of building' does seem a slightly strange word to describe the shape of a plant; it is, no doubt, a handy shorthand term for people in the know, but I try to avoid it as I suspect it mystifies anyone who is not.

Having got that off my chest, I have to say that in recent years there has been an increasing, and salutary, emphasis on plants with structured form and exuberant foliage, especially, but by no means exclusively, as suitable occupants for town or city gardens. Their widespread popularity has been promoted by warmer winter temperatures, which means that those subtropical plants which have large foliage (and there are many) stand a greater chance of survival outside in this country. There is also a more general appreciation of how to nurse slightly tender plants through the coldest months using various *ad hoc* protection measures, such as bubble wrap, polypropylene windbreak material, horticultural fleece, even terracotta drainpipes, as well as straw, dried bracken and compost. What is more, anyone who has a conservatory or greenhouse can store one or two tender exotics through the winter. A number of useful books have been published in recent years and the Eden Project in Cornwall has provided a huge spur to the public imagination. 'Architectural' plants are also firm favourites with television gardeners keen to create absolutely instant televisual impact.

These plants are promoted by garden designers in the indisputable belief that our gardens benefit from a judicious mixture of contrasting elements: hard, soft; floppy, rigid; angular, fluid; vertical, horizontal; dark, light; colourful, sombre; and so on. These elements are necessary regardless of whether a garden is large or small, formally or informally laid out.

Spiky plants like *Yucca cordifolia* (in or out of flower) and the non-flowering New Zealand flax, *Phormium tenax*, draw the eye immediately, so they make excellent focal points, either free-standing or in pots, to emphasise a particular properly architectural feature, like a change of level or an entrance. Both are hardy in sheltered places in sun, and they have the virtue of being evergreen. This is also an important recommendation for the hardy Chusan palm, *Trachycarpus fortunei*, which has large, elegant, pleated, fan-shaped fronds erupting from a fibrous trunk, and yellow flowers in early summer. For very small gardens, however, the diminutive *T. wagnerianus* is the better bet. And there is *Fatsia japonica*, which makes a rounded evergreen shrub with large, glossy, finger-like leaves and sprays of globular, creamy-white flowers (like ivy flowers gone mad) in autumn, and will do fine in partial shade. A variegated form is choicer but not so hardy. Among deciduous plants, no large garden with a pond or bog is complete without *Gunnera manicata*, nor a small garden with pond or bog without the lance-shaped leaves of *Iris sibirica*.

At midsummer, as stiff-necked perennials like globe artichokes and tall eryngiums develop a degree of maturity, it is possible to see why this kind of plant is so useful in borders as well. Formlessness, as in a meadow or perennial planting, can become monotonous, however true to 'nature' it may be. Punctuation marks such as those produced by the flowering heads of *Cynara scolymus* or the angular branching stems of *Crambe cordifolia* are welcome diversions for the eye. For those who are not anxious to promote the 'exotic' look yet still want a variety of forms in their gardens, these perennials offer the answer, at least from midsummer onwards. Among evergreens with structured shape I would rate highly most forms of *Mahonia*, such as M. *japonica*, and the smallest of the pampas grasses, *Cortaderia pumila*; and among deciduous plants, *Cornus controversa* 'Variegata' (even if it is rather slow-growing), which develops horizontal branches as it matures.

The smaller the planting, of course, the less ambitious you should be with your plants of bold or distinctive foliage; scale and context matter. Even in expansive settings, I would err on the side of moderation. For if you are not careful, and get too carried away, your garden could well become as angular as a truculent teenager, and you may then find yourself longing for some visual peace and quiet.

Independent Magazine

Orchid Mania   *11 March 2000*

Are you happy as you are? Do you want life to go on, more or less, as it is now? Do your garden and gardening satisfy your desire to care for beautiful things? If your answers are 'yes', I advise you strongly never to go anywhere near the New Horticultural Hall in Westminster, when the Royal Horticultural Society is holding its annual London Orchid Show. Such events are known to change people's lives.

Before you accuse me of exaggerating grotesquely for effect, there is plenty of evidence that orchids, of both the epiphytic and terrestrial kind, can have an intense impact on those who know them. Even those other huge families of plants, roses and rhododendrons, cannot compare in their capacity for unsettling otherwise perfectly balanced people. No one who has read Susan Orlean's *The Orchid Thief*, about orchid fanciers in Florida, or who knows much about the orchid mania which swept Britain during the nineteenth century, could possibly doubt it.

The first tropical epiphytic (that is, one that uses a tree trunk for support) orchid was not flowered in Britain until the 1760s, and, strangely, caused little of a stir. It was not until a cattleya was accidentally introduced (as wrapping for other plants) in the early nineteenth century that British botanists and gardeners started to pay close attention. The requirements of these early-introduced tropical orchids were so exacting that they suited the ambitions of a horticulturally-obsessed gentry, and extravagant glasshouses were erected to cater for them. Plant hunters were sent to extremely wild and woolly places, both in South America and Asia, to find them. It was a dangerous, sometimes fatal, business for the orchid hunters, who most assuredly did not do it for the money, but it was a fascinating and lucrative business for orchid nurserymen such as Frederick Sander, 'the Orchid King', who founded nurseries on both sides of the Atlantic. Rare specimens were sold at auction for enormous prices.

In 1889 the RHS formed an Orchid Committee to set standards of nomenclature and to award prizes. The Society has been closely involved ever since with the increasingly complicated business of orchid naming, thanks to the capacity of orchids to hybridise even with other genera, creating bi-generic, even sometimes tri-generic, crosses. Fortunately, Frederick Sander had the foresight to set up a register of orchid hybrids in 1901, and this register, now in the control of the RHS, is updated frequently. Three thousand new hybrids are added each year.

The first half of the twentieth century was not an auspicious time for orchids. Two world wars interrupted supplies of the fuel needed to heat glasshouses, so orchid growing and breeding tended to move to the United States and Australia. By the 1950s, however, matters had improved; it was then that the British Orchid Growers' Association founded the London Orchid Show, now run by the RHS. The current explosion in interest in orchids is easily explained by the fact that they are relatively so much cheaper these days, as a result of the development of tissue culture techniques in the 1960s. Orchid propagation before that had been slow and laborious; now it is possible to culture masses of the same clone from meristem cells in the laboratory.

Moreover, as gardens have shrunk, gardeners have seen the advantage of specialist plant growing, concentrating their attention on particular plant families rather than a broad mix. Orchids fit this bill. Cymbidiums, odontoglossums, dendrobiums, paphiopedilums, cattleyas, laelias and phalaenopsis are all tender orchids which can be successfully grown by amateur gardeners, provided they take a little trouble to find out the particular requirements of each genus. And they give value for money, for they live such a long time. Effective insulation materials, together with relatively inexpensive thermostatically-controlled heaters and life-saving automatic vents, mean that amateur greenhouses can provide suitable growing conditions, but even the house or conservatory is good enough, at least for the more amenable genera. Proprietary orchid composts are available which help give confidence to the inexperienced.

However, these are all practical matters concerning cultivation; they do not bear any relation to the love people feel for orchids. If you want to understand that, you will have to meet some. The next London Orchid Show in March could be the start of the affair.

Independent

6

Bulbs

Painted by a Guiding Hand　　　　　*6 March 1994*

It is not a love of hoeing or weeding or digging – pleasurable as these activities often are – which makes us gardeners (for these are only the means to an end) but a desire, even need, to be reminded continually and close to home of the marvels of our natural world.

Take the crocus, for example, which clamours for a reaction from me at the moment – if it is only irritation at the pecking of the petals by the birds. Considering how small a plant it is, this bulb exhibits a powerful number of natural, congruous intricacies. We may argue with each other about whether these intricacies are the result of billions of years of slow painful evolution from a primordial soup, or whether a Guiding Hand

137

painted every petal and forked every stigma, but we would not argue over the result – a flower of such exceptional variety that a lifetime is scarcely sufficient to learn all the shapes of stigmata or the almost infinite variety of featherings and markings on the petals.

There is more to the crocus even than that, however. Its capacity to use its contractile roots to pull itself down to the exact spot in the soil which suits it best, rather than make shift with the level which we in our careless way have ordained for it, seems to me little short of miraculous. How does it sense that it is at the wrong level for its surest survival, and set about putting the matter right?

Moreover, although they do not look capable of it, the spiky leaves of the crocus can push their way through tarmac.This is not altogether surprising if you consider the rocky nature of their native habitats – for most originate in mountainous regions. As wonderful as anything, however, is the way that the petals open out to greet the sun, thus affording a better opportunity for flying insects, coaxed airborne by the warmth of the sun, to pollinate the flower; although this is a physiological response to help ensure fertilisation, it also has the effect of endowing the crocus with a most appealing, because almost human, personality.

In the crocus, the stigma, the pollen-receptive female flower part, is very important for identification purposes. Stigmata are forked and fringed in many species. They vary in colour from golden to bright scarlet – those of *Crocus sativus*, from which saffron is gleaned, for example, are a particularly attractive red.

The bulbs are not, strictly speaking, bulbs at all, but corms. Few care about that. What matters is that the 'tunics' of these corms can also be used to help distinguish between different species. For example, *Crocus ancyrensis* has a reticulate, or netted, tunic, whereas that of *C. chrysanthus* is annulate, which is to say, ringed. (The former, incidentally, are supposedly less

Bulbs

attractive to mice – the great crocus expert E.A. Bowles reckoned it was because the netting got round their teeth!)

Knowing how to identify crocuses does not necessarily mean it is easy to do, because there are dozens of species and hundreds of cultivated forms. Most have smaller (less than 4 inches tall), daintier and less bulbous flowers than the large Dutch crocuses (forms of *Crocus vernus*), which are what most people mean when they use the word 'crocus'. These are the ones planted in their tens of thousands in grass in public parks, where they undoubtedly look their best.

It is no help to know that *Crocus biflorus* means 'the two-flowered crocus', because most crocuses produce two flowers as a matter of course. Reginald Farrer wrote, teasingly, that it was known as the Scotch crocus because 'it belongs to the Mediterranean basin from Tuscany to Georgia'. *Crocus biflorus* has a goblet-shaped flower which is pure white with purple stripes on the outside; *C. biflorus* ssp. *alexandri* differs from that in having the outside of petals more or less completely purple; *C. biflorus* ssp. *weldenii* 'Fairy' is pale lilac instead of purple. All are worth growing, preferably in sunny raised rock beds where they can be seen close to.

The same is true of *Crocus chrysanthus*, which flowers at the same sort of time. The many cultivar forms of this species are enormously rewarding to grow and study because of the range of featherings and ground colour on the petals. Several of the cultivars are easy to pick out, such as the gold and bronze 'Zwanenburg Bronze', the white and mauve 'Ladykiller' and the lavender-blue 'Blue Pearl', but others are more difficult. There is, however, a simple way of establishing whether an unknown flower is a form of *C. chrysanthus* – if you have sharp eyes, that is. Look out for the tiny, delicate, blue-black barbs at the base of the pollen-bearing anthers which surround the stigma inside the flower. If they are not marvellous, then I have lost the power to marvel at anything.

Sunday Telegraph

Brazen Hussies *2 March 2002*

I am never in any hurry for winter to end. I take it in leisurely fashion, savouring each opening hellebore flower, regretting each fading snowdrop and aconite. That is why these mild winters do not suit me at all, for they bring on the dancing daffodils far too early. What is more, shrubs which have no business to be anything but dormant in February are unfurling their leaves. All of a sudden, there is no time to reflect in a slow, pleasurable manner on what has just been, or anticipate what is to come, before the helter-skelter spring rush is upon us.

This painful collision of seasons makes the true late February and early March flowers such as the lesser celandine easy to miss, their subtle allure masked by a thoroughly egged pudding of yolky daffodils. The lesser celandine, *Ranunculus ficaria*, is so-called to distinguish it from the 'greater' celandine, a poppy named *Chelidonium majus*, which it resembles scarcely at all. (If you ever needed a cast-iron example of why botanical Latin names are better than 'common' names for plants, this is surely it.) *Ranunculus ficaria* is closely related to the buttercup instead, and has much of the latter's invasive propensities, so the word 'celandine' usually strikes terror into the hearts of conscientious gardeners. Certainly I would never willingly introduce the wild *R. ficaria* to my flower beds, with its tiny tubers multiplying in the soil unseen, but I do love to see it stretch its bright yellow star petals wide at ground level in meadow, grassy bank or deciduous wood.

Moreover, there are dozens of garden forms with either single or double flowers which are usually far less rampageous than the native species and can, therefore, be admitted to the garden. Indeed, some are quite hard to get to spread at all. They are either garden hybrids, or forms which have arisen in the wild and been found at one time or another by sharp-eyed botanists or gardeners.

'Brazen Hussy' is the best known, with the wittiest name,

and it was found by Christopher Lloyd near his home in East Sussex. It is called 'brazen' because the young, long-stalked, heart-shaped leaves are a shiny purplish-bronze. It has been crossed with a number of others, so that you can now buy 'Coy Hussy', 'Brazen Child' and 'Brazen Daughter' as well. All are fun to collect, although care must be taken to weed out any seedlings which turn up with ordinary green leaves. 'Coppernob' is quite similar to 'Brazen Hussy' but has copper-orange flowers which fade with age. 'Randall's White' is a very attractive pallid form which has creamy-white flowers, blue on the reverse, and green leaves. And there is *Ranunculus ficaria* var. *aurantiacus*, which is a coppery-orange-flowered version, sometimes called 'Cuprea'.

Among the double flowers praise is due to 'Collarette', with a neat yellow flower with a golden anemone centre surrounding a green heart, and green leaves with bronze centres. This has in the past been wrongly called 'E.A. Bowles' or 'Bowles' Double', and can still be found under those names. There is much less confusion, you will be glad to hear, about the charmingly-named 'Double Mud', which has large double creamy-yellow flowers.

Such is the versatility of *Ranunculus ficaria*, and the insatiable hunger of gardeners for novelty, that a good hunt in nursery catalogues or the *RHS Plant Finder* will yield up, among others, 'Mobled Jade', which has foliage marbled with bronze; 'Green Petal', a double with green-striped yellow petals; 'Coffee Cream', creamy-yellow petals with dark brown reverses to them; 'Ken Aslet Double', large, cream, water-lily-like flowers; 'Tortoiseshell', with intricately marbled leaves; and 'Brambling', with single flowers and silver and purple markings on the leaves. And more are being named all the time, it seems.

One of the virtues of the lesser celandine is that it produces its leaves in the winter but dies down by midsummer. It therefore makes a good subject for the front of a deciduous shrub border, covering the ground in the same conditions which hellebores, aconites and snowdrops like, and then disappearing when the shrubs strut their stuff in summer. Should you fear that your carpet of celandines is getting out of hand (as it sometimes can), the judicious and careful use of the systemic weedkiller glyphosate just after flowering will keep it in your control. Otherwise you will have to dig and delve for the clusters of small tubers. Celandines like best a moist soil in semi-shade, but they are very tolerant, so you could plant them in a seemingly unpromising spot like a hedge bottom, and see how they go. Those with very small gardens might prefer to grow the choice varieties in terracotta pots instead. And if next winter is 'normal', in the way the last few winters have not been, they will beat the daffodils to the draw. Which will suit those of us who like to savour our small pleasures.

Independent

Laid-back Narcissi   3 *March 2001*

It is hard to imagine a world in early March, least of all a garden, without *Narcissus cyclamineus* varieties. It would certainly be a dull place without any of these brightly-coloured miniature daffodils, with their distinctive and characteristic swept-back petals, to liven up an alpine bed or warm the cold spaces under deciduous shrubs. They are the stout-hearted if diminutive vanguard of the army of narcissi and daffodils which crowd our gardens in mid and late spring.

The name *cyclamineus* means 'like a cyclamen', a reference to the way those petals are both twisted and reflexed, much as a cyclamen flower's are, although I have always thought the six petals and trumpet or corona together look more like one half of a pulled cracker. When I see these flowers, I am also keenly reminded of a bad-tempered donkey we looked after when I was a child. Jack was a beach animal rescued from the knacker's yard and of uncertain temper; if you went too close to him, his ears would lie flat along his neck, he would turn to chew his flank, and then charge at you. Ever since, the flat laid-back 'ears' of *Narcissus cyclamineus* have brought Jack the donkey to mind. Vita Sackville-West memorably wrote that this flower 'lays its ears back as if frightened or in a tantrum'. In Jack's case, it was probably both.

The species, *Narcissus cyclamineus*, comes from wet lowland areas in northern Portugal and Spain. It has two leaves which grow to about 22 cm tall, the same length as the flower stem, which holds a single, pendent flower. So acutely angled is the flower and so reflexed its perianth segments that it looks as if at any moment it will plunge head first into the ground. This is a bulb suited best to a damp, acidic soil in partial shade, but fortunately its garden hybrids are much less fussy.

So numerous and important are these hybrids and cultivated forms that one of the thirteen sections into which narcissi and daffodils are grouped is devoted exclusively to them (Group 6). Not all the cultivars have perianth segments which reflex right the way back, but it is a sufficiently strong characteristic for you always to know one when you see one. The most famous is probably 'February Gold', not only because it is quite tall and imposing for a *cyclamineus* cultivar (about 30 cm high) but because, especially in the south of England, it flowers in February in mild years. It has a butter-yellow, flared trumpet and slightly lighter-coloured petals.

'February Silver' flowers at the same time but has a pretty creamy-white trumpet and white petals. 'Dove Wings' has a pale creamy-yellow perianth and light yellow trumpet. 'Jetfire' grows to 25 cm tall and has a red-orange trumpet and yellow perianth segments. A popular, strong-growing but later-flowering cultivar is 'Jenny', which has a lemon-yellow corona and lighter, pointed petals, while the equally popular but diminutive 'Jumblie' scores because it is one of the few *cyclamineus* hybrids with more than one flower to the stem: there can be as many as three, golden-yellow, with a deeper corona.'Tête-à-Tête' is similar in size, colour, flowering period and number of flowers, but has petals which are scarcely reflexed at all. 'Beryl' is a good 'doer', multiplying well in grass and producing 20-cm stems of flowers with short, narrow, orange coronas and pale yellow petals.

However, early March does not belong entirely to Group 6 narcissi. Our two native daffodils, the Lent lily, *Narcissus pseudonarcissus*, usually sold in the form called 'Lobularis', is also an early flowerer, as is the closely-related Tenby daffodil, *Narcissus obvallaris*. 'Lobularis' has a pale yellow perianth with a darker yellow, long trumpet, while *obvallaris* is completely golden-yellow. These are well worth looking for, not only for the beauty and neat propriety of their flowers (and for perianth segments which look forward, not back) but because, being British natives, they are likely to find your climate, if not necessarily your soil, congenial to them. No one who has seen them growing on the tops of Devon walls could forget the charms of the Lent lily, but it also grows wild elsewhere, most notably in the Lake District, as the Wordsworths attested.

Narcissus cyclamineus and its hybrids are happiest in a neutral or acid soil but will grow elsewhere in soils which do not dry out easily, especially in late summer. They can all be grown in troughs or pots, in gritty compost, and the dwarfer ones are set off better here than in the open garden. Our native narcissi can be happily naturalised in short grass, as can the larger, stronger *cyclamineus* hybrids such as 'Beryl' and 'February Gold'. They need to be planted deep, however, at least 15 cm underground, to help prevent them running out of available moisture in summer, and consequently failing to initiate flower buds for the following year.

Narcissus of every variety are best planted in the early autumn, but March is the moment to be looking out for them, making lists of 'must-haves' at flower shows, and simply enjoying their cheerful gaiety in the early spring garden.

Daily Telegraph

Consider the Lily   14 April 2001

Is there any plant name which has so many associations for us, so much resonance, as the lily? I don't think so. My plant encyclopedia names no fewer than seventy genera of plants which have 'lily' as part of their common names. A few are true lilies – that is, of the genus *Lilium* – but many bear little or no resemblance to *Lilium* as we know it: foxtail lily is *Eremurus*; kaffir lily, *Schizostylis*; Mexican lily, *Hippeastrum*; torch lily, *Kniphofia*. The list is a long one. Many come from the ends of the earth, named originally by explorers, settlers, missionaries, indeed anyone who did not consider himself a botanist, I suspect, and was happier using vernacular names. Not all these lilies are even bulbs. The truth is that 'lily' is a very, very old word, which probably originally referred to anything that was just a pretty flower. Hence the lilies of the field which, though they toiled not, neither did they spin, still managed to outshine King Solomon.

I have been pondering lilies lately and perhaps you have been, too. After all, in every parish in the land, women (for it is nearly always women, I know) swiftly but deftly arrange the flowers in church in that short space of time between the end of Good Friday, when no flowers are permitted, and the beginning of Easter Day, when every part of the church must be decorated and beautiful. Many of these arrangements of flowers feature so-called 'Easter lilies', *Lilium longiflorum*, which have huge glistening white, very fragrant, open trumpet flowers, and fleshy, ribbed green leaves. They are heart-achingly beautiful.

There are a number of other 'lilies' with Christian epithets. The Lent lily, so-called because of the season when it flowers, is our charming native daffydowndilly, *Narcissus pseudonarcissus*, and there are two types of Resurrection lily (*Kaempferia rotunda* and *Lycoris squamigera*), not to mention three named after saints: St Bernard's lily (*Anthericum liliago*), St Joseph's lily

(*Hippeastrum vittatum*) and St Bruno's lily (*Paradisea*). The Madonna lily (*Lilium candidum*) has a prominent place in Renaissance paintings of the Annunciation, when the Angel Gabriel appears to Mary; in fact, you can find this lily depicted in religious paintings from pre-Renaissance to pre-Raphaelite. White lilies also feature in the iconography of Islam, and were holy flowers to the ancient Assyrians.

There are a number of rather more secular 'lilies', some positively creepy, like the Voodoo lily (which is a strange kind of arum called *Sauromatum venosum*), some fuddling, like the American trout lily (*Erythronium revolutum*), and some just plain sweet, like the pyjama lily (*Crinum macowanii*), which has pink flowers with a dark red stripe on each petal.

Let us go back to *Lilium longiflorum* for a moment, for this Japanese lily, from Ryuku Island and Formosa, was introduced into Britain as late as 1862, but has been a choice glasshouse plant since then. Though not reliably hardy in this climate it is perfectly happy in a conservatory or cold greenhouse, where it will flower in June or July. (The Easter lilies that you can buy from florists at this time of year come from Israel, appropriately enough.) The 18-cm-long flowers are pure white within, except for the golden yellow stamens, and with more than a suggestion of pale *eau-de-nil* green on the outside. They are torpedo-shaped in bud but open into broad, flared trumpets. There can be up to six flowers on a stem, but more usually there are three; these are held horizontally at the top of each 75- to 90-cm-tall stem.

Bulbs of these stem-rooting lilies are well worth seeking out in specialist catalogues for they make magnificent, scented, long-lasting displays if planted in autumn, deeply, in groups of three to a large 30-cm pot, in a loam-based compost such as John Innes No. 2, with extra grit added to help drainage. By 'deeply', I mean at least three times the length of the bulb. They like to be in a very light place, but shaded from hot, direct sunlight; they need feeding regularly with a high-potash feed when in growth; and they should not be allowed to dry out in winter.

These bulbs are available from a few specialist nurseries at relatively modest cost. There used to be a number of named forms about in the trade, but the only one you are likely to come across now is 'White American'. I am told that this lily will also flower from seed in only a few months, which is a very remarkable thing. Unfortunately, I can find no general seed catalogue which lists it, but it is available from specialist society seed lists such as that of the Alpine Garden Society. Otherwise, the best solution I should think would be to buy bulbs first and, when they flower, cross-pollinate one of them (for fertilisation hastens the process of a flower going over) and save seed, sowing it immediately it is ripe. If you live in a sheltered and favoured spot, it would be worth trying these bulbs in a lightly-shaded, humus-rich but well-drained soil outdoors. You may not have flowers for decorating the church next Easter, but you will certainly have something to lift the spirits each summer.

Independent

Familiarity breeds Content   *15 May 1994*

It is a widely held axiom that familiarity undermines the pleasure we take in flowers. The argument runs that if we had never seen winter jasmine or forsythia before, we would be amazed at their beauty; so commonplace are they, however, that we scarcely give them a second glance. Contempt for the everyday is the reason why those people newly bitten by the gardening bug are so conspicuous for their enthusiasm – an enthusiasm which, to our shame, we hard-boiled old sophisticates can find almost embarrassing.

There is an extreme form of this theory, held by some gardeners whose opinion I respect, which goes along these lines:

if you were to read a botanical description of *Taraxacum offici-nale* in a nursery catalogue and not recognise it as the common dandelion, you would fall over yourself to buy it.

Up to a point, Lord Copper. Those cheery yellow, round, fringed flowers on short fleshy stems and with deeply-cut leaves look well enough on a distant road verge, but are too dumpy to be really attractive (except to poets of rare sensibility like John Clare, of course); it is not therefore simply a cultural taboo dating from childhood or a healthy fear of invasiveness which dilutes my enthusiasm for them.

To my mind, there are absolute standards of beauty in flower form and colour. You only have to think of apple blossom. All over the country every year, people must thank their gods that they are alive to see the apple trees flowering so brilliantly in the still sunshine of early May. No amount of familiarity could ever dull the edge of admiration, let alone breed contempt, for this annual miracle.

But to return to the humbler dandelion. The attitude I mention represents a proper, if in this instance misplaced, desire to cast off the cloak of blasé pseudo-sophistication and view common flowers with fresh, unprejudiced eyes. In my view, it is a great deal easier to do this with the common bluebell, another flower most people will not let into the garden. Once known, charmingly, as *Endymion non-scriptus*, now rather more prosaically as *Hyacinthoides non-scriptus*, it is a bulb with spikes some 12 inches tall rising from strappy, smothering leaves and composed of hanging bells of a deep and satisfying blue.

There are several clumps of bluebells in borders in our garden. I suspect they arrived by accident rather than design, for this garden backs onto fields and woods where there are indigenous bluebells, and this plant is a very successful coloniser in conditions that suit it. Both the individual flowers on each stem, and the stems *en masse*, have an appealing freshness to them, which associates well here with the bright and variegated spring foliage of *Euonymus fortunei* 'Emerald 'n' Gold', as well as acid-yellow *Euphorbia polychroma* and all the late white daffodils, like 'Cheerfulness'.

I also love to see them naturalised in grass, for although they are woodland plants, they are surprisingly tolerant of sun. There is a grassy roadside bank near here where the blue and white forms grow in about equal numbers. So close is the bank to a garden that I suspect they were planted deliberately; it is a simple planting, but a most effective one.

Some natives – the cowslip, for example – should find a place in every garden, but the common bluebell is not quite one of those. I know that I cannot allow the bluebells to spread through the borders indefinitely and must soon remove them to wilder regions, in this case a small 'woodland' planting in the outer reaches of the garden. (This cannot yet be dignified by the term 'wood', consisting as it does of four hundred spindly little whips of native deciduous trees, entirely clothed by the latest fashion in *prêt-à-porter* pink protective plastic tubes, but I have high hopes for it in thirty years' time.)

As for the garden proper, I am thinking of replacing the blue-bells with *Hyacinthoides hispanica* (syn. *Scilla campanulata*). If anything, it is taller and stronger-growing, but it seeds less freely, so can be let loose in a not-too-tidy cottage border without fear of the consequences. What is more, I can choose pink and white forms as well as the blue, to make an attractive if undemanding instant colour combination. Best of all, because this bulb comes all the way from Spain it has a defi-nite, if spurious, exotic feel to it. You wait: I shall be singing the praises of *Crepis incana*, the pink dandelion from southern Greece, next.

Sunday Telegraph

Horticultural Hilarity *2 October 1994*

Ever since the dreadful, never-to-be-forgotten day at school when I played the washboard in a disastrous House rendition of Leopold Mozart's Toy Symphony I have not been very keen on artful jocularity. The lack of spontaneity has a way of freezing the smile on my lips. I am quite sure, for example, that I would not have hit it off with Sir Frank Crisp, whose garden at Friar Park near Henley in the early years of this century was full of visual puns and jokes. His rock garden was a scaled-down replica of the Matterhorn, with a summit of alabaster to resemble snow, and had tin chamois 'grazing' on it. A crooked skull hung above the door of the scullery (skull awry, geddit?). Stagy pleasantries like that just make me cross.

But in our last garden there was one horticultural joke which always worked a treat with my sternly non-horticultural children and, indeed, anybody else, child or grown-up, who visited. This was *Arisarum proboscideum*, 'the mouse-tail plant'. Year after year it appeared in spring, in the shade of a walnut tree, as a cover of glossy dark green arrowhead leaves which almost completely masked the strange flowers when they came in May and June. As this plant is a member of the aroid (Lords-and-Ladies) family, the flower consists of a spathe, partly bulbous and white and partly brown and hooded like a Franciscan friar's cowl. But the really fascinating aspect of the flower is the curved tip, elongated into a 'tail' up to 6 inches (15 cm) long, the end of which can just be seen above the covering of leaves. A small child asked to lift the leaves carefully is greeted by what looks like the back end of a mouse scurrying away.

If my plodding description of what is a very charming and unusual plant has not put you off, I suggest you get hold of a few of these and plant them in autumn. In the dry shade of the walnut tree our 'mouse plant' never multiplied, but I am assured that, in damper woodland conditions, it can stray a little. That is no matter if you plant it under deciduous shrubs or in any unpromising place where most plants will not thrive, and then mulch it with leaf mould or composted bark. The tubers may be bought, inexpensively, from a variety of mail-order bulb firms.

While on the subject of horticultural drollery, one of the best or worst examples, depending on your attitude, is another bulb that should be planted in autumn. This is the 'split corona' or, as the nurserymen will have it ,'orchid-flowering' daffodil, of which there are several varieties in commerce. These are the newest type of trumpet daffodil to be developed, the class having been registered only in 1950; the distinctive character-istic is that the trumpet is split into (usually) six pieces, which are pressed back flat against the outer petals.These inner petals are usually elaborately frilled and can be the same colour as the outer perianths, as with 'Cassata', or different, as with 'Lemon Beauty'. A flower head which has been detached from its stalk and leaves is not always easy to identify as a daffodil at all, so anyone with a highly-developed sense of fun can tease visitors with an amusing guessing game. However, what really makes me laugh about these daffodils is that the breeders plainly did not create them as a joke.

Sunday Telegraph

Full-blooded   8 May 1994

Contrary to received medical opinion, anaemia is not a condi-tion confined to mammals; in my experience, gardens also often suffer from it. Its symptoms show up most clearly in spring – potentially the liveliest time in the year – when many gardens are pale to the point of bloodlessness, and the most colourful displays come from plantings of pheasant-eye nar-cissus and pinkish 'Amanogawa' cherries. The simple remedy for this condition is not however, as you might think, a shot of iron, but a dose of revivifying tulip.

Apart perhaps from rhododendrons, roses and irises, I cannot think of a single group of plants which can equal the range of colour to be found among the fourteen classes and four hundred cultivars of tulip. The genus can claim everything from the deepest purple to the most glistening white, and everything except blue in between, including – in the case of the Viridiflora varieties – green. In theory, at least, there is a tulip suitable for every colour scheme, adventurous or subdued.

In practice, however, people are often put off, both by the habit of some types and the way that they are used. If you have recently flinched at the sight of yellow and red tulips planted together in a windswept municipal 'planter', bending over each other like conspiratorial drunks, you may feel justified in giving the whole genus a wide berth.

The flowers of some tulips, especially those of the Darwin group, are not elegant in themselves, being shaped rather like scalped coloured balls; these sit on tall rubber-tubing stems which issue from flaccid leaves. If, as is often the case in public places, these tulips are knitted into a patchwork quilt of mutually detracting colours, without relief from plants of different habit, the result is not entirely satisfactory.

It seems to me important to play to the tulip's strengths, not its weaknesses. Greater use could be made of the many varieties which do have very pleasing flowers. Those in the Lily-Flowered class, for example, have pointed and waisted petals, which give the unopen flowers the look of fluted wine glasses. (I cannot immediately recall a lily with a flower exactly that shape, but there we are.) For sheer *joie de vivre*, there are few flowers in the garden to beat the 'parrot' tulips; even in green bud the crinkling of the petals is evident, and they open in flamboyant and endearing frilliness at the beginning of May. Yet you do not often meet them in gardens.

Nor do all tulips have at least two-foot-tall stems as straight, initially, as a commissionaire's backbone. The early double tulip 'Peach Blossom', for example, reaches only nine inches high and you can scarcely see the stems for the large flowers, which open out flat as they mature. There are even some tulips with attractive leaves, especially those derived from *Tulipa greigii*, which have inwardly-curved, glaucous leaves, striped inside with purple.

The important thing is not to leave tulips stranded like ship-wrecked mariners, huddled in little groups on their own, buffeted by gales and April showers. It should not be beyond our wit to find places for them to grow where the stems and leaves are scarcely visible. There are plenty of perennials which, though not flowering in April and May, will back them up and shelter them from the wind: delphiniums, evergreen grasses, bergenias, together with small deciduous shrubs like *Spiraea bumalda* and *Potentilla fruticosa*. There is a group of red Darwin tulips in my garden (not planted by me, I confess) which is supported and protected by the branches of a hydrangea, the colour enhanced by the shrub's fresh green leaves. Another place for such a group would be just in front of the shrub *Spiraea* × *arguta*, with white flowers in early May.

Tulips should also find a place among the few spring-flowering hardy perennials like *Doronicum plantagineum* 'Excelsum' (the dark purple 'Queen of the Night' would look stunning as a contrast), *Helleborus corsicus* and *Brunnera macrophylla*, or tall biennials like the white and mauve versions of honesty (*Lunaria annua*).

If money is no object and you like to plant masses of bedding plants in summer, why not do as the Dutch do, and give beds over completely to a scheme composed of dispensable bulbs? You could, for example, put the Triumph tulip 'Golden Melody' among the tall *Fritillaria persica* 'Adiyaman' (stately, four feet tall, with grey-green leaves and bloomy plum flowers) and add an underplanting of the blue-violet grape hyacinth *Muscari latifolium*. Then just dig the tulips up and throw them away after flowering.

As for those tulips with striped, flared and feathered petals which can cause problems when planning colour schemes, well, they are just the thing to grow on their own or with groups of colourful polyanthus in deep containers and window boxes, as lively examples of full-blooded spring exuberance.

Sunday Telegraph

A Lost Cause?   1 August 1993

I suppose it is inevitable that having been born and educated in Oxford I should be imbued with the spirit of the place, a spirit so particular that Matthew Arnold was moved to call the city the 'home of lost causes, and forsaken beliefs, and unpopular names, and impossible loyalties!'

I am not quite sure about unpopular names, but I would not quarrel with the others, especially a fondness for lost causes. Charles I, Bonny Prince Charlie, a referendum on the Maastricht treaty, the campaign against uPVC windows – the more obviously doomed, the stouter I am in support. One of the horticultural lost causes dearest to my heart is the colchicum, known erroneously as the autumn crocus or meadow saffron, and irrelevantly but picturesquely as 'naked ladies'. I commend it to you at a time when it is suitable to be planting out its corms, but with no very great expectation that you will take me up on it.

It is not that the colchicum is an ugly plant – very far from it – or that it is unreliable and disease-prone, for it is not. What puts people off is its rather odd propensity for flowering without its leaves in the early autumn, and then in the spring, in time to swamp other plants, pushing up lush green straps which die in a soggy and too-obvious manner in early summer.

This habit is the reason why it is usually (which is to say, not very often) advocated that colchicums be grown in grass, in the same conditions that suit daffodils. The objection is that the effect can look rather mean, for their price prohibits splashing out as you might on a sack of 'Carlton' daffs.

All this seems defeatist talk to me. Certainly colchicums increase only slowly in grass, but it is possible to plant them initially in good soil in the vegetable patch, and after a couple of years dig up and divide the corms, and re-plant them in grass. The leaves can be mown round in spring and, when they start to yellow, can be cut off (not pulled, however, which may damage the nascent flower buds) and the grass mown properly. They are not plants for a neat lawn, it is true, but are well suited to the wildflower 'meadow'.

It is also held against colchicums that they are poisonous. Well, so they are, but most of us do not have livestock grazing in our gardens, and I would be surprised if young children were tempted by them. Anyway, forewarned is forearmed.

The main objection, however, is the fact that the leaves will smother less robust plants in borders. The answer to that is to avoid planting anything permanent too close, but put in low-growing tender perennials to replace the leaves in June when you can cut them down – *Felicia amelloides*, trailing verbenas, small argyranthemums, *Helichrysum petiolare*. These should cover the nakedness of the stems yet will be removed in the late autumn, either by frost or by human agency. Alternatively, as colchicums will stand some shade, plant them in clear ground under deciduous shrubs.

I once saw a mass of colchicums flowering at Felbrigg, a National Trust house in Norfolk. They were tucked in behind a low box hedge at the front of a shrub border and were so thickly flowering that they stopped me in my tracks. It seemed to me an eminently sensible place to put them because, without the bright pink of the flowers to catch the eye, the leaves would not worry you when they started to die.

The most widely grown colchicum is probably the rose-lilac *Colchicum autumnale*, but *C. speciosum*, with a fat pink flower like an oversized crocus (hence the confusion, although the botanists will tell you loftily that they are impossible to muddle because the first has six stamens and the other three, so there), is also well worth growing. It has a rather charming white version, 'Album'. My favourite is 'Waterlily', a large mauve variety with masses of petals. I have seen it at its best grown in pots in an alpine house, because the flowers are easily spoiled by autumn rain. Perhaps the finest of all is the rosy purple *C. agrippinum,* which has fascinating tessellations, or chequering, on the petals; it is one of the earliest to flower, in August.

It is rare to find bulbs which flower so soon after planting as colchicums do; indeed, if you are not on the ball, sometimes they will flower before you get them into the ground. Between the beginning of August and early September is the time they will be sent out by the specialist nurseries, and when you will find them for sale in the better garden centres. Plant the corms 3 to 4 inches (7.5–10 cm) below ground, in moisture-retentive soil, and retire quickly to watch the fireworks.

Sunday Telegraph

Little Short of Miraculous

19 October 2002

There are not many Latin tags which have survived in my memory since my schooldays, but *mirabile dictu* or 'marvellous to relate' is one of them. I must have liked the cadence of it, and though I had very little Latin, I had enough to wish to show it off during my teenage pretentious/facetious phase. Now the phrase comes back to me each September when *Cyclamen mirabilis* first begins to flower in the cold greenhouse, for *mirabile* it is.

Perhaps you know it? I hope so, for it is certainly not uncommon in specialist bulb catalogues and has an Award of Garden Merit from the Royal Horticultural Society to boot. Unlike the stonking big *persicum* hybrids (which we buy at Christmas, when inspiration fails, for elderly relatives who can rarely keep them for very long because their houses are too hot) the whole plant grows no taller than 4 inches. The flowers, giving off a scent suggestive of primrose, are loosely twisted like paper streamers and raggedly toothed at the top, as if some abstemious mouse had nibbled just a few little bits from each petal. These are a delicate pink in colour, with a darker, purple-pink colouring at the base, but there are no bumps (auricles) such as you see in the mouths of other cyclamen flowers.

The leaves, which have slightly rucked edges, appear just before the flowers unfurl, and are heart-shaped normally, matt-green on the upper side but with a lovely pattern of silver, flushed pink when young, encircling the central part. The undersides of the leaves are purple, like those of the commoner *Cyclamen hederifolium*. This cyclamen was the subject of scandal in the 1970s, when huge numbers of tubers were dug up from the wild in Turkey and imported into Europe. Nowadays, however, you will be relieved to know that those which are commercially available have been nursery-grown. And there are even some good forms: the cyclamen experts Tile Barn Nurseries in Kent, for instance, sell three variants, one of which has white flowers ('Tilebarn Jan'), and two ('Tilebarn Nicholas' and 'Tilebarn Anne') with particularly good leaf colouring.

One minute, it seems, there are just a few dead stalks lying on top of the grit in the pot, the next the young leaves are unfurling and the flowers elongating before my eyes. They flower with *Cyclamen cilicium*, a similar species, also from Turkey. At the same time, and in the same greenhouse, a couple of Jersey lilies, *Nerine sarniensis*, emerge from the deadest-of-dead papery bulb tops to stretch their necks and flower flamboyantly within a couple of weeks. This capacity of bulbs, corms and tubers to send up flowers from seemingly dead storage organs never fails to thrill, however often I see it happen. On the same day as the cyclamen emerged, under the Bramley apple tree a dozen *Crocus speciosus* were suddenly in full flower.

Bulbs

When the flowers of *Cyclamen mirabile* finally give way after a few weeks and they set seed, the stems twist into a spiral. This is not so they can shoot the seed some distance, but to bring it down to ground level close to the tuber. Don't ask me why.

I can only think of one other plant, the tender marvel of Peru, *Mirabilis jalapa*, which has a similarly admiring name. Perhaps botanists have always been superstitious about according a plant such an accolade, in case they tempt the wrath of the gods thereby. Or perhaps, more prosaically, they do not make value judgements about plants as often as gardeners do. Whatever the reason, the almost-uniqueness of this plant is one more powerful incentive to grow it.

Daily Telegraph

Look to your Roots

21 October 1990

The garden party is finally over, and the business of clearing up has begun in earnest. Most of the guests, having stayed so late, are somewhat the worse for wear, and the ones feeling particularly fragile will have to come into the house, at least until it is time to prepare for next year's festivities.

For both plants and people the summer party has been hectic and exciting, but at the same time painful and disappointing; seemingly endless at the beginning, but over far too quickly. Many plants, such as dahlias, have enjoyed the generous hours of sunshine, but lack of soil moisture has sometimes restricted the growth of stems, and sometimes their flowers have faded too quickly.

But whether plants have done well or badly, the compère has finally called for 'Auld Lang Syne' and it is time to pack up and go home. The first frosts are upon us and the dahlias must find their way indoors – that is, if they are to be certain to survive the winter.

I say 'certain' because we can all cite examples of forgotten dahlia tubers which have lived through the ensuing mild winter to explode into life the following season. Many gardeners working light soils in the south get them through the average winter just by covering the soil round the stems with dried bracken or ashes. Flying by your coat-tails is no better a precept for gardening than it is for life, however, so once the first frost has blackened the top of the leaves, cut the stems down to six inches or so (just enough to afford a firm grip) and dig the tubers up.

Dahlias use up the food stored in their underground tubers as they grow, and have to make new ones each year. This happens between August and mid October, so there is no sense in leaving them in the ground much longer, particularly as a hard frost might penetrate to the tubers. Digging dahlia tubers has to be done carefully, for they come away from each other rather easily. A spade is a less offensive weapon than a fork, because you do less damage should you slice cleanly through a tuber 'finger' than if you make a hole in it.

The soil should be gently shaken and eased away and a name label, attached by wire or strong string, tied round each stem. Then each plant can be hung somewhere upside down to allow any moisture in the stem to fall out. The obvious place for this, if you are lucky enough to have it, is the slatted wooden staging in a cool greenhouse. Otherwise, a simple construction of chicken wire stretched between short posts in the garage or an airy shed would be suitable. Or you can simply put the tubers in shallow boxes, stems facing downwards.

When they are dry, the tubers should be plunked in a solution of benomyl* because dahlias are very prone to attack from fungal diseases; indeed, some disease is almost inevitable, particularly in cold, moist winters. They will then need to be left to dry for a few hours. After that they can be placed, stem

* Long since taken off the market, unfortunately.

upwards, in tomato trays, bedded in and covered by dry spent potting compost or sand.

Dahlia tubers need to be looked over every so often during the winter and spring because they can rot or shrivel, especially if they are put in too warm a place (they need only be kept safe from frost). If they have shrivelled, prolonged immersion in a bucket of water usually reinflates the tubers. If 'fingers' have rotted, the infected part should be cut away cleanly and the wound dusted with sulphur.

I do not think I am imagining the fact that some of the more restrained dahlias are gaining in popularity as denizens of the flower border – rather than merely as cutting flowers in dull rows in the vegetable garden.* It is true they have very unexciting leaves, but these can be hidden by bulky perennials, and it seems short-sighted to deny ourselves the dahlia's range of colour, flower shape and extended flowering period at the end of summer.

After all, not all dahlias have flowers the size of soup plates and the colour of Outspan oranges. No self-respecting plantsman should do without *Dahlia merckii*, for example, a species with attractive single lilac-mauve flowers and a rangy, almost delicate habit, while some of the Miscellaneous varieties, such as the bronze-leaved, deep-red 'Bishop of Llandaff', are invaluable for a full-blooded late summer colour scheme.

Observer

* Can it really be that I spotted a trend early on?

7

Trees and Shrubs

A Sight for Sore Eyes   *30 December 2000*

Last week, I did something that was more than usually stupid. I did it by accident, of course, but that is often how it seems when stupidity is involved. I was pruning a neglected forsythia (what forsythia is ever not neglected?) by cutting out a number of old, thick, unthrifty stems from the centre of the bush, when I failed to duck or blink to prevent a twig poking me in the eye. Refusing to think of forsythia in the same terms as a whippy, thorny rose, I had not bothered to wear goggles or even a pair of sunglasses as eye protection. Immediately my vision blurred, I wept copious salt tears, and was forced to resort to the paracetamol, for it was painful. Only when I got round to bathing my eye in Optrex did things

Trees and Shrubs

begin slowly to look up. I shall not be so insouciant again
when pruning.

I have been bathing my eyes with Optrex from time to time
all my conscious life, but it was only last week, while assidu-
ously reading the label, that I discovered its magic ingredient to
be witch hazel. I should have known. Witch hazel is a great if
rather astringent healer, first discovered by Native Americans.
The active principle is derived from the leaves of *Hamamelis vir-
giniana*, a large shrub or small tree which is native to Virginia,
as you might expect from the name. In autumn, just before the
hazel-like, slightly corrugated roundish leaves begin to turn
yellow and then fall, it produces yellow flowers composed of
four twisted, narrow petals.

Although hardy, this species is not much seen in gardens in
Britain, mainly because gardeners generally agree that the great
virtue of most witch hazels – apart from the autumn colour of
the leaves, the attractive erect, vase-shaped habit, and the
lovely scent of the flowers, of course – is the fact that they bloom
in the dead of winter, after those leaves have fallen and before
much else is out. There are some slight differences between
varieties, but most witch hazels flower in January and February.

You are much more likely to find the Chinese witch hazel,
Hamamelis mollis, which has downy leaves and young twigs, or
one of the splendid offspring from its match with the Japanese
species, *H. japonica*, like *H.* × *intermedia* 'Pallida', 'Arnold
Promise', 'Jelena', 'Diane', or 'Vezna'. 'Pallida' has larger than
average sulphur-yellow petals whereas 'Jelena' has orange
ones, those of 'Diane' are coppery-red and 'Vezna' has pendant
flowers which are deep yellow, orange-red at the base. 'Arnold
Promise' is popular because it has large bright-yellow flowers
a little later than usual, in late February or early March. Also
quite widely available is the early-spring-flowering suckering
shrub *H. vernalis*, the Ozark witch hazel, best known in the
wonderful form called 'Sandra' which has purple young
leaves and then brilliant autumn tints.

The species *Hamamelis vernalis* and *H. mollis* have leaves which turn butter-yellow in autumn, whereas those of *H. × intermedia* often turn bright orange and red before they fall. This is especially true of dark-flowered forms like 'Jelena' and 'Diane'. I have a particularly soft spot for these two because they were raised at Kalmthout Arboretum near Antwerp in Belgium, a place where I happily worked as a student one boiling hot summer. They are named after the owner, Madame Jelena de Belder, one of the most charming, charismatic and adventurous of all botanist/gardeners, and her daughter Diane.

Why, you must be wondering, are these obviously terrific small trees not as commonplace as pink cherry in every suburban garden, scenting the winter air in every country churchyard, and the centrepiece of the front lawn of every house on 'executive' estates up and down the country? The answer is unfortunately not difficult to divine. Witch hazels are just not for the faint-hearted: they are relatively slow to grow, comparatively fussy as to soil and situation (they definitely thrive best in a deep acid or neutral humus-rich soil which retains its moisture in summer, and in a sheltered but open position) and, yes, they are quite expensive to buy, both because of their slow rate of growth and because the cultivars have to be grafted. But if none of that puts you off and you plant one in the garden, I can promise you that one day, in the not too distant future, you will have a sight for very sore eyes.

Independent

Nuts about Hazels
5 February 2000

It has always been a mystery to me why the male flowers of hazel and birch should be known as 'catkins', which is a Tudor word for kitten. Only willows, and not even all of them, have the intensely silky catkins which justify the name 'pussy willow'. Be that as it may, by the beginning of February the pendulous but unripe green and grainy catkins of the native hazel have been adding subdued colour and interest to my garden for more than a month. Then the catkins turn yellow, because the anthers are beginning to shed their pollen, and if you look carefully you can make out the female flowers – tiny bristles of bright pink stigmata – which are borne on twigs close by.

The native hazel, *Corylus avellana*, the cobnut, has interesting round-oval, corrugated leaves which turn yellow in autumn at much the same time as the nuts, much loved of squirrels, mature. Left to itself it will make a substantial shrub or even a small, many-stemmed tree. However, leaving a hazel to itself is not what has been done historically, and thanks to a greater modern understanding of woodland ecology and conservation (after years when we seemed to have forgotten what we once knew) it is not being done once more.

For the native hazel is one of the prime candidates, along with ash, oak and sallow, for 'coppicing', that forester's trick which takes advantage of a native tree's capacity to regenerate perfectly satisfactorily from short stumps. Coppicing consists of cutting the main stems back hard every few years, so that straight poles grow up from near the base. This truly ancient craft has been resurrected in some native woodlands, partly for reasons of good silvicultural management, partly because native woods can be used for handicrafts, and partly because hazel makes excellent charcoal when burned in the traditional way.

The native hazel has a yellow-leafed form, 'Aurea', which you may come across, but the one most widely grown, for reasons I find almost unfathomable, is the corkscrew hazel, or Harry Lauder's walking-stick, as it used to be known. (Who now remembers Harry Lauder?) This form was found growing in a Gloucestershire hedgerow in about 1863, and somebody with an eye for a curiosity propagated it and introduced it into commerce. Worse luck. It is not too ugly provided that it is regularly pruned, but if the branches are allowed to wrap round each other, like a nest of woody vipers, it is a slightly repellent thing which your eye is all too readily drawn to. Moreover, instead of hanging down neatly as they should, the lamb's-tail catkins tend to poke out in any old direction. I suppose that I am not really a fan of oddities in the garden, and for the same reason I can very much leave alone the contorted willow, *Salix babylonica* var. *pekinensis* 'Tortuosa'. 'Tortuosa' about says it all.

The filbert, much sought-after by connoisseurs of nuts, is descended from *Corylus maxima* from south-east Europe. Except in commercial nutteries, the most common form you are likely to meet is 'Purpurea'. It has a very deep purple leaf, which reddens somewhat in autumn, and also purple-tinged catkins. The leaf can have all the gloomy intensity of a German philosopher, but in the right sunny situation, and in association with orange and blue flowers, say, or shrubs with more feathery foliage, it can be striking indeed. You have to take care when placing this shrub, which like other hazels is unfussy as to soil, even enjoying chalk. It would stick out like a sore thumb in a country hedgerow, and is best kept within the confines of an enclosed garden. You can take advantage of the hazel's tolerance for being coppiced and cut all the stems of this plant back almost to the base every two or three years; in that way, you will get a neater, fan-shaped shrub and excellent foliage.

These hazels, even when they grow up to be trees, have the souls of shrubs. However, there is a garden-worthy hazel, *Corylus colurna*, from Turkey, which always makes a medium-sized or large tree and, without any pruning, is remarkably pyramidal in shape. A mature specimen is a splendid sight, especially as this hazel has large deep green, oval, slightly-lobed leaves which yellow in autumn, and a striking pale, flaking bark. It is very hardy, tolerant of clay and chalk, has similar attractive catkins in late winter to other hazels, and edible nuts. If you have some space, even in a windy spot, and you want to grow something a little different, then this is definitely a tree to consider.

Independent

Mellower Yellow   *10 March 2001*

I love early spring. You love early spring. We all love early spring in the garden. But at this time of year, do you ever experience the faintest bat-squeak of dread, a momentary frisson of trepidation, as the forsythia flowers open? Certainly I find that all those naked brown branches lined with such brazenly obvious golden-yellow flowers can get too much for me, especially on a sunny day. No doubt if there were only one garden in the country where *Forsythia* 'Lynwood' was grown I would exclaim in admiring wonder in March, but since it grows in every street, down every lane, over every wall, I look forward to its annual flowering about as much as I do to the arrival of my income tax demand.

'All right, clever clogs,' you may well say, and with justification, 'if you are so snooty, exactly what else can you suggest, in the shrubby line, which will flower in early March, grow pretty well anywhere, and flower reliably each year?'

It is true that, with the exception of the slightly-later-flowering and equally amiable but just as hackneyed flowering currant (*Ribes sanguineum*), there is nothing so reliable and amenable which is prepared to come into flower just as the snowdrops are losing their grip. Forsythia is the boss in March, there is no doubt of that.

But, and it is a reasonably big 'but', there are a number of others which, though a bit harder to please, deserve at least to be considered for gardens, especially if you can see someone else's forsythia whenever you go out of the front door. *Sycopsis sinensis*, *Stachyurus praecox*, *Corylopsis pauciflora* – these, too, deserve their place in the sun or, in some cases, partial shade.

Sycopsis sinensis is a close relative of the witch hazel, a Chinese shrub found by the great British plant explorer, Ernest Wilson, who sent it back to Veitch's of Exeter, the nursery which had paid for his expedition, a hundred years ago. In that time it has hardly made substantial inroads into the general horticultural consciousness; it has always been a shrub (or, occasionally, small tree) for the enthusiast's garden. Nevertheless, it is offered by at least twelve nurseries nationwide (according to the *RHS Plant Finder*). It has a neat evergreen habit which should recommend it to anyone trying to find plants of substance for the winter garden, with leathery, pendulous, pointed leaves; at this time of year it is bright with clusters of yellow- and red-stamened, petal-less flowers which emerge from round brown felted buds.

It is supposed to do best in a fertile, humus-rich but free-draining soil, in a sheltered place in sun where the soil does not dry out easily, otherwise in partial shade. The great plantswoman, Valerie Finnis, however, grows it with its outermost branches interlaced with those of the Persian ironwood, *Parrotia persica*, in a well-drained but very limey soil on the site in her garden of an ancient limestone village. So make of that what you will. The parrotia, incidentally, is a close relative and flowers at the same time, but is deciduous and has the added benefit of impressive autumn leaf colour. It will eventually grow into a spreading tree, whereas the sycopsis is more an erect, medium-sized to large shrub.

Stachyurus praecox and *S. chinensis* also come from the Far East, indeed the latter was introduced by Ernest Wilson from China in 1908, but they are deciduous, producing their flowers just before the leaves in late February and early March. These flowers, hanging in stiff strings (racemes), consist of little four-petalled bells. They are creamy-yellow in the case of *S. chinensis*, and greeny-yellow in *S. praecox*. These shrubs are both charming in flower, and *praecox* is also notable for its striking purple-red young shoots. These large, spreading shrubs like the same conditions which suit *Sycopsis;* they too will consent to grow on alkaline soils if the soil is well-prepared.

Better known than *Stachyurus* is *Corylopsis*, of which *pauciflora* is the most readily available species; this is a shrub you may well come across in your local garden centre. It never grows as big as *Stachyurus* or *Sycopsis*, so suits the smaller garden, where its masses of primrose-yellow, fragrant flowers, held in drooping tassels, are a ravishing sight at this time of year. These are swiftly followed by oval, hazel-like, corrugated leaves which start off pink and become bright green. You may also come across the taller-growing *C. sinensis*, which is what was once known as *C. willmottiae*. It has a lovely form with plum-coloured young shoots and leaves, called 'Spring Purple'. *Sinensis*, not *pauciflora*, is the species to plump for if your soil is limey.

I can see that none of these large, slow-growing, rather choosy shrubs can possibly compete for the *numero uno* position among early spring-flowering shrubs, but planting even one of them close by should mitigate the dazzling but sometimes repelling forcefulness of forsythia.

Independent

No Conferring: Conifers   29 April 2000

We all have them, don't we? Friends who know it all. Friends who insist on entering pub quizzes, despite your embarrassment; who count up the points they score when they watch *University Challenge* and proudly boast that they can beat Balliol College, Oxford singlehandedly; and who can bring a party to a grinding halt with a recitation of the kings and queens of England and their dates, preferably in verse form. We put up with all this for their many other qualities but, by goodness, we like to catch them out from time to time.

A good way, I find, is to ask them to name three deciduous

conifers which grow in this country. 'Deciduous?' they repeat, incredulously. 'Everyone knows that conifers are evergreen.' Ah, got you there, mate. In fact, there are several conifers (cone-bearing trees or gymnosperms to you, squire) which do shed their leaves each November. And their new fresh green linear leaves, or needles, emerge in mid spring.

The most fascinating of them all, and the one whose name is the most fun to roll round the mouth, is *Metasequoia glyptostroboides,* aka the dawn redwood. Its fascination, and that is not hyperbole, revolves around the fact that for many years it was known only as a fossil imprinted on 200-million-year-old rocks, and was widely assumed to be extinct. However, sometime in 1941 living specimens were found in the depths of central China. This was a most inauspicious moment for a botanical discovery, since China was occupied by the Japanese at the time, so it is not surprising that the tree was not named, nor its botanical description published and circulated, until 1944. (It acquired its specific name *glyptostroboides* because it is related, in lineage and looks, to a very rare Chinese deciduous tree called *Glyptostrobus pensilis*.) In 1948, when war was over, seed was sent to the Arnold Arboretum in Massachusetts, who distributed it not only to botanic gardens but to large private gardens as well, in Britain and elsewhere. As the head gardener of one of these large establishments once told me, *à propos* the seedling which he had planted: 'We practically took its temperature every day and sang it to sleep at night', so fearful was he of losing such a precious tree, about which so little was known.

He need not have worried. In the southern half of England and in Wales, in particular, the dawn redwood has proved not only hardy and healthy but also extremely vigorous, growing initially at a metre a year in the best circumstances. However, it has not turned out to be a menace in the Leyland cypress league, for growth slows down with age, and on the originally-introduced specimens is now only a few centimetres a year, according to the late, great tree expert, Alan Mitchell. It is most attractive and intriguing, making a conical shape, with a trunk which is conspicuously thickest very close to ground level, tapering quickly so that it is quite narrow at the top. With rounded hollows in it, as if it had been punched hard by a giant's fist, the trunk is russet copper in colour, and the outer bark peels in vertical flakes.

The soft needles are not unlike those of yew, but brighter green in colour, and rather flatter; they turn coppery-orange, yellow and even pink in autumn, before falling. You are most likely to find a mature specimen in a public garden, grown singly, although a grove of them is also a most attractive sight. This tree is now quite widely spread in commerce, and you will certainly come across it in tree and shrub nurseries and large garden centres. It does especially well in a soil which retains moisture in summer, and should be planted where the sun will strike it.

The dawn redwood has a relative, the swamp cypress, which can also be found in public gardens and is sometimes mistaken for it. An equally handsome tree, *Taxodium distichum* originates in swamps and damp ground in the eastern United States and makes a rather broader conical-shaped tree in time, with smaller leaves which don't emerge until June. They colour russet-brown before falling. If you ever find this planted near a pond or lake, look out for the knobbly 'knees', correctly 'pneumatophores', close by: they are tree roots which have erupted above ground to allow them to breathe in waterlogged conditions. You may have to search a bit further if you want to buy a taxodium; it comes into leaf too late, and is eventually rather too tall, to be popular as a tree for small or medium-sized gardens.

And what of the third deciduous conifer? At the risk of sounding like a sad person quoting old Monty Python sketches, number three is the larch. The European larch, *Larix decidua*, deserves to be so much more widely planted than it is. It is such a good-looking tree, coming into bright green leaf (the true Emerald Green of the paintbox) in early spring; these needles turn a lovely pure yellow in autumn. The larch grows very fast when young, but slows down when older; it flowers and cones when quite young, and it grows pretty well anywhere, being especially good in a windy spot. It looks best grown in a group, I think. Its deciduous nature means that it does not leave a barren circle beneath it, as is so often the way with evergreen conifers. You can actually grow spring-flowering bulbs and flowers under it. What is more, larches are popular with a host of interesting birds. If you ask your pub quizzer friend, he should be able to tell you: goldcrests, goldfinches, crossbills, redpolls, coal tits, blue tits . . .

Independent

Better Elders   *18 September 1999*

I wonder how much affection we feel towards our native common elder, *Sambucus nigra*? This medium-sized shrub, with its flat cloudy heads of heavily scented creamy-white flowers in May and June, its vinous-purple berries in September and its yellow leaves in October, is instantly recognisable to us all, yet most gardeners give it a wide berth. Speaking for myself, I tolerate it only in the furthest, wildest reaches of the garden, as a concession to the shelter and food it gives to wild creatures, in particular a hen pheasant and her brood, and for the delicious cordial to be made from the flowers. In the garden it seeds around far too freely for comfort, and those seedlings have tenacious roots which require strength to dislodge and have a horrible smell which lingers on the hands. Somehow this shrub never looks quite right even in a hedgerow, for the trunk is coarse, the growth unrestrained and inclined to undermine other plants nearby, and it has leaves which both colour and drop piecemeal through the autumn, giving it a thin, careless look when compared with neat field maples and dense hawthorns.

For many years, however, we gardeners seem to have had a distinct weakness for planting its garden varieties, those selections with yellow, purple, variegated or deeply-cut (laciniate) leaves, for they offer other virtues besides simple good-natured amenability. (The common elder grows almost anywhere, in sun or partial shade, in clay or chalk, and is easy to propagate, rooting very readily from semi-ripe September cuttings.) They are none of them quite so vigorous as the ordinary native, and if pruned every winter can be kept within bounds, and suitable for gardens where there is not much space for deciduous shrubs.

Some are better than others, in my opinion. I have no very great love, for example, for a form called 'Pulverulenta' which has green leaves so mottled and striped with white that it looks quite ill, and is certainly not a good 'doer'. Better as a garden plant is *Sambucus nigra* 'Aurea', provided it is planted in dappled shade so that the golden-yellow leaves are not burned to a crisp by high summer sun. Another you will find quite readily available is the form called *laciniata*, which has the normal green leaves, but so finely cut they look like parsley and give a delicacy quite lacking in the ordinary shrub. Also quite widely grown is 'Marginata', which has a pretty and clean irregular creamy-white edge to the leaves.

The best, if availability and popularity are reliable guides at least, is the brownish-purple-leaved 'Guincho Purple', which you may also find sold under the name 'Purpurea'. This starts off like the native elder with green leaves in spring, but they soon take on deeper, darker tones. Then, as autumn wears on, they turn to red before they fall. Provided it is not too ruthlessly pruned, this shrub has pretty pink-tinged white flowers on purple stalks, in May and June. It is a very useful ingredient in a strong, lively colour scheme where purple, yellow and orange predominate. It has to be said, however, that it is quite unsuitable for boundary hedges or anywhere else bordering on countryside, for it draws the eye ineluctably, almost as much as a copper beech or purple-leaved ornamental cherry will.

Fans of this plant will be very pleased to know that a cross between 'Guincho Purple' and 'Fastigiata' has been recently bred and is available in garden centres. It is called 'Black Beauty' and its raisers have high hopes for it as a shrub for both private and public plantings. It is the first ornamental shrub to come from a specially targeted breeding programme at the horticultural research establishment Horticulture Research International at East Malling in Kent, which was funded by the nursery stock industry via the Horticultural Development Council, and by MAFF [now DEFRA]. Its noteworthy characteristics are that it has darker, more intensely purple foliage than any other, the foliage colour develops very quickly in the spring and is retained until the leaves fall, the flowers are *properly* pink, and with a lemon fragrance, and it has purple-black berries. It is a shrub which will apparently grow up to ten feet in eight years, if left unpruned, but I am sure it can be kept smaller and fresher by cutting back one-year-old growths by half and older stems almost to ground level, sometime in the dormant season, and then feeding and mulching the plant well. I intend to grow it close to 'Guincho Purple' to compare the two, for I think it possible that its unchanging purpleness will eventually grate on me. Only time will tell whether it will prove a fine addition to gardens, but I hope so.

Independent

Brotherly Love at Election Time 16 June 2001

All right, I admit it. I am one of those sad people who mind enough about politics to allow myself to be inveigled into sticking leaflets through doors before an election. Even sadder is the admission that I enjoy it, although in my heart of hearts I know that has much less to do with political zeal than with the opportunity it gives me to look around my neighbours' front gardens.

June is the most perfect time of year for an election. How lovely it is to be out on a warm evening, among the first flush of climbing and shrub roses and the almost overpowering orange-blossom fragrance of the philadelphus. I remember with particular delight this year standing rooted on a doorstep breathing in the scent from the creamy-white single flowers of a large, overhanging *Philadelphus* 'Burfordensis'. This is the scent of summer for me, and it made the rush and press of political events temporarily recede.

Although you only come across it in old gardens now, I have a weak spot too for the small-flowered but highly scented *Philadelphus coronarius*, which has been cultivated in Britain since the reign of Elizabeth I. It was brought to Europe from Constantinople by the splendidly-named Ogier Ghiselin de Busbecq, the Holy Roman Emperor's Ambassador to the Court of Suleiman the Magnificent. He was a flower-minded chap, having been also responsible for introducing the tulip from Turkey. At the same time as he introduced the mock orange he also brought back the lilac, *Syringa*, and as both shrubs have pithy stems which could be made into pipes they were known originally as the 'White Pipe' and the 'Blew Pipe' trees. It is amazing how often you see these two shrubs growing alongside one another in gardens, and indeed for many years gardeners muddled up the names by calling *Philadelphus* 'syringa'.

Some gardeners refuse to grow mock orange on the grounds that it is not a very exciting shrub for eleven months of the year, but unless you have a tiny garden, medium-sized green shrubs are invaluable as a background for more colourful flowers. Moreover, this is an argument often put forward by people who grow ornamental cherry trees and bearded irises, neither of which has any longer flowering season than the philadelphus.

Philadelphus coronarius grows up to 3 metres tall by 2 metres across. The four-petalled, open-cupped, 2.5-cm flowers are creamy-white with yellow stamens. The leaves get to 10 cm long and are mid green and oval, with toothed margins. There is a yellow form, 'Aurea', which does not grow so big, as well as one with white margins to the leaves, 'Variegata'. These days they are more commonly available than ordinary *P. coronarius*, although personally I find the yellow-leafed variety unsatisfactory because if grown in a sunny place (and it will not flower profusely in shade) the leaves tend to brown and crisp. There are also many modern and highly desirable hybrids descended, directly or indirectly, from the original mock orange, such as 'Belle Étoile', 'Burfordensis', and 'Beauclerk'. There are ones with double flowers too, such as 'Virginal' and 'Manteau d'Hermine', although these are not usually as highly-scented as the single flowers. If you have not much space, there are compact varieties such as *P. microphyllus*, 'Manteau d'Hermine' and 'Silberregen' ('Silver Showers').

Philadelphus are very tolerant shrubs which will grow in a wide range of conditions, and continue to flower well even if neglected. They do flower best in full sun but will grow in partial shade, even if the soil is prone to drying out. Pruning is helpful, but not vital every year; it consists of cutting older wood right out after it has flowered. You can do this partly when you cut stems to bring into the house, for these flowers last well in water. In some years, philadelphus can be badly affected by blackfly, but are otherwise likely to be trouble-free. They strike quite readily from softwood cuttings taken in July, or hardwood cuttings in November.

Because they flower as the great spring shrubs are on the wane, philadelphus are best placed with shrub roses in large beds where they can spread to full stretch. They make excellent companions, because they are difficult to push around, for the vigorous Penzance briars (forms of *Rosa rubiginosa*) and other species roses, and the creamy-white flowers are also set off well by climbing and rambling roses such as creamy-pink 'Constance Spry'. But they do well towards the back of large perennial borders, too, and can be effective as a flowering hedge.

While doing my leaflet rounds, I reflect on the botanical name of the mock orange – *Philadelphus*, meaning 'brotherly love' in ancient Greek. Perhaps a singularly inappropriate symbol, for election campaigns can be testy and fractious, but it nevertheless gets my vote.

Independent

A Creeping Story   *29 July 2000*

'That's it,' I said in June. 'I have had enough. More than enough.' More than enough, that is, of the Virginia creeper on the front of the house. For seven years, since we moved here, I have battled with this many-tendrilled monster each summer. Planted (not by me, I hasten to add) far too close to the front door on the north side of the house, by the end of June it is enfolding unwary postmen in its clinging, damply-leafy embrace, masking the windows and creating a Stygian gloom in the house, tightening its grip on telephone wires until people have to bellow down the line to make themselves heard, insinuating its long curling young stems under the already crumbly stone roof tiles, causing builders to suck their teeth, shake their heads and raise their quotes. Twice a summer at least it must be severely curbed, which takes hours of labour and requires some vertiginous ladder work.

Of course, *Parthenocissus quinquefolia* is a splendid plant in many ways, with its red young stems from which arise bronzey-green new leaves and curling tendrils finished with dinky sticky little sucker-pads, and the vigour to make great, thick curtains of foliage consisting of large green leaves made up of five oval leaflets. The leaves colour the deepest scarlet in early autumn, setting off the grey-yellow limestone of the house walls most becomingly, until a sudden wind or frost dumps the leaves on the ground and a maze of brown twiggy stems is left to clothe the house until next spring. The autumn colour together with the 'self-clinging' capacity of this decidu- ous climber are what recommend it to us gardeners, but surely none of that is sufficient recompense for expansionist tenden- cies which would have done credit to the Russian Empire in its heyday? This is a climber that suited tall, stately houses in the days when skilled gardeners cost five shillings an hour and had the time, and heart, to clip and prune and barrow away. It is far too vigorous a plant for a low two-storeyed house owned by busy people. Hence the outburst early in the summer, when I swore that I would pull it up with my bare hands, if need be.

Have I done it? Well, er, no. Not yet. A few days after my howl of frustrated protest, a pair of birds began to make their nest among the folds of its foliage curtain. And not just any birds, but spotted flycatchers, summer visitors all the way from North Africa. These charming birds are not rare, although I rather think I haven't seen so many in recent years, but they like specific conditions: open woodland, parks, gardens in countryside or suburb which can offer at least a few mature trees and shrubs. There they were, sitting on a philadelphus twig a few feet from the house wall, small grey-brown birds with straight beaks and dark stripes on cream breasts and heads, flicking their tails ceaselessly, watching out for passing insects, which they catch on the wing. Whenever I looked out of the kitchen window my eye would be attracted by their short, swooping flight as they secured their prey or disap- peared behind the leafy arras, safe and secure from any roaming sparrowhawk, overbold magpie or patient cat with baleful intent.

In July we went away for a holiday and I accepted, sadly, that the flycatchers might well not be there on our return. For I remember so well one summer morning, some ten years ago, looking out on the garden and an open-fronted nesting box which flycatchers had colonised, and watching transfixed as a mother taught her fledglings to fly. She darted around them in obvious encouragement while they stood on the edge of the box like nervous divers on a springboard, waiting for the moment when instinct would overcome fear. That day we had tickets for a test match and had to leave; by the time we got home, the lesson had been learned and the family were gone. That is why I knew, this year, that when we drew up the drive the front garden would be still, bereft now of that mesmerising, magical flycatcher flight.

Since I cannot bear to deprive flycatchers of a possible home in years to come, and would be also sorry to lose that wonderful Virginia creeper autumn colour, I have decided to plant *Parthenocissus henryana*, a close relation of *P. quinquefolia*, instead. Not nearly so often seen, the so-called 'Chinese Virginia creeper' differs from the more common one in having attractively variegated leaves with distinctive chalk-white and pink central veins down each of the three or five 'finger' leaflets. The variegation is most vivid if it is planted in partial shade, as it would be. It colours reliably and well in autumn. Best of all, it is not so vigorous; it grows more slowly and to a maximum height of ten rather than twenty metres. I shall plant it further away from the front door and, as it establishes itself, gradually cut back and eventually dig up the original. In that way the spotted flycatchers should not be inconvenienced, and I just might keep my cool in June.

Independent

Arresting Advice   *10 October 1993*

For some people these days, the garden serves more as a barrier to an unfriendly world than as a place of beauty and spiritual refreshment. There are respectable historical precedents for this, of course. The medieval enclosed gardens (*hortus conclusus*) in western Europe and the Persian 'paradise' gardens were designed to keep out ravening beasts and, symbolically, the fear and horror that stalked the outside world. Now, it seems, we feel the need for protection once more.

I was once arrested, as it were, by a news item concerning advice given house-owners by Essex police about deterring burglars. They had apparently advocated planting a variety of thorny shrubs in the garden, either as hedges or as impenetrable barriers in front of drainpipes and under windows. The species suggested as suitable were some of the commonly-available types of berberis (*Berberis julianae, B. × ottawensis* 'Superba', *B. × stenophylla*, and *B. gagnepainii*) together with *Mahonia × media* 'Winter Sun', gorse (*Ulex europaeus*), pyracanthas, *Hippophäe rhamnoides*, hawthorn, and three roses – *Rosa* 'Frühlingsgold', *R. rugosa rubra* and *R. rugosa* 'Blanc Double de Coubert'.

The idea was not new. On their own initiative, and usually after they have had one intruder come through a downstairs window, some garden owners I know have planted prickly bushes. However, this was the first time I had seen the practice given official backing and publicity.

On the face of it, the idea makes admirable sense. But much as I – like every other householder – hate the idea of being burgled and wish to protect myself against it by whatever means I can, I would pause for a moment's reflection before going out to buy, and plant, a living palisade as spiky as a bored teenager.

The problem is that not only are some of these plants decidedly more attractive than others, but they are all mighty thorny. The householder who is also a keen gardener should remember that the biter can be bit. Anyone who has ever backed into a berberis while weeding head down in a flower bed (or indeed anyone who has not, but has a lively imagination) will know how painful and infuriating it can be. This, of course, by no means rules out these plants as unsuitable, but it does mean that we need to handle them with care and, except in the case of hedges, plant them only where they are isolated from us by other plantings. It is not just burglars who may find their clothes and flesh torn by barbs.

Fortunately, several of these plants, especially the berberis, will stand close clipping with equanimity, which is especially helpful if you need something for planting under a low window. Pyracanthas can be clipped into a tall thin shape to protect the bottom of a drainpipe. All the common forms can achieve ten feet, which is plenty. They are also evergreen, which is an advantage in a way, but does mean they should only be put in front of plastic drainpipes requiring little or no maintenance.

Berberis darwinii does the part of deterrence excellently; it is just a pity that it has rather unattractive orange flowers; *B.* × *stenophylla*, which has golden-yellow ones, is marginally preferable. I like *B. thunbergii* 'Atropurpurea' (similar to *B.* × *ottawensis* 'Superba' but smaller) the best because the leaves turn from purple to glowing red in the autumn, but you are then left with bare spiny twigs in the dormant season. Those with prickles on their leaves as well as stems, such as *B. gagnepainii*, are painful to weed round and through, but are useful if you require an evergreen for the task.

All types of *Rosa rugosa* are desirable, especially for an informal flowering hedge. I would certainly not quibble with the choice of 'Blanc Double de Coubert', even if rain can sometimes brown the white handkerchief flowers, but I think 'Scabrosa' a better bet than *rubra*, and the paler pink 'Fru Dagmar Hastrup' preferable to either.

I do wonder, however, about the introduction into our gardens of *Ulex europaeus*, the common gorse, which such a campaign might encourage. It is not widely available in nurseries, interestingly enough, even though it is a native, thriving particularly on acid heathland. The problem with it (apart from the blindingly golden flowers, which are not easy to place, yet are out for most of the year) is that it cannot abide a dry spell and, if put in the droughty conditions generally obtaining under the eaves of a house, most definitely will not thrive.

On the other hand, I wholeheartedly applaud the recommendation to plant 'Winter Sun', one of the large evergreen winter-flowering mahonias. Even if a burglar got past the sharp points of the leaves, its beautiful, innocent, scented flowers would surely bring about a change of heart. On reflection, perhaps the greatest benefit of planting a selection of these plants is that they might do as much to tear a burglar's thoughts away from stealing as they will to tear his trousers.

Sunday Telegraph

Going Native   *23 October 1999*

What a precious thing a sunny day in early October can be. Picking bright red apples against a backcloth of bottle-green leaves and azure sky is almost the most pleasant activity you could devise. Except, perhaps, gathering elderberries, blackberries, sloes and haws from the hedgerows and shaws in the countryside, marvelling the while at the gleaming polished scarlet of the rose hips and the bloomy deep purple of sloes, while yellowhammers and dunnocks flit in and out and Red Admiral and Peacock butterflies spread their wings in the sunshine.

There is no reason on earth why almost all gardeners, wherever they live, should not plant hedges composed of common native plants as boundaries to their own gardens, rather than putting up with rampant Leyland cypress or a soulless fence. If farmers can make them stock-proof, it is certainly possible to make them dog- and child-proof by occasional, consistent pruning. What is more, native hedges look just as good in suburban or urban gardens as they do in the country, and their benefit for wildlife is, if anything, even greater.

If you think your neighbours might object (although why on earth should they, except possibly because of the thorns?), an alternative is to plant an internal hedge instead, perhaps to mark off one part of the garden from another, or to hide the compost or dustbins; or plant native species in your shrub borders, and allow them to grow how they will. Just because there are any number of foreign plants suitable for growing in our gardens does not mean that you must ignore the British ones; especially if you are keen to attract wildlife, which has co-evolved with wild plants and knows where to go for both protection and sustenance.

Last winter I planted a native hedge of young bare-rooted two-foot-tall 'whips' in a line on the garden boundary. I chose a mixture of species suitable for my alkaline soil that included hawthorn, blackthorn, the European spindle (which comes into leaf early and has colourful red and orange fruits), field maple (whose leaves colour reliably yellow in autumn), the wayfaring tree (actually a shrub called *Viburnum lantana)*, the common hazel, the guelder rose and the dog rose, together with a few English oak and ash. More than half the plants consisted of only two species, *Crataegus monogyna*, the quickthorn or may, which flowers in May and whose fruits are haws, together with *Prunus spinosa*, the blackthorn, which flowers in early April or late March and produces sloes. A hedge made up predominantly of these two knits well together, and will stand hard clipping if required. I avoided green beech because I garden on clay, which does not suit it, and common alder, because I live in an area of meagre average rainfall and a low water table. Needless to say I did not plant any brambles, for I take a devotion to native plants only so far, and no further. Much as I love the fruits, I hate the promiscuous and thorny seedlings in my flower beds.

I prepared the soil well, planted the whips at the level at which they grew in the nursery, and laid a weed-suppressing permeable mat around their bases. I planted them quite closely, about a foot apart, and in a single row rather than a staggered double row, which would have made too wide a hedge for my purposes. All except the already branching dog rose were encased in pink polypropylene tubes known as 'tree shelters', to act as mini-greenhouses, and help protect them from the strimmer, the rabbits and weedkiller spraydrift for the first season, until they are established and before they are trimmed. (Beech should not be put in these tubes, incidentally, as they do not flourish.) Being native, the plants rooted easily and well from a late autumn planting.

People worry about pruning hedges, but it is not much of a problem. I want a tall, informal country hedgerow, so after about three years of conscientious trimming to encourage the individual plants to break from low down (as they are all eager to do), I will leave them alone. If, however, you would like a semi-formal or informal hedge restrained in height and width, you will need to take a little more trouble. Of course, you won't want to cut it when birds might be nesting in spring, or risk removing nascent fruits, whether for you or the birds, by clipping in summer. The best compromise solution is to trim the hedge in early winter, when you have time on your hands. You can use a hedge trimmer provided you also wear goggles and thick gauntlet gloves, for those thorns can be wicked, or you can do it the slower, meticulous way with secateurs and Grecian curved saw. In spring you will have a neatish hedge, yet there will still be flower enough to give you autumn fruits. You could not say that of a Leyland cypress hedge, could you?

Independent

Millennarian Zeal   *6 November 1999*

The moment of truth has finally arrived. We have been talking for ages about planting a tree for the Millennium, and now that the trees are losing their leaves and retreating into dormancy, the best time for putting a new one in the ground has come. Now (well, some time in the next four months, at least, when the soil is neither sodden nor frozen) is the time to act.

At a point in the next two weeks, all being well, I shall be planting a small *Tilia cordata* 'Winter Orange', which I bought in the spring in a 2-litre pot from Bluebell Nursery and which I have nurtured ever since. The 'small-leafed lime' is a very handsome tree when mature, genuinely native, and of astonishing longevity; it is reputed to last a thousand years, if left to itself (which it almost certainly won't be, the way things are going in the countryside at present). It has tiny scented yellow-green flowers in spring, which the bees love, and good orange-yellow autumn colour. The cultivar name 'Winter Orange' refers to its orange young stems and twigs in the winter, although when in leaf it is well-nigh indistinguishable from the 'ordinary' lime.

That is not the end of my efforts, for next spring, as soon as the soil begins to warm up, I hope to help plant a young yew (*Taxus baccata*) in the village churchyard; this yew was donated by the Conservation Foundation, as part of its admirable 'Yews for the Millennium' initiative. This small but sturdy sapling in a pot has been propagated from one of the most ancient yews in the country, guaranteed more than two thousand years old. That kind of longevity is truly humbling.

Once we have all planted specimen trees in our gardens, our churchyards, our urban community spaces, our pocket parks, our school playgrounds, will we assume that we have done our duty and marked the Millennium properly? I rather hope not, for I cannot help thinking that this is an appropriate time for a bit of joined-up tree planting, by which I mean creating an avenue consisting of a number of trees of the same species.

The tree avenue has a long history in Britain. It was already well-established as a feature of garden and park design by the early seventeenth century. In 1656 John Evelyn noted in his Diary with admiration the early maturity of the avenues planted by the first Duke of Buckingham at New Hall in Essex, especially the quadruple (!) avenue of lime trees which led up to the house. At least until the beginning of the twentieth century, the avenue has been seen as a way of aggrandising a drive or road leading to a house of consequence, or to bound a woodland ride or point to a far vista. Limes have always been the favourite, but sweet or horse chestnuts, beeches, weeping spruces, specimen Leyland cypresses, even monkey puzzle trees, have had their devotees. The only strict rule is that all the trees, whatever they are, should be the same.

I appreciate that the times are out of joint for planting grandiose avenues again, but I wonder if there is really something so very ridiculous about planting a small-scale one, comprising medium-sized or small trees. I have it in mind to plant, in my garden, a short avenue of *Malus tschonoskii*, with eight trees lining each side of a broad grass path (30 metres long by 10 across) which leads from the garden gate to the boundary and is parallel to the low churchyard wall, and therefore visible to churchgoers on Sundays. This form of ornamental crab apple from Japan is commonly planted to great effect in suburban streets, making a naturally erect shape, with pink-flushed white flowers in spring, red and yellow fruits and brilliant, sumptuous leaf colour in autumn.

I may, however, plump for the slightly smaller but also narrowly upright *Malus* 'John Downie', which has much the same virtues as *M. tschonoskii* but is also a common denizen of the countryside, so that it will not fight with its surroundings in the way the more exotic crab might. Or perhaps I will go for that wonderful whitebeam *Sorbus thibetica* 'John Mitchell', whose intensely silver-haired young leaves unfurl from the vertical and look at a distance like gleaming magnolia flowers, before they open out. If the space were broader, then it would be no contest: it would have to the upward-growing form of hornbeam, *Carpinus betulus* 'Fastigiata', which naturally develops a 'flame' shape, about 12 metres tall by 6 metres across at maturity. Whatever I choose, the plants must be genetically identical to each other – that is, propagated vegetatively rather than from seed, which might introduce a degree of variability. All that I need for the task, therefore, is a trustworthy nursery to buy them from, a large tape measure, some bamboo canes, a spade, some home-made compost – and plenty of millennarian zeal.

Independent

Prickly Customers   *18 December 1999*

It is possible, if you are a gardener, to convince yourself that you like the winter. I certainly have. The lawn may be shaggy, the borders sodden and brown, the trees bare and exposed, but nonetheless I can find plenty of cheering compensations. The catkins on the hazels are lengthening, the snowdrops have nosed above ground, the hellebores are about to unfurl, *Viburnum* × *bodnantense* is scenting the air deliciously, the scarlet twigs of *Acer davidii* gleam in the sun, and the stems of *Rubus cockburnianus* are at their most intensely white.

Mention the words 'ornamental bramble', which this is, and most sensible people blench. The reputation of some species of *Rubus* for invasiveness is perfectly well deserved, and all of them exhibit a marked degree of vim and vigour. They are, with only a few exceptions, extremely prickly, and they have the capacity to root at their shoot tips, so they are natural makers of thickets. If there is one thing that we gardeners find difficult to cope with, it is a prickly thicket. So, as the saying goes, you don't have to be mad to plant them, but it helps.

In fairness, even the most tidy gardener would have to admit that there are a number of 'ornamental' *Rubus* (as opposed to fruiting ones like blackberry, tayberry, loganberry, Japanese wineberry or raspberry) which have lovely flowers. 'Benenden' springs immediately to mind. Others, like 'Betty Ashburner', have a prostrate habit and so make good ground-cover in inhospitable soils and situations, although *R. tricolor* can act like an over-excited, show-off child at a party who doesn't know when to stop. A few, notably *R. cockburnianus*, *R. biflorus* and *R. thibetanus*, have the most lovely stems in winter.

The one I grow is *Rubus cockburnianus*, which I insist on pronouncing 'coburnianus', like the port wine shippers, because it sounds better and is almost certainly correct, although I probably earn a reputation for pretentiousness in the process. This deciduous shrub originates in the plantsman's paradise of western Szechuan in China, and was introduced by the great English plant hunter E.H. Wilson in 1907. Its growth is like that of a raspberry, in as much as it has biennial stems: they grow one year, and produce flowers the next. These stems arch in an attractive way and can be as much as eight feet long.

And what whiteness! The shoots are always white, where the bloom has not been knocked off them, but at this time of year, without the leaves to mask them and with the added spur of lower temperatures, they look as if they had been whitewashed by a master decorator who has achieved the finest, most even finish. This whiteness overlays deep purple, so that from a distance and on a grey winter day the stems look ghostly mauve. If you cut them for Christmas decoration there is no need to reach for the silver spray paint, although you will have to mind the prickles.

This shrub has rather interesting diamond-shaped leaflets, green above, silver below, which yellow before falling in autumn. The purple flowers are insignificant. It is supposed to bear black fruits, but my shrubs don't go in for that. There is a relative, *Rubus biflorus*, with larger, white flowers, round yellow fruit and a more erect habit (so, less likely to have shoots which can touch the ground and root). This arrived in Britain from the Himalayas in the early nineteenth century, and was for many years the white-stemmed species most widely grown. However, it was *R. cockburnianus* which gained the

RHS Award of Garden Merit, and so is more widely available in nurseries these days. Some swear by *R. thibetanus*, especially the variety called 'Silver Fern' whose stems are a more bluish-white, with ferny leaves which are silvery above as well as below. This is another of E.H. Wilson's introductions.

The trick to living happily with these ornamental brambles is to prune them as if they were autumn-fruiting raspberries, by cutting (with gloves, if you value your skin) the old canes close to the base in late winter or early spring, and thereby making space for the new ones growing up. You sacrifice flowers and fruit this way, but that is a small matter; since the colour is best on very young canes, and moreover abrasion of one stem on another tends to remove the waxy bloom, this method ensures the whitest stems in winter. If you are growing this shrub in a restricted space, it makes sense in summer to snip back any shoots that look as if they might arch over and touch the ground, in order to avoid any danger of thicket-making. Alternatively, if you have a wild and woolly place in the garden, as I have, where you are happy to let them go, you need do nothing at all. Except take pleasure in them on winter days.

Independent

8

The Kitchen Garden

An Ill Wind?   22 September 2001

It seemed about as ill a wind as there could be. The highest
autumn and winter rainfall since records began brought extensive flooding in its wake, and with it loss, expense, future
uncertainty and real despair to villages and riparian towns in
many parts of the country. It has been deuced hard to think of
any benefit resulting from such a disaster.

But not impossible. For such extraordinary weather has been
partly responsible for an *annus mirabilis* for tree fruits in my
garden at least and, from what I can gather, in many other places
too. I have marvelled at the bright scarlet clusters of berries thick
on the rowan trees along dual carriageway verges, the flame of
crab apples on a neighbour's 'John Downie', and the way the
'Victoria' plums have dripped pink-red from bending branches
before falling. It is not just here in the Midlands; the Brogdale

Horticultural Trust in faraway Kent also reports an exceptional year.

The spring blossom of every kind of top fruit – apple, rowan, crab, medlar, quince, plum, pear, cherry, hawthorn, even elder- berry – was magnificently prolific. This was thanks to a con- catenation of complex factors, in particular no spring frosts to speak of and sufficiently favourable weather conditions the season before to ensure good flower bud initiation. But this blossom was also delayed by about a fortnight by the wet winter, giving extra time for the pollinating bees to take wing, which benefited especially the early flowerers like plums and pears. Then warm, settled weather in June, combined with unusually ample moisture in the ground, ensured rapid cell division, leading to fruit of good quality. Nor was there, pro- portionately, a very substantial 'June drop', the natural dis- carding by the tree of infertile or imperfect fruitlets.

It is true that in places fruit trees have suffered as a result of winter waterlogging, for roots will die in the end if they cannot breathe; certainly there is talk of some West Country cider apple orchards having to be grubbed, and in my own garden, which has a desperately heavy soil in places, a number of bird cherry trees have faltered, showing distinct signs of attack by *Phytopthora* root rot. Nevertheless, in my conversations with gardeners this season the talk has been of how surprisingly well hardy plants have survived the inundations, and what terrific growth has resulted from consistent soil moisture.

There is something deeply, atavistically satisfying to us in harvest, however far removed we are from want. Just as a Home Counties pony-owner will sigh with profound relief when enough hay to see Toffee safely through the winter has been delivered, and a householder with central heating as well as fireplaces will fidget until the firewood is safely stacked, so gardeners visibly relax when they have their Bramleys safely stowed in boxes or trays – even when they know that many will fetch up on the compost heap, flabby and flaccid, in spring.

Of course, prodigality can be a nuisance. If you have a good harvest, the chances are that your neighbours will have one too, and will press windfall apples on you with a steely determination which brooks no denial. The trick, I suppose, is to copy commercial growers and plant fruit trees which are grafted onto dwarfing and semi-dwarfing rootstocks, growing them either in restricted forms, like cordons or espaliers, or in a mini-orchard setting. They are less prolific but easier to pick, need less space, and are swifter coming into bearing, provided the soil is fertile. For myself, I have a mixture of these and large, mature trees, which give me problems of plenty but whose crooked, individual shapes add potently to the atmosphere of the garden.

The atavistic satisfaction we feel in home-grown plenty even touches my resolutely non-gardening husband. I discovered him in our 'orchard' (I use the quotation marks advisedly) very early the other morning, dressed in a suit and preparing for a long drive to work. He had gone to seek refreshment and relief from daily care in scrutinising the ripeness of the damsons, marvelling at the prolific medlars and tutting at the tardiness of the quinces. His pleasure in a plum *au point* or a well-ripened, eccentrically-named apple is touching, but his close attention imposes a burden of responsibility on me, in particular that of picking and storing the fruits carefully and at the right moment. This year, so large is the potential harvest that I shall be drawing up a timetable of when to pick what. All should be well, provided that a truly ill wind does not beat me to it.

The Spectator

The Apple of my Eye   17 October 1993

When we move house, most of us cling with all our might to some small object of value – a jewel case, perhaps, or a set of love letters or even a favourite kitchen knife. This is despite the removal men's determination to separate it from us into a box marked 'Oddments 3', whence it will only emerge weeks or even months later. Although we do not really fear its loss, we are taking no chances.

The object I clung to when we moved was a young 'Barnack Beauty' apple tree in a pot. This was the only complete plant, as opposed to small divisions or cuttings, which I had dug up from our old garden. So important was it to me that its removal was formally enshrined in the contract we signed with the purchasers.

My attachment to that tree must seem a little odd. You may wonder why I could not simply go out and buy another one? I could, but only with difficulty, for this tree came all the way from Kent, there being no source for it that I could discover here in Northamptonshire.The reason why it is so precious to me is that the variety was bred in 1840 only a few miles from where we lived before, and only a few more from where we are now. Yet despite the fact that it is well suited to the local lime-rich soil and low rainfall, I rarely come across it in local gardens.

My 'Barnack Beauty' is, for me, a marker of this locality; not so obvious, perhaps, as the Collyweston stone roof slates and Barnack stone, but important nevertheless. In so many ways, our attachment to locality has become seriously weakened. Just as we are losing our regional vernacular architecture (modern houses look the same whether you live in Salford or Stamford), so we have little sense now of regional diversity in plants and gardening. This insignificant apple tree represents my tiny individual attempt to reverse the trend.

Gardeners and environmentalists are aware of the threat to regional particularity, and are fighting a rearguard action. Coincidentally, one of the symbols of the movement is the apple, because in the old days, before we could all travel where we liked, many apple varieties were only grown very locally. One of the moving spirits is the charity Common Ground, which held its first annual Apple Day in October 1990, aimed at bringing to the public's attention the helter-skelter loss of orchards (150,000 acres in thirty years) and apple varieties.

I have just been studying Common Ground's Apple Map. Apart from being attractive and colourful – the kind of picture that should be framed and hung in the kitchen for study and edification in idle moments – it marks the origin of hundreds of the six thousand varieties that have arisen in this island over two millennia, and describes dozens of them.

Most of us know, I would guess, where 'Bramley's Seedling' and 'Cox's Orange Pippin' arose, but I for one had no idea that the hybrid apple 'Newton Wonder' was discovered growing out of the thatch of the Hardinge Arms at King's Newton in Derbyshire. Even if it is only legend, that knowledge has deep-ened my appreciation of this wonderfully prolific and long-keeping apple. Another keeping apple, 'Hunt House', was taken on long sea journeys out of Whitby, and 'Lane's Prince Albert' is so called because Henry Lane planted it immediately after helping to cheer Queen Victoria and Prince Albert through the streets of Berkhamsted in 1841. The map under-lines the fact that the apple is stitched into our cultural and social history.

I found my 'Barnack Beauty' illustrated and described on the map, which was cheering. However, marked close by was one that I had never heard of before. This was 'Lord Burghley', which arose, naturally enough, on the Marquess of Exeter's estate at Burghley, outside Stamford, only a mile or two from Barnack.

The Apple Map describes 'Lord Burghley' as 'Firm, yellow, juicy with a slight pine flavour. Pale yellow, flushed with red. Attractive.' My edition of *The Plant Finder* tells me that it is listed by three nurseries which deal in mail-order plants. No prizes for guessing what my first purchase for the new garden has been.

Sunday Telegraph

Quince-essential   12 October 2002

Spindle bushes, Japanese maples, Virginia creeper, chrysanthemums, Michaelmas daisies, salvias, rudbeckias, verbenas,
penstemons, English roses: the garden is bright with autumnal
scarlets, oranges, yellows, burnt umbers, pinks and mauves.
But what is it that draws me out into the garden on a sunny,
sharp Saturday morning? A nondescript little tree in the
orchard with faded leaves, crooked trunk, and scattered fruit
hanging from its haphazard branches.

This is a quince tree, whose pear-shaped fruits are turning to
a pale yellow and are now ready to pick, although not to eat. It
is 'Vranja', a Serbian variety which I bought some years ago
from Reed's Nursery in Norfolk, along with a specimen of the
slightly earlier 'Meech's Prolific'. What surprises me a little is
that I value these two scruffy trees almost as much as I do, say,
the indispensable and stately *Crataegus persimilis* 'Prunifolia'
whose fruits and leaves are just colouring now.

On 21 September I picked all the 'Meech's Prolific' (rather a
misnomer this year, it must be said, since it is having a bit of a
year off after the stupendous crop of 2001), and placed them on
one of the window sills in the church for the Harvest Festival.
The slanting sunlight through the clear glass touched the
furred skins and turned them to gold. Knowing how popular
quinces always are at the auction of produce after the service
made me feel a little better about marching along the streets
of London in the huge crowds gathered by the Countryside
Alliance when I should have been in church.

The exact timing of picking does not really matter, since
these are fruits which go on ripening off the tree, but I try to do
it before the winds really start to blow. Quinces are not fit for
anything until November at the earliest, and even then they
cannot be eaten as you would an apple. They are as hard as
nails, and gritty as sandpaper. We put them in cardboard boxes
in the shed, and it is the purest pleasure to wander out there on

a Sunday morning in December to select a fruit to add, in chunks, to an apple pudding, because of the scent which rises up when you open the box. The vast majority of our quinces, however, are made into jelly, which is not only delicious but has the rich red translucence of a garnet, or light port wine. With its slight astringency, it is a much more satisfactory accompaniment to lamb than the more conventional redcurrant jelly.

The quince trees flower here in May, with the most delightful single pinkish-white, open-cup flowers set against downy, grey-green foliage. These flowers have the advantage of being self-fertile (as well as being capable of pollinating pear blossom) so the set is usually quite good, and I soon find little furry fruits among the by now dark-green and hairless leaves. By early October they are hanging like large ripe pears, 4 to 6 inches long, on thick stalks; unless abraded by twigs or leaves, they still have a soft, thin fur on the skin.

All this makes me puzzle why quinces are so comparatively rare in gardens, certainly rarer than pear trees, which cannot be relied upon to flourish except in favoured districts or against warm walls. Ironically, if it were not for the quince, pears would not flourish at all, since the two most common pear rootstocks are Quince 'A' and Quince 'C', 'A' making a rather larger tree than 'C'. I grow both quince and pear in this cold, dry corner of the East Midlands, and I know which is the more rewarding.

Daily Telegraph

Sloe to Please   *18 November 2000*

At every organised and sociable outdoor activity I attend in winter, from horse races to rugby matches, there is a good chance that someone will offer me a slug of sloe gin 'to keep out the cold'. This offer will usually be accompanied by a lot of confidential chat concerning its making – from the sloe-picking to pricking, sweetening, steeping and keeping – and will sometimes include a hint that it contains a special ingredient, which is a closely-guarded family secret, of course. This detailed explanation is rather wasted on me, since all the sloe gin I have ever tasted has reminded me of cheap cough medicine, but it pleases me to think that there are still people about prepared to take such trouble over a drink.

What I find most amusing is that one or two of the sloe gin makers I know would be hard pressed to tell you even the family of plants to which sloes belong, let alone what their flowers look like in spring. I don't especially blame them, for there seems little connection between *Prunus spinosus*, the blackthorn, with its rough leaves, spiny spurs and bright white single flowers in April, and the hard waxy blue, then black, half-inch round plums which we call sloes in autumn.

In the Midlands where I live, blackthorn is a very common feature of country hedges, so common indeed that bad weather in late March or early April is often called a 'blackthorn winter'. If you are a sloe gin enthusiast, you might like to grow your own blackthorn in a hedge composed of native trees and shrubs, or you could find a place for it in a not-too-neat shrub planting on a poor soil, for it will always rather make a suckering bush than a tree. But there are other hedgerow fruits seen much less often which also have a certain allure, partly for making alcoholic toe-warmers or jams and jellies, but mostly simply for the look of them.

The most picturesquely named is the bullace, *Prunus institia*, which you will still occasionally come across in an old-established farm hedge. It is usually dark purple, bloomy and easily mistaken for a sloe, although about twice the size. Bullaces are impossible to find in garden centres, but you may come across 'Shepherd's Bullace', 'Black Bullace' or 'Golden Bullace' (also known as 'White Bullace') in a specialist fruit tree nursery. It would be a pity if these old varieties died out altogether, especially as, like sloes, they are popular with wildlife in winter.

The French version of the bullace is the mirabelle, which you sometimes see in shops for a short season in September, under the name 'Mirabelle de Nancy'. They are not quite round, dusky yellow, and are a bit bland in taste, but do well in cooking, I find. They are similar in appearance to the cherry plum or myrobalan (*Prunus cerasifera*), which are yellow, red or purple in colour, and are again supposed to be good in cooking. Our domestic plum (*P. domestica*) descends from a cross between the cherry plum and the blackthorn, long ago. However, the ordinary myrobalan is not much grown these days, except as a vigorous rootstock on which to graft plum varieties. Far better-known are the myrobalan's purple-leafed forms, *P. cerasifera* 'Nigra' and 'Pissardii', the first with pink flowers and red young leaves, the second with white flowers. I don't know about you, but I find that the unrelieved deep purple of the mature foliage of these spreading small trees, often grown in suburban streets, grates on the nerves.

Closely related to the bullace is the damson, so-called because it originated in Damascus. This, brought to Europe during the Crusades, really is a tree worth growing for its fruits in September. 'Merryweather', the most commonly planted, is self-fertile, which is a great advantage with plum-type fruit trees because they flower earliest of the main tree fruits, when pollinators are not always active. It has very large fruits for a damson; in fact, it is considered in some quarters to be a culinary plum. It is blue-black in colour, with a yellowy-green flesh. Later-maturing is the smaller 'Farleigh', which is partly self-fertile and will crop heavily if it has suitable plum neighbours that flower at the same time, like 'Oullins Gage'. You may see 'Shropshire' (also known as 'Shropshire Prune') offered; this is not such a heavy cropper, but thought by many to have the best taste of all. Although damsons are rather out of fashion, they are worth considering for an orchard, or even for planting in a mixed hedge, as they are hardier than plums and quite wind-resistant. And, for those not frightened of a bit of fiddling work, there is always the opportunity to make damson jam, damson cheese and, of course, damson gin. Just don't ask <u>me</u> for the recipe.

Independent

Happy to be Caged In   *19 August 2000*

I don't know at what point in your life you first realised that you were fully grown-up, but for me the moment came when I finally acquired a fruit-cage. Despite already possessing a 'with-profits' pension plan (whatever that may be), a John Lewis account card and an ancient Volvo, not to mention a husband, teenage children and a Labrador, I have never managed to convince myself that I was anything other than a gawky adolescent inside. Until this summer, that is. Now I have a fruit-cage, I know I have finally reached adulthood.

I am so thrilled with this fruit-cage that I go out in the evenings just to stand and look at it, even though it is – until the winter planting – quite devoid of life. The dispassionate eye sees a two-metre-high tubular aluminium rectangular structure, covered in an unexceptional black polypropylene netting; all it contains is an expanse of manured and dug-over soil divided by a path composed of secondhand paving flags, on one side of which are four tall wooden posts connected by wires, awaiting raspberry and other canes. I, however, who am not the slightest bit dispassionate, see in it a thing of beauty and a joy for a very long time.

If you have never struggled year after year to grow soft fruit – by which I mean strawberries, raspberries, blackberries, loganberries and other funny hybrid cane fruits, currants and gooseberries – successfully in the open garden, you cannot possibly appreciate my enthusiasm for this utilitarian structure. But if you have, your heart will beat with sympathetic fellow-feeling. You will know that I no longer need to wrestle with netting draped over plants to keep birds away from the buds in the winter and the fruits in summer, which only seems to serve to trap them inside, and also proves conclusively the malevolent intent of inanimate objects. Nor do I have to set up 'humming wire' and ugly flapping plastic bags in the vegetable garden, to try to preserve members of the brassica family – cabbages, broccoli, Chinese leaves and so on – from the ravages of pigeons.

From sour experience, I can say that you should consider outlay on a fruit-cage sooner rather than later if you like soft fruit (or brassicas, come to that). And who does not? Red, white and black currants and all berries are the most worthwhile of all fruits to grow yourself, because they are easily bruised and travel very badly, so they are always expensive and only fitfully available. You rarely see affordable white currants for sale, for example, yet a more delicious treat, when eaten raw with a little sugar, cannot be imagined. We toil at growing lettuces and tomatoes for the sake of their inimitable freshness, but a fresh and sun-warmed raspberry is better, and the stuff of which happy childhood memories are made.

What is more, there has probably never been a better range of varieties available to amateurs, combining breadth of season with good flavour and even, sometimes, disease resistance. It is possible, for example, by canny choice of cultivars and where space is not a problem, to grow raspberries and strawberries which will fruit from late June until late September. There are yummy red dessert gooseberries, like 'Martlet', which are resistant to American gooseberry mildew. And, for a confined space, there is a compact form of blackcurrant, called 'Ben Sarek', which you can even use to make a dwarf hedge, for blackcurrants are not so bothered by birds as other fruit.

Fruit is without question worthwhile, but the truth is inescapable, although writers try to escape it: growing soft fruit – even with the luxury of a fruit-cage – takes a bit of time, trouble, and study. A complex description of, say, spur-pruning cordon gooseberries may well be followed by a breezy exhortation to 'have a go'. I think it best not to be too ambitious, initially. The easiest way to grow currants and gooseberries is as simple, old-fashioned bushes, even though these are wasteful of space, and graduate to the cordons, standards and fans suitable for the ornamental *potager* or a confined space as interest and knowledge increase. Find a comprehensible, user-friendly instruction manual, such as Dr David Hessayon's *The Fruit Expert*, and take it out into the garden every time you attend to the fruit, until all becomes clear. It's not so expensive that it will matter too much if it gets mud splashes on it.

Out in the garden each evening, my mind's eye fills the new fruit-cage with neat rows of strawberries, glistening scarlet above golden straw, and flame-shaped blackcurrant bushes, dark purple against green. I can even see myself picking strigs of shining redcurrants and ivory-pink, translucent white currants, together with full-blooded loganberries and dusky crimson raspberries, to place on a white china plate for the 'collection of fruits' class at our local flower show. You can still have fun, you know, even when you are grown-up.

Independent

Autumn Bliss *13 July 2002*

It is not possible to open a gardening magazine in early autumn without finding an article praising the virtues of ancient cultivated varieties of fruit, especially apples, and the importance of growing them. Thanks to Apple Day in October, thinking gardeners are keenly aware of the importance of preserving our nation's heritage of tree fruits, not only for reasons of genetic diversity but also for their historical and regional resonances.

There is also increasing emphasis in some seed catalogues on 'heritage' vegetables, especially potatoes and tomatoes, and I happily have a punt on a few of these each year. As a general rule, the taste of most old varieties is stronger and often more satisfying than that of their modern successors, but with the exception of 'Newton Wonder', which is one of the most beautiful and prolific of apples, more often than not the price you pay for taste is a comparatively poor yield, and prodigious ailments.

There are occasions when modernity has a distinct appeal – especially at that moment in the summer when I am picking soft fruits, for I am the grateful beneficiary of breeding work done on raspberries in recent years at the Scottish Crops Research Institute at Invergowrie and Horticulture Research International at East Malling. The SCRI has developed a number of excellent heavy-cropping, pest-resistant cultivars in their 'Glen' series since the first one, 'Glen Clova', was released in 1970, while East Malling developed the first commercially-available 'primocanes': that is, raspberries which fruit in late summer and autumn on canes which have grown up that season.

The summer-fruiting 'Glen Clova' made such a hit because its yields were 30 per cent higher than anything else grown at the time. Since then several more varieties have been released which are even more prolific, and notable for their resistance to raspberry aphid, a debilitating pest which spreads an even more debilitating virus. Frankly, I cannot see much reason for any private gardener to grow anything other than 'Glen Moy' for June cropping and 'Glen Ample' for early July. They are full of taste, easy to gather (which is to say they come off the plugs easily, and the canes are without spines), and a pleasing shape, size and colour.

The best and most famous autumn raspberry is 'Autumn Bliss', which has both transformed commercial raspberry growing by extending the season substantially and cheered up home gardeners no end since it was first introduced in the early 1980s. Named, slightly bizarrely, after Sir Arthur Bliss, 'Autumn Bliss' starts fruiting in August, and in my garden last year did not leave off until November, when the berries finally took on a rather musty taste. If one could become blasé about raspberries, then last November I was in danger of doing so. The canes, which grow from the base after the late-winter pruning each year, need little support from wires and stakes, and apart from a spring topdressing with sulphur chips to help lower the pH of my alkaline soil a bit, and an organic mulch, the only work I do is pull up suckers between the rows to prevent the rapid development of a raspberry thicket.

The humble autumn raspberry also teaches a fundamental lesson about pruning which no successful gardener can really duck. It is this: that shrubs which flower before midsummer must be pruned after they are over if they are to have time to initiate new flower buds before the following spring, while shrubs which flower after midsummer must be pruned the following late winter. Primocane raspberries are therefore quick, not slow, growers. When old canes are cut down completely in February (which could not be simpler, incidentally), new canes grow up fast enough to make flower and set fruit within seven months. Summer-fruiting ones, on the other hand, make their biggest spurt of new leaf and cane growth at the same time as they fruit (which can be a bit of a nuisance, because the leafage masks those fruits), and the new canes must be tied in on horizontal wires when the old fruited canes are cut down in August.

The other great virtue of autumn-fruiting raspberries is that birds do not go for them with the single-minded determination with which they attack summer fruits. There is so much else in the berry line for them to eat in autumn that you need bother with no more than a bit of impromptu netting. If that. I am even considering growing a thicket of this raspberry in one of the wilder reaches of the garden, and simply taking a hedge trimmer to the old canes once a year. Autumn Bliss? You bet.

The Spectator

Seedy Doings in the Herb Garden   *27 July 2002*

It was not until I started looking around the garden recently for things to enter in horticultural classes at our local village flower show that it hit me. By 'it', I mean my sad neglect this year of the herbs in my garden. I found, to my shame, that I was in no position whatever to make up a decent vase of them for displaying publicly to my friends and neighbours. Peas, of course; raspberries, sure; blackcurrants, certainly; roses, perhaps; but herbs, definitely not. With the exception of rose-mary, tarragon and mint, my herbs were becoming as seedy as a Soho dive.

The vast majority of common culinary herbs flower in mid-summer and begin to look decidedly washed-out and straggly once they have done so. The flowers are rarely distinguished and, moreover, thrive at the expense of the foliage. This is the reason why I have never yielded to herb enthusiasts' recom-mendations to make a separate 'herb garden'. Instead, I mainly grow herbs for convenience rather than aesthetics, close to the back door, in a sunny border and in well-drained soil. Here they are useful, and pleasant enough in spring, but I plant bulbs and annuals among them so that their later shortcomings go unnoticed.

Neglecting them as much as I have this year is a rather uncharacteristic failure on my part, for I am, in the general run of things, as committed to cutting off heads as Lewis Carroll's Red Queen. This is because I know how much it rejuvenates plants in the middle of summer to lose their seed-heads, espe-cially if those seed-heads are not worth keeping. Perhaps it was the almost torrential rain in early July this year that kept me from the herb border, or just a thousand other things which somehow seemed more important at the time. Next year, however, I intend to do better, if only because there are presently hardly any decent thyme leaves to harvest, now my plants are so taken up with flowering. The other advantage of cutting off the flowers and flower stems is that the plant is spurred into producing some new and fresh leaf and stem growth, which is useful both for the kitchen and as propagating material.

Dead-heading is not necessary in the case of those herbs which are naturally biennial, of course, as fresh plants have to be raised each spring. From time to time I still come across people, who are put out when their parsley runs up to flower and loses its charm and efficacy as a herb. But like chervil it is a biennial, and is programmed to flower in its second summer; in fact, even meticulous and frequent dead-heading won't prevent biennials dying out at the end of the season.

There is much to be said for sowing parsley deliberately at this time of year, so that you have a good supply for winter. After all, there is no time when you do not need this herb, and remembering to freeze chopped parsley in ice-cube trays is more than this particular flesh and blood can bear. Sowing parsley now in a well-watered drill in a cold frame, or in a container, is a perfectly sensible stratagem. This is a particularly good time to sow chervil, too, for it grows quite well in the autumn. Dill, which is an annual, can also be sown up until September provided, as with all the others, it is kept well watered in dry weather. As for basil, which is a tender herb, it is not too late to sow a few seeds and keep the resulting seedlings in pots in a light place indoors, pinching out the stems as they grow to make the plants bushier.

If you want none of this bother, it is of course as easy as anything to grow annual and biennial herbs in informal patches, rather than in rows. Chervil, dill, borage, fennel, lovage and parsley can all be left to self-seed, but in most cases you will have to put up with some rather rank umbelliferous flowers first, and also be diligent with the hoe in spring to stop things getting out of hand.

Several shrubby herbs, such as thyme, rosemary, bay, sage and winter savory, can be propagated now from semi-ripe cuttings. And summertime is also a good moment for propagating mint by potting up divisions if you want good supplies later on in the year. I use the roots from the outer extremities, and thereby also prevent the mint from spreading too far. Herbs like mint would never have become so popular, regardless of their culinary merit, if they had not been easy to grow. But I have learned this year that there is a difference between a plant existing and a plant really thriving. And it is the gardener who makes that difference.

Independent Magazine

Coming a Cropper   13 March 1994

There is a topic of horticultural moment which is almost guaranteed to make gardeners look shifty and shuffle their feet, and that is any mention of a cropping plan for the vegetable garden. This is because the devising of a detailed plan is an arduous, time-consuming and often fruitless task, which few of us attempt with much enthusiasm.

When I was a young horticultural student, my year group was given charge of a plot of land, divided equally among us, to make parcels about a quarter the size of an allotment. Our job was to grow vegetables to the best of our abilities for a whole season, and our first task was to make a cropping plan which would ensure the most efficient use of the plot. We were to be marked on this and, later, on how our cultivations and produce lived up to this statement of intent. 'Successional sowings' and 'intercropping' (the sowing of quick-to-mature vegetables among slower ones, for example lettuces between rows of parsnips) were the buzz words. Evening after evening I toiled, making elaborate calendars which never quite dovetailed, my heart sinking at the thought of all those turnips and swedes which I would never eat and might have difficulty palming off on my flatmates.

The Kitchen Garden

Even when the plan was finished I cannot say I had complete faith in it, because I had not been told the most important information – namely, what had been grown on my particular plot for the previous three years. I was unable, therefore, to take specific advantage of my predecessor's pea crop, and the nitrogen left in the soil as a result, to give heart to my spinach.

Integral to a successful cropping plan is a four-year rotation of the main types of vegetable; this, as we know from countless practical manuals (not to mention half-remembered history lessons about 'Turnip' Townsend and the Agrarian Revolution), is self-evidently a Good Thing. A sensible crop rotation maximises fertility and also helps prevent the buildup of 'host-specific' pests and diseases. The way it works, put simply, is this: a crop of legumes (peas, beans and so on) is followed by brassicas and other green leaf vegetables, then by root vegetables and members of the potato family, and finally by onions and their relatives. Quick-growing salad plants are used as intercropping, but in different places each year.

That is the theory. In the event, so close together and relatively small were those plots that rotation to discourage pests was useless, just as it is in many gardens. Carrot fly, for example, can fly several yards, which may well represent a substantial part of many vegetable plots. In addition, some of the worst afflictions remain viable for a far longer period than four years, twenty years being not unheard-of for club root and potato cyst eelworm, and at least seven for onion white rot.

On the virtues of crop rotation for promoting fertility, however, there can be no argument. Growing the same type of plant intensively on the same ground for years will diminish yield as sure as God made them li'l green tomatoes.

Onions are supposed to be an exception, but there is a problem with that. Many is the time I have stood looking judicial at the side of an allotment while a chap tells me that he cannot think why his onions should have succumbed to white rot or onion fly. When I tentatively suggest that it might have

206

something to do with his having grown them on the same land for many years, he looks offended and replies 'I was always told that you kicked your wife out of your bed before your onions out of theirs', or earthy words to that effect. We can only hope that one positive result of the present morally confused climate will be healthier onions.

The joker in the pack with my student plot was the weather. As I recall, my best-laid plans went agley because of the unusual growing season, so that they had to be revised radically as the summer went on, causing my marks to dip extravagantly. Although I started off in fine style, eccentric weather conditions ensured that none of my crops ever took the time to come to maturity the books and catalogues told me they would; successional sowings started to bump into each other, like cars on a fog-bound motorway. The intercropping intermingled.

I would not like to leave anyone with the impression that a cropping plan is a waste of time. Far from it. I have learned after many years of vegetable growing that, although I can remember what I grew *and* where last summer, the year before and the one before that have slipped through the grille of memory. If thought out now, and amended as the season unfolds, a plan should prove an invaluable *aide-mémoire* and guide for next season, even if it turns out to be a work of fiction for this one.

Sunday Telegraph

Summer Offensive   10 July 1994

Vegetable gardening is not unlike conducting a military campaign. It goes very well to begin with – trenches are dug, immaculate drills are done, courage is high – but then momentum is lost and things start to get bogged down. Gaps appear in the ranks; food and water run short. Bringing up reinforcements is necessary but not easy, for obstacles such as dry soil, hot sun and shorter days get in the way. The troops who have done all the initial work become demoralised, and attention shifts to other fronts.

However, although the situation is desperate, it is not serious. It may be too late to sow peas, because (with the exception of a few resistant varieties like 'Cavalier') they will almost inevitably succumb to powdery mildew, and the heat of the July sun coupled with dry soil will probably put paid to spinach, which bolts quicker than a frightened cavalry charger in these conditions, but there is much that can be done to plug the gaps and raise morale.

Among the vegetables which not only can but should be sown at this time are the Oriental brassicas which have become so popular with cooks in recent years. If sown before the longest day, many are likely to run up to flower prematurely. Chinese broccoli, mizuna greens and komatsuna are exceptions, but also do well if sown now. Pak choi is the best known Oriental vegetable, but you will also find on sale the seed of mustard greens, headed Chinese cabbage, mizuna greens and mooli radishes. It must be understood, however, that these vegetables are breakfast, dinner, lunch and tea to the larvae of the cabbage white butterfly, so either you must spend your evenings picking these caterpillars off, or you have to spray with derris. Moreover, because of the enormous amount of leaf they make, none of these vegetables does well in dry or poor soil.

Winter radishes can also be sown now; the best known is 'Black Spanish', which comes in two forms, long or round; the skin is black, the flesh white, the taste hot and peppery. These radishes are hardy, so can be left in the ground, or lifted and stored in December.

Although there is still time to sow lettuces, it is best to plump for those which can claim some resistance to downy mildew, such as 'Debby' or 'Dolly'. Alternatively, try endive, which is another salad vegetable which may bolt from spring sowings but will stand some frost. There are two types, crinkly-leafed and broad-leafed; both must be blanched when nearly full grown, because the leaves are rather bitter-tasting. Blanching is not difficult; it simply means upending a large pot or bucket over the plant, to whiten the leaves and improve the taste.

Spinach would not be passed fit at this time of year, it is true, but its comrades, spinach beet and Swiss chard, are ready to be called up. They may not have quite the delicate lush taste of spring spinach, being something of a good chew, but they are very slow to run up to flower if sown now, and are pretty hardy as well. Indeed, you can harvest them through the winter.

As part of the late summer offensive, I do recommend you have a shot with spring cabbage, which can be sown in August to provide green leaves in the 'hungry gap' of March and April, and also Japanese onions. It is rather critical at what time the latter are sown. The second week of August in the north, one week later in the Midlands, and the last week of August in the south is usually recommended. This may seem like a military precision which is out of place in Civvy Street, but if the onions are too large before the winter they will bolt in the spring, and if too small they may succumb in harsh weather. 'Imai Early Yellow' will mature from late June, with 'Senshyu Semi-Globe' coming in two weeks later.

If the soil is very dry when you intend to sow these late-comers, draw out a deeper than usual drill with a hoe, water the bottom of it well, then line it with peat or peat substitute, which you can then water and onto which you can sow the seed. This should retain enough moisture to allow the seed to germinate and make its roots. Cover the drill with dry soil to inhibit evaporation from below. If possible, make the drills in the shadow of runner beans or Jerusalem artichokes; these stalwarts will shade them until removed in the shorter colder days, when the young plants will need all the sunshine going. There really is no need to feel alarmed by the state of the vegetable garden in July: instead, we should summon the courage to say, like Marshal Foch: 'My centre is giving way, my right is in retreat: situation excellent. I shall attack.'

Sunday Telegraph

Showing Off 20 July 2002

You need the soft hands of an opening batsman to gather fruit and vegetables successfully. Sensitivity and lightness of touch are the key, but I am usually found wanting. Harvesting raspberries, red currants, peas and broad beans, in particular, is a powerful challenge to a slovenly, clumsy, pressured soul like mine. Raspberries and currants can, in a hurried moment, be so easily squished to a pulp, and as for broad beans, do you pull or push? If you pull, you risk yanking the whole plant out of the ground; if you push, nothing happens except that the pod bends in the middle.

Harvesting has been preoccupying me lately, since it was our village show last Saturday and I was keen to enter several of the horticultural classes and support the show. Have you ever met anyone, by the way, who claimed that they exhibited at flower shows for reasons of vainglory, unhealthy competitiveness or a desire to show off to their neighbours? Or even just to measure their level of expertise or take pleasure in perfection? Certainly not. We are, one and all, 'just supporting the show'.

The same day, however, I had been asked to help judge the horticultural exhibits at our local town flower show, and I knew I would be on the *qui vive* for examples of slapdash harvesting. So, when collecting pea pods I was careful not to rub off the bloom, and I took the scissors up to the fruit cage to cut the raspberries' stalks, for the hulls must be left intact. I dug a whole row to find four evenly-matched, scab-free potatoes, and washed them with a sponge to preserve the soft skin.

You could be forgiven for thinking that if I am let loose to judge at local shows, I must be a successful competitor, too. Not so. Unless the class is very small, in which case I feel cheated, I usually come second or worse. Experience and knowledge are helpful, sure, but personality matters more. The slovenliness and carelessness which characterise my harvesting for the kitchen often do for me on Show Day as well. That, and the presence of too many other distractions through the season. The most successful exhibitors dislike television and hate holidays. Consistent evening work and meticulous attention to detail are the keys to success.

Despite my shortcomings I go on trying, for the discipline it exerts. I still feel the need for some character formation. And I am convinced that it is beneficial for children. When my daughter was eight, she won a cup at a local show for amassing most points in the children's classes. Jam tarts, cheese scones, fruit cake, unusual animal made out of a courgette, 'model garden': she made them all. I remember her picking cosmos buds for 'cabbages' in her 'vegetable garden' and borrowing a compact mirror for the 'pond'. And I remember, too, biting back a reproof as my feet crunched on the sugar scattered across the kitchen floor. Yet now, just out of her teens, she is a most accomplished cook. Surely the seeds of that interest were sown more than ten years before? I like to think so.

So how did I do? A first prize for potatoes, which pleased me more than I can say, and also for five strigs of fat, shiny 'Ben Conan' blackcurrants; an honourable second for my raspberries and loganberries. But nothing at all for my beautifully uniform and silky but, it would seem, immature peas. In Eliot's words, 'Between the idea and the reality, between the motion and the act falls the Shadow.' The Shadow did for me, all right.

Daily Telegraph

9

Friend or Foe?

Knowing All There is to be Knowed   15 December 2001

Sometimes I think I married Mr Toad, after all. Not in appearance, I hasten to add, for although my husband is just as handsome as Toad he is rather thinner, and has a quieter taste in waistcoats. Nor is he boastful – far from it. There is a resemblance, however, in his propensity for deeply-felt but sometimes rather short-lived enthusiasms. Patristic theology, fly-fishing, wood burners, the early music of The Doors, twentieth-century British oil-paintings, the poetry of Les Murray, sports cars: these are all things which at one time or another have caught my husband's fancy and engaged his intellect.

Now it is the turn of bee-keeping. Not that he keeps bees, you understand, but he fully intends to do so next year, and is presently engaged in that peculiarly delicious early stage of an enthusiasm, 'finding out *all* about it'. We once went on a fishing holiday to Scotland, and I have never forgotten with what care, as a beginner, he read the hotel's fishing book (which had entries going back to before the First World War) in order 'to find out all about it' and, in particular, to discover just exactly which flies were most successful on that stretch of river. He has never suggested a fishing holiday since.

The bee-keeping enthusiasm started in Cornwall this summer. We visited a bee 'centre' where we watched a murky video in Australian about 'queen management' and talked to the centre's owner about how the beginner should begin. This information was reinforced by more extensive chat with expert amateur beekeepers at the Royal Cornwall Show. We became conversant with the horrors of varroa mite, the importance of swarm control, the challenge of rape-flower honey, the iniquities of mice and wasps. We admired the clarity of the honey and the purity of the beeswax on show. We bought an illuminating volume (*Bees at the Bottom of The Garden* by Alan Campion) on the subject.

Once home, my husband made contact with the county bee-keepers' association, only to discover that its 'swarm coordinator', who would provide us with our first bees next summer, was a friend of ours, a saintly clergyman of the old school, famous for the beauty of his garden and the abundance of his honey. All we need do at present, therefore, is buy a couple of second-hand hives, as well as the indispensable if inelegant protective clothing of veil, boiler-suit and white wellies, a smoker, a hive tool and possibly a small centrifuge for extracting the honey, and wait for May to come round.

I am of course delighted, as any gardener would be, and keen to encourage him. I know exactly where the hives should be placed: at the end of the paddock, with the hive opening facing south, and close by a recently-planted boundary hedgerow of native shrubs. I am hoping that the abundance of hawthorn blossom will keep the bees content, and discourage them from foraging further afield among the surrounding fields of rape. In due season I hope they will find their way to the orchard and vegetable garden to improve pollination there. Not only will our garden benefit but also, I am hoping, those of our neighbours, even the smallest of which boasts at least one fruit tree.

Honey bees are demonstrably A Good Thing in every possible way, and likely to prove fascinating to my cerebral husband because of their complex social organisation. Moreover, they are much harder to keep these days, as a result of the depredations of varroa mite, so that the number of beekeepers in Britain has dropped by almost half in the past ten years, and the price of honey has risen proportionately. (I am reliably told, incidentally, that living in a town is no bar to keeping honey bees; certainly I have a good friend who used to have hives in her garden in Highbury.) What better occupation on a sunny afternoon, for a thoughtful Toad who dislikes gardening and loves honey, than tending bees in the fresh air?

There are, however, two questions which nag away at me. First, will he be over his apiarian fever by the time we acquire our hive of bees next summer? And, even if he is still keen, will it conflict with one of his other passions, which is driving a crimson-coloured Countax (C Series) ride-on lawn mower with foot-pedal-controlled hydrostatic transmission, electromagnetic clutch and three contra-rotating blades? I cannot bear to think what might happen were he to zoom around a corner in the paddock at breakneck speed, as is his wont, and drive slap bang into a beehive. The poetry of motion! O bliss! O my! O . . . . . . aaaagh! O poop-poop!

The Spectator

Making a Beeline   *10 August 2002*

It is far worse than I could have ever imagined. When I wrote last autumn about my husband's desire to keep honey bees, I felt confident that it would be a short-lived, Mr Toad enthusiasm. However, stung (no pun intended) by the documentary evidence of my lack of faith, he has plainly determined to turn bee-keeping into a lifelong obsession. Within a few days of his being given two colonies in April, one of them had swarmed, coming to rest conveniently in a nearby hedge, and he managed to deal with it safely and successfully. After that, there was no stopping him.

His waking hours are spent worrying about varroa mite and wax moth, and he does not keep his anxieties to himself, unfortunately. If you think a few well-chosen horticultural Latin names can bring a dinner party to a grinding halt, try scattering your conversation with 'brood chambers', 'propolis' and 'queen excluders'. Normal words like 'foundation', 'super' and 'comb' take on strange meanings; in that respect, bee-keeping is as bad as gardening.

I have been careful to lend a sympathetic ear – especially since he claims that half the reason for keeping bees is to improve the pollination of blossom in the orchard – but nothing more, for I dread the sunny afternoon when I shall be asked to leave the safety of my borders, don all the ridiculous and sweaty kit and go to the hives to do something mysterious, difficult, and possibly painful. Especially since these bees seem quite batey and I have already been stung, when I made the mistake of going to talk to my husband who was walking back to the house from the hives, followed by a number of bees doing the apiarian equivalent of 'Who are you looking at, Jimmy?'

There has, however, been one wholly beneficial side effect: I have learned a great deal more than I knew before about the species of bee which inhabit the garden. This is principally as a result of my husband inviting me to accompany him outside in the early mornings, while still in our dressing-gowns, to watch the furious, almost frenetic bee activity on a patch of single-flowered Shirley poppies I grow close to the house. We watch them collecting pollen on their legs in smooth, heavy yellow lumps, which sometimes seem to make it difficult for them to take off again. Although the honey bees are numerous, these poppies also play host to a number of species of worker bumble bee, known inaccurately and demotically by us as 'orange bums', 'white bums' and 'buff bums'. In fact, as I have now discovered, if you want to get interested in bumble bees you have to learn their Latin names, for the colour of bum is only one of several diagnostic features. The ones we get in the garden, as far as I can identify creatures which do not believe in keeping still, are the widely-distributed *Bombus lapidarius* (black body, orange 'tail'), *B. pascuorum* (reddish-brown thorax, known as a 'carder' bee), *B. hortorum* (white 'tail', scruffily hairy), *B. lucorum* (white 'tail') and *B. terrestris* (queen has buff 'tail', workers white 'tail', shorter-haired than *B. lucorum*).

Looking back, I remember how much I enjoyed watching bumble bees in the early spring when only the much larger queens were about, looking for nesting sites and forage; they are the Lancaster bombers of the *Bombus* world – slow, noisy, but wonderfully sturdy and impressive.

I used to think, in my careless way, that there were three types of bee: bumble, honey, and masonry. In fact there are 267 species of native bee (of which the 'domesticated' honey bee is not really one, as it comes from Asia originally); most species are solitary, like the red mason bee, which is, incidentally, many times more efficient as a pollinator than the honey bee. Some, like bumble bees, are social, in that they club together in nests. Closely related are cuckoo bees, which lay their eggs in bumble bee nests. Bumble bees nest just under the ground, often in old mouseholes or, if they are carder bees, on the surface. It occurs to me that the tussocky long grass in our young tree plantation, usually cut only once a year, must be an ideal nesting site for them.

Which is cheering, since we are told constantly that many of our native bees are in serious decline, mainly due to habitat extinction or degeneration. Long-tongued bumble bee species are particularly on the slide. This decline can only be stopped if gardeners and farmers concertedly grow plants with nectar-rich, long-tubed, single flowers, such as those of the pea and deadnettle families (legumes and labiates). Besides the Shirley poppies, other good bee plants in my garden are *Nepeta*, *Verbena bonariensis*, lavender, clovers (we don't cut the lawn short), foxgloves, *Delphinium* species, and cultivated thistles.

I would not tell my husband this, of course, but the short-tongued bumble bees, like *Bombus terrestris*, are excellent pollinators of apple blossom, perhaps better than honey bees. What is more, they rarely sting. And, most importantly, promoting their welfare does not usually turn a normal, sensible, rational person into a monomaniac.

The Spectator

Butterfly Couch   7 July 2001

When I tell people that I am prepared to accept a certain amount of couch grass in my garden, they look at me as if I have finally parted company with my trolley. After all, couch grass, twitch or *Agropyron repens* (as we don't call it) is generally considered to be among the very worst of all weeds, up there in the Hall of Infamy with ground elder, bindweed and horsetail. Its soil-creeping rhizomes have points as sharp as arrows which can push their way through the hardest, driest, most compacted clay soil, and a piece as small as a centimetre is capable of producing green grass blades and will soon romp away with all the explosive and misdirected energy of a two-year-old.

Moreover, in leaf it looks so similar to many other, better-behaved grasses that it is hard to spot it for what it is in a meadow planting until it flowers (and you have to be a bit of a botanist to identify it even then), and it is impossible to eradicate with weedkiller without killing everything else as well. The only way to keep it under control when it creeps into borders is by frequently digging it out, and in lawns and orchards by close mowing, which it dislikes.

So I had better explain myself. Couch grass acts as one of the hosts for the eggs and then caterpillars of a number of native British butterfly species, notably the Wall Brown, Gatekeeper, Meadow Brown, Ringlet and Speckled Wood. While couch has been largely eradicated from arable farmland by efficient husbandry, verges and gardens (especially slightly scruffy country ones like mine) on fertile soils remain important habitats for it. I have a small 'meadow' where it thrives on the fertile clay, and creeps into the flower borders whenever it gets a chance. This is not a source of shame to me, particularly; couch is such a formidably well-adjusted plant, as happy in its milieu as a TV presenter in the Groucho Club, that it would be foolish for me to think that I could ever get rid of it completely, and for good. And by way of compensation, I do see a healthy and heartening population of these butterflies each summer, which adds enormously to my enjoyment of the garden and, at the risk of sounding both soupy and pious, to my sense of being in harmony rather than conflict with the natural world.

In the last decade or two there has been much welcome emphasis on encouraging butterflies into the garden by providing nectar plants which suit them. Buddlejas, Michaelmas daisies and *Sedum spectabile* are the plants that we grow in the hope of seeing Peacocks, Small Tortoiseshells, Red Admirals and others in summer. As butterflies spend most of their time in restless and inconsequential, if appealing, flight, the best way of examining these beautiful creatures is to encourage them to alight on a plant to feed.

However, providing food for the adults can only ever be half the answer. These food plants are exotic, non-native plants, having been introduced into this country some time in the last two hundred years or so, which is the merest blink of the eye in terms of butterfly evolution. They have not, in the jargon, 'co-evolved' with these plants, and cannot therefore be expected as a matter of course to think them suitable for providing sustenance for Junior. The truth is that these Peacocks and small Tortoiseshells are still going to lay their eggs on stinging nettles if they can find them, as they have for millions of years. Indeed, a large nettle patch in the vicinity (even if not actually in your garden) is the best precondition for seeing a satisfactory range of butterflies.

Only one or two butterflies are really picky, it must be said. The Brimstone, for example, will only lay its eggs on the leaves of the buckthorn, *Rhamnus,* a native plant not often seen, and the Holly Blue lays its eggs in spring on holly, and in summer on ivy. Mercifully for all those readers who wondered whether I was about to suggest introducing couch grass into their gardens, butterflies like Wall Browns and Gatekeepers will lay their eggs on a number of coarse grasses, of which couch grass is only one kind.

Most gardeners can accept the idea of leaving a patch of these grasses, beneath apple trees, say or even a crop of nettles behind the fire-heap, but even relaxed gardeners have a problem with helping out the Small Copper butterfly, whose larva food plants of choice are docks and sorrel, the Painted Lady which likes thistles, and the Orange-Tip which favours Jack-in-the-hedge and charlock. I suppose that, in the end, it all depends what you consider a garden is for. I know what I think.

Independent

Red Alert
27 April 2002

'The Creator', said J.B.S. Haldane 'if He exists, has a special preference for beetles.' In which case, He is a great deal more broad-minded than the average gardener. Ladybirds and ground beetles apart, we hate the lot of 'em. Vine weevils, wire-worms, chafer grubs, bark beetles, shot-hole borers, viburnum beetles, pea and bean weevils – all are beetles of one kind or another, and all are a nuisance at the least, and devastatingly damaging at the worst. This year, in the list of the top ten pests about which members asked scientists at the Royal Horticultural Society's Gardens at Wisley, beetles came in at numbers 2, 3, 6 and 8. Worst was the vine weevil, not surprisingly, but following hard on its heels was the lily beetle.

The lily beetle? What on earth is that? may well be the reaction of readers in the north and west of England, as well as in the Celtic fringe. For *Lilioceris lilii*, often known as the scarlet lily beetle because of its colour, is not a native but was first established in England in 1940, in a garden in Chobham, Surrey, having come over from the Continent. It is moving north and west and has been sighted in Lancashire, the Midlands and Devon, but as it only flies in hot, dry weather, preferring to crawl otherwise, its progress depends on the vagaries of the British climate. As anyone who remembers the Battle of Britain will tell you, the summer of 1940 was one of cloudless skies; it seems it was not just the Luftwaffe which tried to invade southern England from Europe that year. Mercifully, my garden in the East Midlands is still free of lily beetles, but I remember them well from my time working at Wisley, and acquired a healthy respect for their destructive capabilities.

The lily beetle, once seen, is never forgotten. The adult is 8 mm long, with a bright red body, black legs and head. Beetles start to emerge from their winter rest in the soil in early spring, and the females lay up to three hundred jelly-bean-shaped eggs on the undersides of leaves of lilies and fritillaries, mainly near the plant's base. These hatch in ten days into fat, brown-red, black-headed larvae which eat the foliage and flowers voraciously and, charmingly, cover themselves in their own black excrement, which makes picking them off a less than pleasant task. As they favour the underside of leaves, they are not always easy to spot. The adults also eat leaves, and in bad infestations lilies can be completely defoliated. This weakens them, and rather undermines the point of growing them. The larvae then pupate and emerge later in the summer as adults, to supplement the numbers of adults which overwintered. It is depressing. Indeed, I know people in the south-east of England who have given up growing lilies as a result, and that is a great deprivation.

Some help is, however, at hand. Although generally it is difficult to pierce the hard elytra (carapace) of a beetle, larvae are more vulnerable. Bio Provado Ultimate Bug Killer (containing the very effective new insecticide imidacloprid, mixed with methiocarb) is now recommended for use against lily beetle, as well as the scale, red spider mite, aphids, whitefly, thrips and mealybug which do such damage in greenhouses and conservatories. It is formulated as an aerosol spray, and is therefore relatively expensive, but ideal for plants in restricted circumstances, such as lilies in pots. Egg-laying stops at the end of July, so spraying is a waste of time after mid August. Organic gardeners will have to use their fingers and thumbs on the eggs, larvae and adults as soon as they are seen, and lay down newspaper to collect the adults which fall belly-up on the ground when disturbed.

In Europe, the lily beetle is kept in natural check by six ferocious parasitic wasps. Two of these (*Tetrastichus setifer* and *Lemophagus errabundus*) are able to live in our colder climes and parasitise the larvae but are not active for so long in the summer as the lily beetle larvae, so the population reduction may not be enough to make a significant difference. Andrew Salisbury, an entomologist at Wisley, is presently carrying out research on these parasites and other aspects of the lily beetle question, but the work is in its early stages, and it is not yet known whether these wasps could ever be reared commercially for sale to gardeners as a biological control. Until we know more, we can only admire one of God's most beautiful and successful creatures while reaching, without compunction, for the sprayer.

Independent

Snake in the Grass   *17 November 2001*

I cannot tell you what a relief it is that the days are short and cold. In other years, the putting up of the bubble insulation in the greenhouses, the storing of the apples, the planting of the tulips, the clearing of the borders would be tinged with a quiet sadness, speaking as they do of the slow dying of the year. This November, however, things are different.

It all began on a day in late August. By chance I was away, so Cynthia, who works with me in the garden each Tuesday, winter and summer, was on her own. She was walking along beside the orchard to the compost bins, which are under her meticulous and constant care. Suddenly (as she reported to me in broken sentences later that day) she caught a glimpse of a young grass snake, distinctive for its olive-green colouring and the yellow band around its neck, basking in the longish grass. She confessed to shrieking, and I do not disbelieve her. I would have shrieked, too.

For weeks afterwards, both she and I could barely bring ourselves to go into the orchard, let alone lift the wooden lids of the compost bins, for fear of what we might find, especially after a gardening friend told me she had once found a nest of grass snakes curled up asleep in her compost bin. (Another friend told me that she has grass snakes in her garden that climb onto the top of her yew hedges to bask, which information I have been strangely reluctant to pass on.) We vied with each other for the privilege of pushing the wheelbarrow, whose raucous squeak from an unoiled axle was usually a powerful irritant. No longer. It was our protection from what we might find in the long grass of the paddock on the way to the fire-heap. Only when October came, and we could be reasonably sure that any grass snake would be hibernating, did we finally relax.

Natrix natrix, I have discovered after visiting a lot of spine-chilling, jitters-making naturalists' websites, gets its name because it likes to swim, and indeed is rarely found very far from water. We have no pond, as it happens, although we fully intend to dig one, once we can fish the idea out of the Too Difficult and Expensive file where it presently resides. However, there is a farm ditch beyond our boundary which periodically fills with water, and there are certainly plenty of sunny banks, long grass, rubbly stone walls, toads, frogs, small mammals and general lack of disturbance, all of which grass snakes like. And we have compost heaps, which are favourite places for them to lay eggs, being both warm and secure. They hibernate between October and March, and lay eggs in June and July which hatch in August and September. Males can grow to three feet long, females to five. It is likely that Cynthia saw a young one which had hatched in the pile of garden rubbish waiting to be composted.

She is adamant it was not a slow worm, which we may also, unwittingly, be harbouring in the garden. Slow worms have fewer markings and, as every schoolchild knows, a slow worm is a lizard without legs. However, the distinction is an idle, irrelevant one if, like Cynthia and me, you are herpetophobic.

Before you start thinking sly thoughts about women and snakes, I would just like to say that we are ladies of a certain age who were brought up to think that snakes were nasty, slimy, slinky things, and we were not taken to zoos as children, to be wreathed in writhing serpents, like Laocoön and his sons. That said, even the naturalists advise against handling grass snakes, although they are harmless, not only because they don't like the pressure (apparently), but because they show their displeasure by excreting a foul-smelling liquid all over you. No danger of that in our garden, I can assure you.

Of course, in a way we are both very pleased. The presence of snakes or lizards in the garden is proof that we have perpetuated, even if we have not created, an environment which suits wild creatures. For most of us, unless we are farmers or fieldsportsmen, gardening is the only means by which we interact intimately with Nature. If we are sensible, we are happy to neither control that wildlife nor even know its every way. And we cannot possibly be fussy about what we foster. Although I am frightened of coming across a snake or slow worm, I am pleased that they choose to live here, especially as naturalists seem generally agreed that their numbers are in sharp decline.

Curiously, the more amphibian websites I visited, and the more colour photographs I studied, the less I feared to look upon them. I was relieved, it is true, that lack of the appropriate software prevented me from seeing action film of a grass snake swimming, but in time I became almost inured to stills of curled-up serpents. Who knows, I may even get round to oiling that wheelbarrow axle, some time in the next ten years. Whether Cynthia will ever be able to find a spare moment to tend the compost bins, come the spring, is another matter.

The Spectator

Weeding in the Dark   *9 June 1991*

Weeds, like sorrows, come not single spies, but in battalions. They form an enemy host with a choice of weapons, both physical and psychological, at their disposal. Some detachments gain ground by sheer aggression while others, frailer but more cunning, work by stealth. Like any enemy, they can be relied upon to be consistently beastly; their habits are far more dependable than most of the plants on which I lavish attention.

Friend or Foe?

They have played a constant and recurring part in my gardening career. In my childhood, harassed grown-ups jealous of my mooching idleness would find some unattractive, weed-related task to 'occupy' me. When I first took to gardening of my own accord, in my late teens, I discovered that this childhood fagging had ensured a broad working knowledge of weeds and their ways, even though I knew no common names beyond groundsel, bindweed and shepherd's purse. Weeds continue to absorb me, and no doubt a day will come when their vitality will out-match mine.

In my own garden – and sometimes even in other people's – my close involvement with them means I barely have eyes for anything else. Someone will say 'How pretty your border looks', and in genuine surprise I realise that they are admiring the flowering asters while all I have seen is the insidious creeping tendrils of bindweed. As there is no such thing as a weed-free garden, I should be careful not to let weeds grow as rankly in my psyche as they do behind the garden shed.

It has to be said, there are years when I am almost grateful to them. After the winter digging, late spring brings a pleasant change of task, and fine days find me happily on my knees at the edge of flower beds, digging weeds out cleanly with a hand fork. Even the white roots of bindweed are not yet encased and brittle in a baked summer soil, but can be drawn gently from a yielding earth.

With a border fork there is still a chance of bringing up most of a dandelion's taproot, and the groundsel has yet to release its swansdown on the evening air, ready to sprout almost as soon as it touches earth. It is pleasant, too, to slow down to the pace of weeding, letting one's mind run on, unrestricted by the rigorous demands of pruning or planning.

April and May are the months when this raggle-taggle army threatens to overwhelm me by sheer force of numbers – until I can lay down a thick organic mulch barrage to contain and neutralise them. This year, however, a dry, windy May halted the mulch-laying before it was half done, for a thick mulch keeps rain out as well as moisture in. I anticipate a long hard summer of weeding, if we do not soon have some appreciable amount of rain.

Although a Dutch hoe works best on dry soil, I rarely use one. There are few people (and I am not among them) who can hoe without nicking the stems of favoured plants, let alone without beheading interesting self-sown seedlings. In the kitchen garden hoeing between rows of seedling vegetables is useful, but it is the weeds among, rather than between, which constitute the most direct competition to the vegetables, and these must be picked by hand. Hoeing, to be successful, has to be done on a dry, warm day so that the weeds quickly shrivel, since groundsel, for example, can root afresh in damp soil.

There is one source of consolation for the hard-pressed gardener. As most weeds are only native plants which happen to be too rampant or dingy to be wanted in the garden, you can confidently expect that different ones will thrive in different soils and localities. It is rare to find *Rumex acetosa* or *Rorippa sylvestris* in an alkaline soil, and mare's tail (*Equisetum*) does not flourish in dry places. Dog's mercury, a native woodland plant, mostly grows in shade, while common ragwort prefers open spaces. The most successful weeds, of course, are those perennials, like ground elder, with catholic tastes in soil and site and the ability to regenerate from little pieces of root.

The real answer to successful mechanical eradication of weeds, I am told, is not hoeing or hand-pulling, or even thick mulching, but digging over the soil in the pitch dark. Researchers at the University of Erlangen in Germany have discovered that if garden soil is dug over in September at night, weed seeds (both on and under the soil) will rarely sprout. This is because the germination of most weed seeds is triggered by light. I am indebted for this information to *Gardening from Which?*, which concluded its report by lamenting that those gardeners who live in urban areas may have problems finding sufficiently dark conditions for this remedy to succeed, owing to the ubiquity of street lighting.

Those of us in the country might be able to think of other problems, such as tripping over one's spade or digging the same piece of ground several times over, not to mention becoming well and truly spooked. I commend this suggestion, however, to all lion-hearted, weed-obsessed insomniacs.

Observer

The Villain of the Piece   *14 September 2002*

Rarely has my garden been so well weeded at the end of August as it was this year. There is nothing like opening your garden to visitors for an afternoon to concentrate the mind. I have no doubt that most, if not all, of the people who came round were generous-spirited, but anyone who is a gardener notices weeds in other people's gardens. It is not malice, simply experience. So for a week beforehand I hoed and I pulled and I dug and I barrowed, searching out every insidious milkweed or hidden sow thistle. I was particularly careful to hoe soil that seemed 'clean', in order to pick up any tiny weed seedlings which would make their presence felt in a few days. I was shored up during this labour by the thought that I would not have to do a great deal more weeding for the rest of this season.

How could I have thought anything of the kind? A week later I was forced outside again to hoe off the groundsel which appeared as if from nowhere, and in some cases was sufficiently well-grown to be almost flowering. I have always considered this the most poisonously awful of all annual weeds, but I reckon it has surpassed itself this summer, thanks to refreshing early August rains.

How do I hate *Senecio vulgaris*? Let me count the ways. Although it is supposed to flag a bit in summer (though plainly not this year), groundsel can be relied upon to sprout at any time, winter or summer. Indeed, three generations can be expected in a single year, which makes it what the botanists call 'an ephemeral'. Hah! It is about as ephemeral as Third World debt. Moreover, if hoed off when in flower it still has the capacity to go on to set seed, and this seed is as fine as thistledown, so is easily dispersed by the wind. Were you ever – theoretically – to get rid of the groundsel in your garden, therefore, in a twinkling it would be reinfected from next door. If the weather is wet the seeds become sticky, in order that they can be carried hither and thither on your wellies. One flower head can produce a thousand seeds, and once those thousand seeds are dispersed, germination will continue for at least five years. The old saw about 'One year's seeding, seven years' weeding' is not far off the mark.

This is not the end of its villainy. Although the rusty spots often seen on the fleshy stems of this weed only do harm to the plant (although not so you would notice), groundsel is also a symptomless carrier of verticillium wilt, which causes wilting and death of foliage and stems. Great. So not only do you have a prolific and unsightly weed in your garden that is quite impossible to eradicate permanently, but it can threaten the health of your trees, shrubs, fruit trees and perennials too. If you grow cucumbers, you won't want to know that groundsel is also the alternate host for this vegetable's powdery mildew. Worst of all, groundsel can harbour chrysanthemum leaf miner, a serious pest of commercial horticulture.

I rather wish now I had not embarked on this exercise, for it has frightened me half to death. Should I ever open the garden again, I shall be mighty tempted to use dichlobenil granules (Casoron G-4) as a pre-emergent weedkiller, to zap the groundsel as they germinate. That should tip the balance of power my way. Well, a bit.

Daily Telegraph

A Load of Rot *21 November 1993*

One of the stranger features of being a committed gardener is that hardly any subject, however overtly unpleasant, seems to be out of bounds, even in the politest company. Few people turn a hair if you mention farmyard manure, fungal pustules, bacterial decay, or pseudocopulation. Certainly no one is affronted by the mention of the words 'brown rot'; instead, it is treated with all the grave consideration which it deserves as one of the great wreckers of pomicultural ambition. As I have recently taken over a garden containing several fruit trees, I find the subject has a more than theoretical fascination at the moment.

Brown rot (*Monilinia fructigena*) is probably the most instantly recognisable of all plant ailments. It affects most of the types of fruit we can grow in our gardens, but particularly ripe and ripening apples, pears and plums. It spreads first over the surface of the fruit, then affects the tissues beneath, causing a general brown disintegration which is not pleasant to handle. It is accompanied by a sweet but overblown smell. On badly-affected fruits, concentric rings of cream-coloured pustules can often be seen. When these burst, fungal spores are released into the atmosphere to be carried on the wind or rain to infect other fruits. However generous the fruiting, much will simply go to waste if brown rot is allowed to spread – as it will, like wildfire, especially to any fruits which have been punctured, bruised, scarred, or otherwise impaired. The closely related fungus *Monilinia laxa* causes blossom wilt and spur blight, as well as minor cankers.

I am not the most careful of gardeners in the general run of things, because while my ambition is infinite my time is not. I have no sooner embarked on one task than my attention is grabbed by another equally, if not more, pressing. There are days when I flit about like a bee in a summer border. But there is one job which I pride myself I do with enormous care, and that is the harvesting and storing of fruit.

Recently a dry afternoon found me, with fingernails newly clipped and filed, on a step ladder among the boughs of a large 'Bramley Seedling' tree, carefully removing apples and trying to ensure that the stalks were left intact as I did so. I then placed them in a box with as much gentleness as if they had been eggs. I even separated picked apples from sound-looking windfalls.

The effects of brown rot are well known, even among people who do not grow fruit. After all, it gave rise to the saying about one rotten apple infecting the whole barrel. We hardly have any excuse, therefore, for taking chances with such a venerable adversary. Instead of simply throwing fruit hugger-mugger into a cardboard box, we should separate them from each other, laying them out individually on shelves in an airy frost-free place (or on trays in the back spare room) or – if we wish to store them for longer – wrapping them in greaseproof paper or the pages of the colour supplements and placing them in shallow boxes.

Brown rot is, in fact, simply first among equals in a whole host of rots – white rot, dry rot, wet rot, and soft rot – which affect plant life. Many have picturesque names: gladiolus core rot, bacterial soft rot, bitter rot, carrot black rot, grey mould rot, onion neck rot, potato dry rot. Even if we do not know all the names, we know the decidedly unpicturesque effects when we see them. The list, if not endless, is sufficiently long to put the fear of God into conscientious gardeners.

The books talk optimistically about preventive measures for brown rot – namely, protecting the fruit from pest, disease, and mechanical injury. That means anything from wasps, frost and hailstones to my fingernails. However, speaking as someone who has at least a tenuous connection with the Real World, I can say that preventing the spread can never be entirely possible. All that can be achieved is to keep it in bounds by discarding rotten fruits in the fire or dustbin and storing sound fruit individually.

The dried-up 'mummies' which hang on after the ripe fruit falls, and which serve as a source of infection for the following year, should also be removed, and the trees pruned well in winter to remove cankers and dead wood, where the fungus also overwinters. In short, the best way of controlling brown rot is to attend to – and I surely need make no apologies for mentioning such a delicate subject – our personal garden hygiene.

Sunday Telegraph

Reaping the Whirlwind   4 November 2002

I laughed out loud. I couldn't help it. My garden, the Monday before last, looked like a cartoon I once saw in a book on the 1929 Wall Street Crash, depicting stunned bankers lying dazed on the floor with dollar bills fluttering all round them. Except in this case it was plants which were stunned, and leaves which were fluttering all round. The funniest sight was a row of maturing Brussels sprouts which were leaning against each other at the same acute angle, as if a Divine hand had been demonstrating the Domino Theory using my brassicas as an example. Elsewhere, bizarrely, a *Salvia farinacea* had been uprooted completely from the border and left to wither on the lawn ten feet away.

As for *Salvia* 'Black and Blue', I have waited all autumn for it to flower, which it has steadfastly refused to do this year despite the fact that it is growing in the warmest, most sheltered, most directly south-facing corner of the house border, for some reason simply growing taller as time goes on (eight feet at the last count). During the gales the leaves were stripped away, leaving the square stems bare, and the still rather embryonic flower buds were found several feet away across the terrace. I am not sure that this plant will retain its favoured position next year. Indeed, I am tempted to remove the tall, bare stalks this very minute.

What was interesting and rather heartening, however, is how well the young trees I have planted over the last nine years fared. Although between ten and fifteen feet tall, not a single one was downed, even though the gales, crossing the flattish farmland to the south-west first, hit them with the most tremendous force. But of course, they were all planted as 18-inch tall, bare-rooted, maiden (that is, branchless) 'whips'. I am convinced of the virtues of planting bare-rooted, as opposed to containerised, trees in a clay soil like mine, and the younger the better, provided that you can protect them in their early years from rabbits, deer, and careless ride-on-mower operatives (who shall remain nameless). I have never needed to stake any of them, and they are much the better for it. I wonder how many trunks of trees growing in gardens, parks and streets snapped off at the top of their stakes a week ago last Sunday.

In the garden proper my efforts at staking clumps of chrysanthemum or aster could not match the force of 70 mph winds, and canes fell, link stakes burst and strings broke all round the garden. Moreover, sturdy perennials which I normally never expect to have to stake, like *Cirsium rivulare* 'Atropurpureum', looked shaken and stirred by the experience. As for those Brussels sprouts, we pulled them upright again, and supported them with stout bamboo canes, feeling as if we had somehow been transported from the East Midlands to the east coast of Scotland, where such things are commonplace. Only the perennial grasses looked as if nothing had disturbed the even tenor of their ways, for their habit of growth is almost uniquely suited to allowing winds to pass through them without damage. Since many of them are prairie plants, this is hardly surprising. Perhaps if global warming is a reality, and autumn gales of such magnitude become the rule, we should look even harder at the perennials of prairies and steppes, such as *Stipa, Festuca, Echinacea* and *Rudbeckia*, to provide both colour and a welcome stability at this time of year. And we should definitely give up on highly artificial constructs like Brussels sprouts.

Daily Telegraph

10

A Miscellany

Give Him the Tools   *30 October 1994*

Gardeners can be divided neatly into two groups, in my experience: those who tackle every aspect of the garden's development and maintenance, and those who feel it necessary to
concern themselves with only one facet, usually the care of the
lawn, or the compost heap, or the garden machinery. It is interesting to me how many members of this last group, the garden
specialists, can also be filed under the heading 'husbands'.

My husband is a typical example. Until recently, he has
always felt himself to be of most use in the garden when
employed in a helpful, hands-off, advisory capacity; for
example, in exhorting me earnestly not to waste the precious
moments when weather and soil were favourably conjoined
for planting, lest another season be lost. His practical partici-
pation was restricted to – well, just restricted.

But that was before we found, a year after we moved house, that we could no longer pretend we had a smallish garden, with appropriate and adequate tools to match. In short, we must bite the sparking plug and buy a ride-on tractor mower for the lawns and paddock, as well as the grass between the trees which I managed to plant last January (thanks, I might say, to some urgent and helpful reminders to 'get on with it'). We needed something which would leave a good finish on a lawn, yet was strong enough, and with high enough blade settings, to take on grass left to grow until wild flowers or bulbs were over. As there was no permanent human help to be had at that time – no, not even for ready money – we were going to have to make do with mechanical servants.

Now, I have never made any secret of the fact that I slept peacefully through my machinery lectures as a student, and am hazy these days even about the difference between diesel and two-stroke, so the idea of acquiring expensive and complicated pieces of machinery held only anxiety for me. I had reckoned, however, without my husband's Scalextric mentality.

Before I could say hydrostatic gear transmission, there was a 'man coming round' to give me a test-drive. Weakly, I listened to advice from this cheerful soul about how to take off the cutter deck (you must be joking, I thought), uncouple the grass collector to put on a dump truck, drain the oil. But despite all this, even I could see that this machine might solve a few problems.

The juggernaut of progress could not be stopped, in any event. When my husband came home from his cerebral labours, with one bound he was in the driving seat and away. And, although no less busy at work than usual (the reason, of course, why he had been prevented heretofore from playing a very active role in the garden), each evening of the fine balmy days of early October saw him reducing the rank grasses of paddock and garden to the consistency of green shag pile carpet. Although at first he scalped with all the enthusiasm of a Native American brave, he soon learned to manoeuvre the tractor efficiently, even elegantly, over uneven ground.

Since this tractor has headlights (a stroke of genius, in my opinion, on the part of the manufacturers), his presence was advertised, as the light faded, by two arcs of light. When he told me that he had taken off the cutter deck to check for possible damage to the blades after hitting a big stone, I knew that we had entered a new era of horticultural co-operation.

In a sense, what we bought to achieve this happy state of affairs is not all that important, for it is the feel-good factor which really matters. (I know that my brother affects to object to his excellent machine because it dares to call itself 'The Suburban'.) As a matter of fact, we chose a Countax K 14 Twin Tractor with a 38-inch triple rotary blade cutter (which achieves a range in grass height from half an inch to three and three-quarter inches), powered grass collection, and a roller to give the all-important lawn stripes. We bought it because it is made in Britain, represents good value for money, and is unlikely to clog on wet grass because the clippings are brushed, rather than blown, into the collecting box. And it is a lot of fun.

What my husband has discovered, with this tractor, is a way of helping without being bludgeoned constantly with examples of his (perfectly understandable) ignorance. Gardening, with all its questions about 'When shall I prune it?' and 'How do I take cuttings?' and 'What is its name?', can be disheartening for people who are too busy to learn, yet fearful of the scorn of others. My husband's rapport with this machine has ended all that. I wish I had realised years ago that garden specialists become such in order both to simplify their lives and to deflect criticism; that all my husband was waiting for was to be given the tools so that he could finish the job.

Sunday Telegraph

Rainy-day Gardening

6 May 2000

You can tell when spring has sprung, because gardening catalogues arrive by every post or flutter from every opened magazine. I don't mean nursery plant brochures, but garden
hardware catalogues which offer everything from hose-reels to
self-watering cloches, wheelbarrow planters to propagating
units, and a mass of 'lifestyle' items as well. They are a pleasing mixture of the whimsical, the inspirational and the unself-
consciously mundane. This year mail-order firms must be
rubbing their hands, for the wettest April since the year
Napoleon marched on Moscow has confounded and frustrated
the best intentions of millions of gardeners, who have been left
on their precious days off work twiddling their thumbs inside
as the rain spatters on the window-panes. Mail-order catalogues, usually a bit of a nuisance when there is so much to be
doing outside in spring, have this year proved something of a
welcome diversion.

The moment I tear the plastic wrapping off one of these
brochures, I am lost. As if by magic, I have a credit card at the
ready to order any number of small gadgets which might – just
possibly – make gardening easier, more successful or more
agreeable for me. Over the years I have acquired a paving-
stone-weeder knife, a daisy grubber, a seed sower, any number
of widgers and dibbers, cane caps, wigwam grips, lawn
aerator sandals, copper pot labels, and a handy scoop. (Scoops
and the like are always 'handy', and ideas invariably 'bright'.)
Of these, only the widger and scoop get daily use in the spring;
the rest sit on shelves or in plastic pots in the shed waiting
vainly for the next outing, like abandoned relatives in an old
people's home. Some gadgets, like the lawn aerator sandals, I
could never get to work properly; instead of walking briskly
and purposefully over the grass, I staggered and lurched as if
through quick-drying cement. Over the years I have wasted
quite a lot of money buying items which either flaws in my per-

sonality or their inherent inutility have ensured that I never use to the full.

Although I ought to be like a reformed drunk, aware of my own proclivities and trying hard to put temptation behind me, I still read these catalogues, I still fill in the order forms, and I still sometimes even send them off. If truth be told, I am not ashamed of it. Show me a woman who is immune to the charm of the galvanised steel 'traditional' watering can in glossy cobalt blue coating, or the allure of a soil thermometer, and I will show you someone without romance or adventure in her soul. Although I cannot quite bring myself to spend £99.95 on a traditional Victorian Lantern Cloche, or £79.50 on a frost-resistant simulated bronze polyresin deer, I would not dream of sneering at anyone who did, for I know what it is to be caught up in the excitement of long-distance acquisition. And as a result of these colourfully illustrated brochures, we are all well-informed about what is available in the hardware and 'lifestyle' line. Few if any garden centres can boast such a range.

Most of these mail-order firms have been quick to develop associated websites, with online brochures using the same details and even the same photographs as the postal ones, and secure credit card facilities. And there are a number of special offers available to encourage you to buy online. Now there is e-commerce, we do not even have to wait for a twice-yearly fix of gardening catalogues. All we need is a rainy day.

Independent

Saving the Planet   20 June 1993

One green bottle,
Drop it in the bank.
Ten green bottles,
What a lot we drank.

Heaps of bottles
And yesterday's a blank
But we'll save the planet,
Tinkle, tinkle, clank!
    Wendy Cope, 'A Green Song', from *Serious Concerns*

Here is a thoroughly modern dilemma: how do we consume as inconspicuously as possible without obsessiveness threatening to ruin the point, or laying ourselves open to ridicule? In the horticultural world, the most fervent planet savers are those who practise 'organic gardening'.

This requires that you garden 'naturally', avoiding the use of artificially produced fertilisers and manures in favour of naturally-occurring and renewable ones, and recycling garden waste by encouraging it to decay to usable compost. The soil rather than the individual plant is fed, for according to organic practitioners, the best promoter of a healthy and vigorous garden is a fertile soil. Chemicals, and pesticides in particular, are ruled out because they upset the natural balance which can come to exist between predator and predated in the garden.

Not surprisingly, there is a purist and a not-quite-so-purist view. Some organic gardeners are happy to use one or two pesticides, such as derris, because they are naturally occurring and of very short persistence. The purists argue, however, that derris is non-specific, killing beneficial as well as harmful insects, so they prefer to use nothing but mechanical means of controlling undesirables.

Organic gardening requires a shift away from conventional attitudes, many of them borrowed from commercial agriculture and therefore inappropriate. Greenfly, for example, need only be kept under reasonable control by tits, ladybirds and hoverflies; they do not need to be eliminated, for in the organic garden some damage to plants is accepted as inevitable. It is no accident that organic principles are most widely practised in kitchen gardens and allotments, where look is less important than edibility.

Purist organic gardeners have a genuine, even earnest, desire to leave as light and plain a footprint as possible on the sands of time. They enjoy the satisfaction of triumphing, unaided, over adversity. I admire – and envy – them for their consistency and steadfastness, while at the same time finding their smugness irritating.

But in one important regard they make life easy for themselves. Whether they realise it or not, they have found a way of avoiding the aesthetic difficulties inherent in making a really attractive garden. Emphasising the non-threatening nature of garden management can absolve them, in the eyes of others as well as themselves, from other duties. If they do not use systemic weedkillers to kill perennial weeds, no one can blame them for covering the soil with old carpet or black polythene, however tatty it makes the garden look.

Artistic and 'green' considerations are not necessarily incompatible, of course, but my experience of committed organic gardeners leads me to doubt that the look of the garden is ever of more than secondary importance to them. After all, you have to learn to view your garden in a particular way not to bridle at the sight of fleshy garlic planted close to rose bushes, or cut-down lemonade bottles over young delphiniums.

Moreover, it requires a difficult juggling act to encourage beneficial creatures at the expense of pests (especially in the case of wasps, which are both), choose disease-resistant flower varieties and 'companion species', and place plants only where they are bound to thrive. Devising attractive colour schemes as well must often seem one dam' thing too many.

I am impressed by organic gardeners' deep knowledge of the way plants and animals interact; with their attempts to find acceptable alternatives for peat; and with their stalwart defence of the virtues of hard work. But I am a horticultural fellow-traveller, constitutionally unsuited to embracing any Big Idea wholeheartedly. Conscious always that there are other voices in other rooms, I have not the single-mindedness to join the Organic Party.

I mostly use plant-extract fertilisers, but if there were no such thing as liquid seaweed I would not ignore a manufactured source of potash instead. I have mostly given up peat, but that is partly because I have horticultural reservations about it. I practise companion planting, but only in the kitchen garden, for I cannot be doing with tomatoes and French marigolds in my flower borders.

The important question to ask, in gardening as in life, should be 'What is it all for?' Organic gardening too often seems less a means to an end than the end itself. I want a beautiful and productive garden, but I prefer to try to achieve it with the help of a limited number of non-persistent chemicals than to make all the sacrifices required by a stern ideology.

Sunday Telegraph

Not Found in Every Swaps Tin   *12 September 1993*

As a child, I collected stamps. Not just any kind, but twentieth-century British Commonwealth, and in particular those belonging to far-flung islands: Mauritius, Gilbert and Ellis, Virgin, Pitcairn.These were attractively colourful, except for the sober and restraining head of His or Her Majesty, but, most important, they were not to be found in every friend's swaps tin. For me they had more cachet than the ten-a-penny CCCP triangular stamps of Yuri Gagarin which other, less discerning souls collected; indeed, on early trips to London, which always included a visit to Stanley Gibbons, I might pay a whole pound for one of the higher denominations.

These days I am no different, except that now I answer the siren call of unusual plants rather than stamps. My greatest

excess was an oh-so-special hellebore seedling I bought at a
Royal Horticultural Society show for £12;* the only regret I
have is that I did not buy two.

The reasons why some plants are uncommon are numerous,
but may be simplified thus: they are difficult to grow, they are
unfashionable, they are ugly or disagreeable, they are only
recently introduced, or they are unlucky.

Keen gardeners do not want to grow ugly or dowdy plants,
on the whole (although they sometimes end up with them,
nevertheless), but they are attracted by difficult plants, unfashionable ones, and those which have recently been bred or, even
better, found in the wild. Above all, they hanker after something which is not in everybody else's swaps tin.

There is nothing reprehensible about this – indeed, the desire
to possess something highly unusual, even unique, from a per-
sonalised number plate to a van Gogh, is a motive force behind
much human action; it is only reprehensible if you steal rare
plants (and people do) from other people's gardens, nurseries,
botanic gardens, or native habitats.

Too sincere a devotion to unusual plants can be confining, of
course, for the gardener often needs the common, dependable,
workhorse plants to cover up when the uncommon ones are
slow to grow or quick to die, and to help make satisfying planting schemes. Nevertheless, there should be room in most
gardens for a few, especially if you like sharing your finds with
friends.

Plants actually on the edge of extinction must be saved if
possible, on that we all agree. Not only can they be a very
important gene resource, but conservation of species is *bonum
in se*, as the lawyers might say. This is well recognised by the
National Council for the Conservation of Plants and Gardens,
the NCCPG (with the accent very much on the P, not G), which
over the last twenty-five years has done a great deal to make

* A lot of money in 1993.

the gardening public aware of the losses already sustained and liable to be sustained in the future, and to encourage us to search out what is lost or neglected, so that we have the greatest possible choice for our gardens.

One measure of the success of the NCCPG (which is, incidentally, organised in county-wide groups) has been the mushrooming of nurseries whose owners use the fact that they grow 'unusual' plants as an important selling point. They often hold a National Collection of a particular genus, so they are repositories of a great deal of information and advice. As so many similar plants are grown in the same place, these collections can be used as bases for botanical and horticultural research work; because the holding of a National Collection confers on the holders a number of obligations, their approach is very much more rigorous in the matter of plant-naming than is usually the case in larger, more general nurseries. Perhaps – who knows – you may discover for sale the horticultural equivalent of a Penny Black or, at the very least, a Pitcairn Islands 1s. 6d. I hope so.

Sunday Telegraph

Roses get fruity   26 June 1994

I sometimes wonder whether we really care about the scent of roses, even though we pay such lip-service to the virtues and attractions of fragrance. It is so common to find scented climbers placed on draughty east walls, and Old Roses planted in large open spaces where the wind is untempered by hedge or wall, that one can only conclude that we do not much care about it.

This may be a feature of a general uneasiness about how to deal with scent. We cannot even describe it effectively. For such a rich language, English has precious few words devoted to scent, and we must grope towards what we mean by imprecise comparisons. The problem is compounded by the fact that flower scents are often concatenations of many different esters, so that there are undertones of this and overtones of that. It is this complexity which helps make descriptions of scents so subjective. One man's tea is another man's tar.

At this season it is fun to play 'smelling games', trying to describe the scents of roses one comes upon in public and private gardens. Most gardens can boast enough roses to make this an enjoyable diversion from gardening. It occurred to me on a rose outing recently that the key to why so many roses have a fruity fragrance is that they are closely related to many of the fruits we grow in the garden. I am not quite sure why this was not blindingly obvious to me long ago; perhaps because roses do also sometimes smell of citrus fruits, and these are definitely in a different family.

I thank God for this scent. Burying my nose in a fruit-scented rose gives me as much pleasure at this time of year as burying it in a glass of a fruity rosé wine. More even than the lavender smell of 'Madame Isaac Pereire' or the myrrh of 'Constance Spry', I long for the fruitiness of 'Madame Hardy' and 'Nymphenburg', 'Ferdinand Pichard' and 'Madame Lauriol de Barny', 'Bredon' and 'Leander', 'Chanel' and 'Silver Jubilee', 'Albertine' and 'Max Graf'. From that list it should be plain that in most rose groups there are varieties which smell of apples and raspberries, but this attribute is especially notice-able among Rambler roses, which descend from *Rosa wichu-rana*, and among the sweet briars.

Rosa rubiginosa, now more correctly called *R. eglanteria*, is our native sweet briar or 'sweet eglantine'; it has long been grown and gets an honourable mention, along with 'sweet musk-roses', in *A Midsummer's Night's Dream*. Its great virtue is that the leaves smell strongly of unripe apples when crushed, or after a shower of rain on a hot day.

In the 1890s Lord Penzance, a grandee with a botanical bent, developed a race of hybrids called the Penzance briars, which he mostly named after characters in Walter Scott novels. These appear to be thoroughly out of favour a hundred years on, presumably because they are thorny, some are prone to blackspot (what isn't, in the wrong conditions?), and they flower only once. I have seen these Penzance briars trained as fans on horizontal wires, which seems to me to be a negation of their true vocation in life. This is either being grown among a group of 'old' and 'new' shrub roses, where their short flowering season will not matter and they can produce their red hips in autumn and their foliage scent any time; or as a constituent of a deciduous 'country' hedge, along with hawthorn, blackthorn and field maple.

David Austin Roses offer fourteen cultivars, most with single scented flowers and nearly all bred by Lord Penzance. Not surprisingly, I am keen to grow one called 'Greenmantle', which is single and pinkish-crimson in colour, with a white eye. I fantasise about creating a thicket towards the outer regions of the garden with it, adding the dark crimson semi-double 'Anne of Geierstein', the pink-flushed white 'Flora McIvor', and the double pink 'Manning's Blush', for subtle variety's sake. *Rosa eglanteria* has single pink flowers and is the most strongly scented of them all in flower and leaf, but it is especially vigorous, growing to eight feet tall and across. It can be trimmed, however, provided you have impermeable gloves.

There are other fruity scents besides apple to be found in the rose garden. 'Adam Messerich' and 'Ferdinand Pichard', for example, smell more of raspberry; if you fancy bananas, you should try *Rosa dupontii* and *R. longicuspsis*, while *R. bracteata* can offer lemons. Perhaps my absolute favourite is the Chinese restaurant tinned-lychee smell of the pinkish-white climbing rose 'Madame Alfred Carrière'. Where there is the will, together with a certain amount of space and plenty of shelter to hold the scent, one could have a veritable fruit salad of fragrance. Well, why not?

Sunday Telegraph

Nothing Serious in Mortality   3 October 1993

Lately I have been in philosophical mood as I contemplate the removal of two long-established shrubs – an *Abutilon vitifolium* and a *Hoheria sexstylosa* – which have recently, and almost coincidentally, died.

The abutilon has been threatening to do something of the sort for some time. A branch died in the spring, but after some quickly applied saw work I believed I had saved the day. But, whatever the problem, it was too well established to be halted. The hoheria died far more quickly. Like Solomon Grundy, it took ill on Thursday, was worse on Friday, and died on Saturday. In both cases, the leaves turned first to brown rags and then dropped grudgingly to the ground

In general, we gardeners have a markedly scientific approach to our gardening these days. We are far better informed than our forebears about how it is that plants grow, and are neither phased by photosynthesis nor foxed by chemical symbols on fertiliser bags. But let a seemingly healthy plant die on us, and we feel bewildered and affronted. The reason for this must be that gardening literature, no doubt unwittingly, gives the impression that trees and shrubs hold the secret of eternal life. Plant death, except where it arises as the result of fatal disease or accident, seems a subject hedged round with as many taboos as our own mortality.

We are taught to take care initially, but if a plant gets over the shock of planting the presumption is that it will go on for ever. That is hardly rational; we certainly do not expect it of our pets, for example. But because plants do not become smelly, arthritic and white-muzzled, or otherwise show signs of age, we do not expect them to hand in their dinner pails.

In fact, there are a number of indicators which we should heed. Dieback of branches is the most obvious, yet strangely it is not an infallible one. I knew my abutilon was at risk when a branch died, but if it had been an ash tree I might not have worried. 'Stag-headed' deciduous trees (that is, those with dead upper branches), according to no less an authority than Professor Oliver Rackham, are not necessarily unhealthy and likely to die.

A poor flowering or fruiting the season before may signal distress, but is hardly an invariable indication; a more certain sign is leaf droop, especially if the soil is moist so that drought can be discounted.

Plants which are on the boundaries of hardiness in this country are generally the most vulnerable, for any cold winter will test them severely. However, that fact can be masked by the length of time it takes for imminent death to manifest itself. Although the abutilon and hoheria are both considered rather tender, last winter was probably too mild to worry them, growing as they did against sunny walls. In any event, it is not always the cold itself which kills; a slightly tender shrub may survive many degrees of frost because it is tucked up under a blanket of snow, but succumb to cold winds in March because they desiccate it.

Important and often arbitrary killers of trees and shrubs are pests and, most particularly, diseases.There are a number of diseases which can kill (honey fungus, Dutch elm disease, fire-blight, silver leaf), and several more which will weaken a plant to a point where it is in danger of dying (bacterial canker, coral spot). A thorough post-mortem may well yield clues.

Establishing the cause of death may also help us prevent a spread to other plants. When I remove my two poor shrubs, I shall take a good look for the tell-tale 'bootlaces' which announce the presence of honey fungus, a likely suspect.

Chemical weedkillers, carelessly applied, can be life-threat-ening, even for shrubs, as can any mechanical or animal-induced 'ring-barking' of small trees.

However, one should never underestimate the extent to which death is inexplicable except in terms of the variable life span of plants. They differ enormously in their natural longevity. Among trees even of the same species there is great disparity, because they are affected by their environment and by how quickly they grow when young. Some species do generally last longer than others, however: limes are longer-lived than beech, yew and pines will outlast spruce or larch.

Native trees, not surprisingly, often live longer than introduced species: not only have they evolved to thrive in the climate, but they have found ways of surviving even when their top hamper is threatened by old age or disease.

Shrubs can be very puzzling. Ceanothus, for example, is a large shrub but is rarely long-lived, ten to fifteen years being a good innings, whereas roses, which are smaller, can go on for twice that time, or more. In the artificial environment of the garden wild fluctuations are inevitable, and a plant which lives many years in your garden may not do nearly so well next door. My abutilon and hoheria had both lived for a decade, so the answer to the puzzle may simply be that the natural and due time had come for them to be gone to their long home.

Sunday Telegraph

Gone Gardening   *9 April 1988*

I had a much-loved uncle who whenever any of his nieces or nephews stayed with him as a child would itemise all the interesting things to do, and end the list with: 'Or there again, we could go fishing.' Fishing was the ultimate but unattainable ideal, only to be dreamed of but more fun than any real possibility.

These days I feel much the same about gardening. If anyone asks me, which is rarely, what I would most like to do at that moment, the answer is always 'gardening'; but the chances are nearly as remote as that fishing expedition of long ago. Snatching time for gardening from the jaws of other commitments is not easy. Some years ago there was a folksy advertising campaign aimed at selling garden equipment, whose slogan was 'Let's go gardening'. Thousands of people like me must have muttered 'Chance would be a very fine thing.'

The problem is that gardening is not something you can take up and drop in an instant, like knitting; it requires preparation both of oneself and, sometimes, even the garden. Although especially important for busy people, gardening does not accommodate itself to their self-inflicted limitations. For one thing, during half the year, and often very much more, old clothes, coats and stout footwear must be sought out and put on. The time (not to mention the sheer mental and physical exertion) required to put together everything needed, from secateurs to indelible pencil, may well take much of that available for the task in hand. There is not a great deal that can be done about this, except to buy waterproof overshoes, which are easier to put on and take off than wellington boots, and to hide a trug basket of useful small tools from the family, in the greenhouse or shed.

If you have young children, time is so fractured anyway that often any attempt to garden seems scarcely justified. My solution was to invite every child of suitable age in the district to come and play (earning myself considerable, although quite unwarranted, praise from their mothers) so that my children were well distracted in the garden and did not kindly offer to help me prune the roses or hoe between the carrots.

The most time-consuming task in the garden, they say, is deciding what job to do. I have certainly spent precious minutes as the dark clouds gathered debating whether I should be weeding the rock-bed or splitting the primroses. I should convince myself that what I do matters less than doing something. After all, I find deep satisfaction in spending even ten minutes washing a few plant pots or sprinkling bone meal around the daffodils – not because these tasks are intrinsically very interesting but because I have thereby stolen a march on all those elements conspiring to keep me away from my garden.

Once I have managed to find my way into the garden, I live in fear of the telephone ringing. It follows me like a tiresome clinging chum whose friendship I first courted and now wish to reject. As a concession to living in the twentieth century I have a cordless telephone which I take into the greenhouse if I absolutely have to. However, as the distance from the house ensures that I hear everything through a thick aural fur I might just as well not bother.*

Like many gardeners, and despite the fact that I should know better, I am not always expert at seizing the moment. I have in the past gone out to douse my apple trees in a tar oil winter wash, only to discover them already broken into bud; I have intended to prune the wisteria but then decided, on inspection, that it was a task best done in a fortnight. Two weeks later, I have forgotten all about it in the rush to do something else. Seeds which are not part of the orgy of spring seed sowing, like Chinese cabbage, lamb's lettuce, sweet Williams and wallflowers, have been left over from year to year because I had no infallible memory jogger. I find now that a small wall-planner chart with the main tasks scribbled in early in the year helps to overcome this. If you follow that advice, you may find that the mower is serviced for the first time in years.

The Spectator

New Millennium Resolutions   1 January 2000

Even those of us who have set our faces resolutely against Millennium hype (and may – oh, the shame of it – have almost been tempted to have a quiet night in on New Year's Eve) know that history divides up into centuries. Whether we like it or not, in years to come we will think of twentieth-century gardening trends separately from those of the twenty-first

---

* Mercifully, there is no reception for my mobile phone in the garden.

century, and will express surprise if they turn out to be rather similar. Now that we have splashed our way across this shallow, narrow Rubicon, our perception of gardens and gardening is bound to be altered by viewing them from a slightly different place, whether they themselves change much or not.

In fact, I think they will. Gardening practices are indicators of social and economic change, and there is a great deal of that about. It is reasonably safe to predict, therefore, that in the next few years gardens will become much more important to us as havens of peace and right-thinking in a frenetic, over-complex, sometimes corrupt world. Simplicity will be an end in itself. Plants will be appreciated more for what they can do than what they are, and in many gardens the numbers used will drop markedly. Lawns and other labour-intensive areas of the garden, will be ditched in favour of high-tech but ideologically pure kitchen gardens. At the same time, gardens will increasingly be seen far more as simple refuges for threatened wildlife than as playgrounds of creative individualism. Technology will be harnessed more effectively to counter climatic shortcomings, in particular in saving water and protecting crops; computers will be used to control the optimum temperature and watering regimes even in small amateur greenhouses. The use of artificial fertilisers, pesticides and weedkillers will be as frowned upon in twenty years' time as smoking in restaurants is now.

The plants used will also vary, if projected climatic changes come about. In the south, especially, the use of drought-tolerant, frost-tender plants is likely to increase at the expense of hardy ones needing a lot of water. So it will be out with the rhododendrons and in with the prickly pears, and our gardens may take on a more southern-hemisphere look. Meanwhile, increasing winds in the north may do for many trees there.

Small-scale general flower shows and the public exhibition of excellence in flowers and vegetables will lose ground further, as leisure pursuits proliferate. Shows which continue to thrive will be under the auspices of specialist societies. Small gardens encourage specialists: you don't need much space to grow rare alpines or exotic orchids under glass, only know-how, time, and occasionally money. And there will be plenty of all that in the next century, especially if we are encouraged to retire at forty.*

At the same time, never-before-experienced general levels of prosperity will put a even greater premium on space, already often limited. Larger gardens, easier to manage with ever-more sophisticated machinery and readily accessible 'hard land-scaping', will once again become potent status symbols, as they were a hundred years ago. That said, it is possible that the proposed loosening of planning controls concerning redundant farm land may have the effect of increasing the size of gardens for new houses in rural areas and on the edge of suburbs. I hope it does, for contemporary houses are all too often shoe-horned into minute plots which make life very difficult for would-be gardeners, not to mention games-playing children. At the same time urban schemes, especially community gardens, should, and I hope will, proliferate, to the general good.

Of developments that I should like to see in the century ahead, rather than simply anticipate, the end of the present preoccupation with 'compact' (by which is meant 'dwarf') plants would suit me very nicely. In concentrating on the finite horizontal extent of gardens, we forget that there are 90 million miles vertically above them. The use of predominantly 'compact' plants leads to dull, flat gardens lacking structural contrast. At the same time, I hope seedsmen will recognise that, say, busy lizzie seed in a mixture of colours which includes everything from salmon to carmine is unlikely to be successful when translated to the border.

* Since I wrote this, the pensions industry has suffered enormous reverses, and we are now told we must work to the age of seventy. Sigh.

Another idea which appeals strongly to me, although its merits are unlikely to strike the Treasury quite so forcibly, is the granting of tax relief to all those private individuals who wish to employ gardeners below retirement age. There is no social stigma attached to working in someone else's garden these days, quite the reverse, so this measure could not possibly herald the return of degrading 'domestic service'. Professional gardeners rightly have a proper appreciation of their value and worth, but there would be far more of them if their potential employers were not so heavily burdened by income tax and could contemplate paying them a decent wage.

Most fervently I hope that, in the next century, the contemporary notion that there is something attractive and desirable about making a durable garden in the space of a weekend will die a natural death. It is certainly possible to do it, and there are situations when it is appropriate, but such an ambition denies any garden owner with a feeling for the soil and for plants almost all pleasure in the process. And that pleasure can be potent indeed. However the next century turns out, I wish you plenty of enjoyment in your garden.

Independent

Conversion Tables

For the various Imperial and Metric measurements which appear in the text. These are gardeners' approximations only.

Inches	cm (approx.)
1	2.5
2	5
3	7.5
4	10
5	12.5
6	15
7	17.5
8	20
9	22.5
10	25
12 (1 ft)	30
18	45
20	50.5
24 (2 ft)	60
30	75
33	85
36 (3 ft)	90
90 (7 ft 6 in)	230

Metres	approx. yards	approx. feet
8	8.75	26.25
14	15	46
15	16	50
25	27	82
50	54.5	164
110	120	360

Feet	metres (approx.)
5	1.5
8	2.5
10	3
20	6
30	9
65	20
80	25
100	30

Temperatures °C	°F
20 =	68
15 =	59
10 =	50
0 =	32 (freezing)

Pounds	kilograms
15	6.8
40.5	18.3
74	33.5
710	322
3.5 tons	3.8 tonnes

- 1½ oz. per sq. yd. = 10 gm per sq. m approx.
- 22 yd = 1 chain = 20 m
- ³⁄₁₆ in ≃ ⅛ in ≃ 4 mm

Index

Index

bay, 204
beech hedging plants, 183
bee-keeping, 212–17
Bees at the Bottom of the Garden (Alan Campion), 213
Beeston, Nottingham, Millenium Sculpture Garden, 15–17
beetles, 219–22
Belder, Madame Jelena de, 163
Bellis, 108
Berberis
    B. darwinii, 180
    B. thunbergii 'Atropurpurea', 180
    B. thunbergii 'Helmond Pillar', 44
    B. × *ottawensis*, 179, 180
    B. × *stenophylla*, 179, 180
Bidens, 57
    B. 'Golden Goddess', 101
biennials, 107–9
Biggs, Matthew, 18
bindweed, 68, 225
bird cherry trees, 190
blackcurrants
    'Ben Sarek', 199
    'Titania', 82
blackthorn *see Prunus spinosus*
Bliss, Sir Arthur, 202
bluebell *see Hyacinthoides non-scriptus*
Bluebell Nursery, 184
Blyth of Rowington, Lord, 14–15
Bodnant, North Wales, 36
Boots Company, The, Millenium Sculpture Garden, 14–17
borage, 204
Botton, Alain de, 64
Bouteloua gracilis, 128
Bowles, E.A., 139
brambles, ornamental, 186–8
Bressingham Plants, 21
British Clematis Society, 124
British Orchid Growers' Association, 135
Brogdale Horticultural Trust, Kent, 189–90
brown rot, 229–31
Brunnera macrophylla, 153
    B. m. 'Hadspen Cream', 116, 117
    B. m. 'Langtrees', 117
    B. m. 'Variegata', 117
buckthorn *see Rhamnus*
Buddleja, 77–8, 218

B. alternifolia, 32
    pruning, 78
bulbs
    long-lasting, 59
    ordering, 54
bullace *see Prunus institia*
Bulwick, Northamptonshire, 28, 30
bumble bees, 216, 217; *see also* honey-bees
burglar-proofing, horticultural, 179–81
butterflies, 100–1
    cabbage white, 208
    encouraging, 103, 218–19
    and weeds, 217–19
Buxus
    B. microphylla, 46–7
    B. sempervirens 'Suffruticosa', 46–7

Calamagrostis, 128
Campanula
    C. pyramidalis, 130
    C. × *media*, 108
Canterbury bells *see Campanula* × *media*
Carex elata 'Aurea', 126
Carpinus betulus, 47
    C. b. 'Fastigiata', 185–6
carrot fly, 206
Caryopteris × *clandonensis*, 77–8
Castle School, Thornbury, 20
catkins, 163–4
Ceanothus, 59, 247
    C. 'Zanzibar', 84
celandine, greater *see Chelidonium majus*
celandine, lesser *see Ranunculus ficaria*
Chaerophyllum hirsutum 'Roseum', 121
Chamaecyparis lawsoniana 'Green Hedger', 47
Chatto, Beth, 99–100
Cheiranthus, 108
Chelidonium majus, 140
Chelsea Flower Show, 19–22, 24, 25, 120
chervil, 204
Chiltern Seeds, 101, 111
Chionochloa, 128
    C. rubra, 128
Chrysanthemum 'Cottage Apricot', 57
chrysanthemum leaf miner, 228
Chusan palm *see Trachycarpus fortunei*
Cistus, 59
Clare, John (poet), 148
Clayton, Mr (head gardener), 112, 114

Index

Index

Index

Index